THE BEDFORD SERIES IN HISTORY AND CULTURE

Twenty Years at Hull-House

with Autobiographical Notes

BY JANE ADDAMS

Related Titles in
THE BEDFORD SERIES IN HISTORY AND CULTURE
Advisory Editors: Lynn Hunt, *University of California, Los Angeles*
David W. Blight, *Yale University*
Bonnie G. Smith, *Rutgers University*
Natalie Zemon Davis, *Princeton University*
Ernest R. May, *Harvard University*

THE BEDFORD SERIES IN HISTORY AND CULTURE

Twenty Years at Hull-House

with Autobiographical Notes

BY JANE ADDAMS

Edited with an Introduction by

Victoria Bissell Brown

Grinnell College

BEDFORD/ST. MARTIN'S
Boston ◆ New York

For Bedford/St. Martin's
History Editor: Katherine E. Kurzman
Developmental Editor: Jen Lesar
Production Supervisor: Dennis Conroy
Project Management: Books By Design, Inc.
Marketing Manager: Charles Cavaliere
Text Design: Claire Seng-Niemoeller
Index: Books By Design, Inc.
Cover Design: Richard Emery Design, Inc.
Cover Photo: Hull-House. The University Library at the University of Illinois at Chicago. Jane Addams Memorial Collection, Wallace Kirkland Papers. *Jane Addams.* Jane Addams Collection, Swarthmore College Peace Collection.
Composition: G&S Typesetters, Inc.
Printing and Binding: Haddon Craftsmen, an R. R. Donnelley & Sons Company

President: Charles H. Christensen
Editorial Director: Joan E. Feinberg
Director of Editing, Design, and Production: Marcia Cohen
Manager, Publishing Services: Emily Berleth

Library of Congress Catalog Card Number: 98-87518

Manufactured in the United States of America.

11 10 9 8
j i h g

For information, write: Bedford / St. Martin's, 75 Arlington Street, Boston, MA 02116
(617-399-4000)

ISBN-10: 0–312–15706–1 (paperback)
          0–312–21817–6 (hardcover)
ISBN-13: 978–0–312–15706–7

Acknowledgments

From *I Came a Stranger: The Story of a Hull-House Girl.* Copyright 1989 by the Board of Trustees of the University of Illinois. Used with the permission of the University of Illinois Press.

Foreword

The Bedford Series in History and Culture is designed so that readers can study the past as historians do.

The historian's first task is finding the evidence. Documents, letters, memoirs, interviews, pictures, movies, novels, or poems can provide facts and clues. Then the historian questions and compares the sources. There is more to do than in a courtroom, for hearsay evidence is welcome, and the historian is usually looking for answers beyond act and motive. Different views of an event may be as important as a single verdict. How a story is told may yield as much information as what it says.

Along the way the historian seeks help from other historians and perhaps from specialists in other disciplines. Finally, it is time to write, to decide on an interpretation and how to arrange the evidence for readers.

Each book in this series contains an important historical document or group of documents, each document a witness from the past and open to interpretation in different ways. The documents are combined with some element of historical narrative — an introduction or a biographical essay, for example — that provides students with an analysis of the primary source material and important background information about the world in which it was produced.

Each book in the series focuses on a specific topic within a specific historical period. Each provides a basis for lively thought and discussion about several aspects of the topic and the historian's role. Each is short enough (and inexpensive enough) to be a reasonable one-week assignment in a college course. Whether as classroom or personal reading, each book in the series provides firsthand experience of the challenge — and fun — of discovering, recreating, and interpreting the past.

Lynn Hunt
David W. Blight
Bonnie G. Smith
Natalie Zemon Davis
Ernest R. May

Preface

Twenty Years at Hull-House was a widely read and widely praised book when it was first published in 1910, and it has stood the test of time, becoming a "classic" text in the history of the American progressive era. Works do not become classics, however, unless they continue to have something to say to readers from different eras. In the case of *Twenty Years at Hull-House,* readers continue to discover its relevance to contemporary concerns with immigration, urban poverty, community organizing, and the relationship between the rich and the poor.

Jane Addams was already the most prominent woman in America when she published this book, and her decision to wrap her political philosophy in an accessible life story proved very attractive to the American reading public. This was not Jane Addams's first published contribution to the era's national debate over laissez-faire capitalism, government regulation, socialism, labor unions, immigration, or women's public role. By 1910, she had already published three books and close to one hundred articles and had delivered countless public addresses on a wide variety of issues. Though she regarded herself as a "slow and bungling writer," it was, in fact, Addams's talent as an engaging author — not her position as the head resident at the Hull-House Settlement of Chicago — that won her the unique public authority on social questions which she enjoyed by the turn of the century.[1] In the years following publication of *Twenty Years at Hull-House,* she would publish another seven books. All of Addams's books were praised, but this memoir of her first two decades at Hull-House was by far her most popular.

Ever since it was first published, the secret to this book's success has been Addams's talent for crafting political parables that sound like

---

[1] Jane Addams to Irene Osgood [Andrews], December 3, 1908. Jane Addams Memorial Collection, University of Illinois, Chicago. See, too, Jane Addams to Hamilton Holt, May 1, 1904, in which she tried to postpone the due date on an article she was writing for Holt's magazine, *The Independent,* on the grounds that she wrote "so slowly and painfully." Also in Jane Addams Memorial Collection, University of Illinois, Chicago.

personal anecdotes. This makes *Twenty Years at Hull-House* a slippery little book. It is easy to get drawn into the anecdotal details and to over-look the political philosophy they are delivering. For that reason, I ap-proached this new edition as a teacher intent on guiding my own stu-dents toward seeing this book as a political treatise that Addams wrote in order to further her reform agenda. I know from my own experience that Addams's seemingly casual language can distract us from recogniz-ing her very serious purpose. It is my hope that the Introduction will aid readers to see Jane Addams as a conscious, careful writer; she "fussed over the book" when she was writing it, she fretted over the fact that she had "never written so slowly on anything," and she experienced great "distress of mind" on the eve of its publication. In the end, she was deeply gratified by the book's success.

This abridgement of *Twenty Years at Hull-House* includes every one of the book's eighteen chapters in condensed form. Care has been taken to preserve the message Addams sought to convey in each chapter and to maintain the narrative and ideological integrity of the book. To enhance modern readers' sense of the historical context in which the book was written and first read, the text has been annotated and several additional primary documents are included in this edition. Some of these docu-ments, such as the Hull-House Weekly Program and Florence Kelley's magazine profile of Hull-House in 1898, are intended to expand the pic-ture of settlement house life. Others, such as Edward A. Ross's racialized treatment of immigrants and the socialists' critique of Addams, are meant to show that Jane Addams lived in a contentious world, that not everyone agreed with her views, and that her opinions were part of na-tional debates about wealth, immigration, and women's rights. Included as well are a chronology of Jane Addams's life which serves as a useful reminder of the breadth of her activities within and beyond Hull-House and, finally, a bibliography that suggests the depth of historians' interest in Addams's life and times.

ACKNOWLEDGMENTS

I am most grateful to Kathryn Kish Sklar and Thomas Dublin for con-necting Bedford/St. Martin's interest in this edition of *Twenty Years at Hull-House* with my interest in Jane Addams. Their confidence in my work on Addams is a continual source of encouragement for me. At all points along the way, the editors at Bedford/St. Martin's have been en-thusiastic and helpful, and I wish to express my particular thanks to

Katherine Kurzman and Jen Lesar for their clear and insightful guidance. My endeavors in introducing and abridging this volume were greatly aided by the thoughtful editorial advice I received from Maureen Flanagan, Michigan State University; Lois Rudnick, University of Massachusetts–Boston; Mina Carson, Oregon State University; Kathleen Kennedy, Western Washington University; and two anonymous reviewers. Each reader contributed valuable criticisms and suggestions and I have endeavored to reflect their wisdom in these pages. Finally, I would like to thank the students in my Progressive Era seminar at Grinnell College for reading the manuscript and contributing their very useful perspective to the revision process. Will Lee-Ashley, Ariane Kissam, Joel Foreman, MLE Davis, and Alegre Bussetti spoke for the student reader in their critiques of the manuscript and, I believe, spoke well. As always, Jim and Elizabeth Brown and Carter Smith have offered spiritual, intellectual, and physical support to this project. Their unflagging interest in Jane Addams and their cheerful inclusion of "Miss Addams" into our household afford me the integration of professional and personal life that Addams knew was essential for health and happiness.

Victoria Bissell Brown

Contents

APPENDICES

PART ONE

Introduction:
Jane Addams Constructs
Herself and Hull-House

I am not so sure that we succeeded in our endeavors. . . . But Hull-House was soberly opened on the theory that the dependence of classes on each other is reciprocal. — *Twenty Years at Hull-House,* pp. 79–80

I learned that life cannot be administered by definite rules and regulations; that wisdom to deal with a man's difficulties comes only through some knowledge of his life and habits as a whole.
— *Twenty Years at Hull-House,* p. 109

As the very existence of the state depends upon the character of its citizens, therefore if certain industrial conditions are forcing the workers below the standard of decency, it becomes possible to deduce the right of state regulation. — *Twenty Years at Hull-House,* p. 135

Twenty Years at Hull-House describes the social problems that existed a century ago in this country. Even so, it grapples with questions that are still pertinent today: Is poverty a result of individual failure or failures of the economic system? Do immigrants enhance or burden the American commitment to democracy and prosperity? Do women bring a distinctive set of female values to civic life? Can white, native-born, economically secure Americans ever really understand, much less help, those who are struggling to survive?

Jane Addams offered her answers to those questions in this 1910 memoir, and those answers reflected the attitudes of the Progressive Era in which she was a central figure. If poverty was the fault of the system, she reasoned, then the system needed to be reformed. If poverty was the fault of the individual, the individual's family needed to be helped. If immigrants were given a fair chance and a decent welcome, their experiences could greatly enrich political and economic life. So, too, if women's experiences with the daily business of survival were respected, their knowledge could serve the community. And if comfortable, well-meaning Americans were willing to listen as well as talk, willing to learn as well as preach, then, yes, they could help those struggling to survive.

Addams couched this argument in a narrative that traces her individual journey to life in a Chicago "settlement house" and her collective experience after she arrived there. Just a few years before Addams published this life story, one popular U.S. magazine dubbed her "the first saint America produced." [1] But *Twenty Years at Hull-House* is not by or about a saint, nor is it even a thorough account of Jane Addams's life story. Instead, it is a carefully crafted statement of Jane Addams's political philosophy, which she made attractive to her readers in 1910 by framing it with her "autobiographical notes." Although important and instructive, the notes were selected and shaped to serve Addams's political mission.

The deceptively simple stories in *Twenty Years at Hull-House* were all designed to make a complex argument. At every turn in the book, Addams was saying that a society that calls itself democratic must make possible the participation of all its members; the wealthy have no monopoly on political wisdom or social ethics. In Addams's opinion, peaceful dialogue across the lines of class, ethnicity, and gender would have to replace conflict, brute force, and repression if American democracy was to survive urban industrialization.

In 1910, when Jane Addams embedded this argument in *Twenty Years at Hull-House,* she was already the most respected woman in the nation. As head resident of the most famous of America's 400 settlement houses, Addams had expanded Hull-House beyond the original house to include thirteen brick buildings encircling a playground and occupying an entire city block in the Nineteenth Ward on Chicago's west side. She had become a national leader in labor mediation, child labor legislation, housing and sanitation reform, vocational education, immigrant welfare,

---

[1] Jane Addams was first called "the first saint America has produced" by John Burns, the British labor leader and M.P. The phrase then appeared in the title of an article about Addams in *Current Literature* 40 (April 1906): 377–79.

woman suffrage, and consumer lobbying. During 1909 alone, the year in which she was hurrying to complete *Twenty Years at Hull-House,* Addams participated in a White House Conference on the Care of Dependent Children, a Child Labor Conference, meetings of the International Association for Labor Legislation, the Municipal Suffrage for Women League, and the National Peace Congress — and was the first woman elected president of the National Conference of Charities and Corrections. In 1913, three years after the book's publication, *The Independent,* a popular magazine, asked its readers to name "the most useful Americans." Jane Addams ranked second, behind Thomas Edison and ahead of Andrew Carnegie.[2] As a popular national representative of progressive ideas, Addams had persuaded a great many people to listen when she challenged Carnegie's assumption that the richest men in the society were the most "fit," or that great accumulations of individual wealth and power were necessarily signs of a healthy democracy.[3]

In keeping with its Progressive Era, egalitarian ethos, *Twenty Years at Hull-House* is not about Jane Addams's individual rise to fame and influence in the United States. It is about a settlement house that was established in an "industrial quarter" of Chicago to provide social and educational services to the thousands of poor and working-class "neighbors" crowded into the streets and tenements around it. It is a story of immigrants and workers, children and families — and of the middle-class women and men who chose to live as "residents" in the settlement house in order to serve the neighborhood. When the book was written, Addams and Hull-House were so famous, and the social context so well known to her readers, that she could presume a level of acquaintance with the enterprise that today's readers cannot possess. The purpose of this introduction, therefore, is to describe the conditions in Chicago in the late nineteenth century that stimulated undertakings like Hull-House, to describe the various political streams that fed the river

[2] "The Most Useful Americans," *The Independent* 74 (1 May 1913): 956–63.

[3] Andrew Carnegie, "Wealth," *North American Review* 148 (June 1889): 653–64 and 148 (December 1889): 682–98. The essay was included in a collection of Carnegie's writings entitled *The Gospel of Wealth and Other Timely Essays* in 1900 (New York: Century Company) and the editors of the *North American Review* were so keen on this essay that they republished it seventeen years later under the title "The Gospel of Wealth," 183 (21 Sept. 1906): 526–37 and 183 (7 Dec. 1906): 1096–106.

William T. Stead, a Christian social reformer and journalist from Britain who was highly critical of America's concentration of wealth, was actually the person who dubbed Carnegie's philosophy "the gospel of wealth." Stead intended to compare Carnegie's position unfavorably with the "social gospel," but Carnegie and the editors of the *North American Review* embraced the title as their own. Addams discusses Stead's visit to Chicago in 1893 in chapter 8 of *Twenty Years at Hull-House.*

of progressivism, and to link Jane Addams's own history to the flow of social activism that Addams and her colleagues regarded, with pride, as the Progressive Era. The purpose of these introductory comments is also to demonstrate that beneath the smooth surface of Addams's semi-autobiographical narrative lies a complex, determined political argument made accessible by its personal tone.

GROWING UP IN THE GILDED AGE

Jane Addams was born in 1860, one year before the start of the Civil War. She died in 1935, in the midst of America's worst economic depression. Her life spanned the country's transformation from a rural, agricultural society to an urban, industrial one. Jane Addams's ideological journey, from elitism to egalitarianism, from a romantic image of herself as a "hero" to a democratic image of herself as a social servant, very much reflects her generation's journey away from their parents' Yankee faith in unfettered industrial capitalism and toward a progressive faith in the state's ability to regulate industrial capitalism in the name of democracy.

Addams was born in the little farming village of Cedarville, just outside Freeport, in northern Illinois's Stephenson County. She grew up there, the youngest of five children, living in the town's biggest house, which was owned by her father, who was the town's richest and most important man. John Huy Addams owned the flour mill in Cedarville and was president of the Second National Bank of Freeport and two Freeport insurance companies. But it was his investment in the Galena and Chicago Railroad that made him rich and his efforts to ensure that the railroad would come through Freeport that made him a respected figure in the county. Like most of his neighbors, John Addams began his pioneer life in northern Illinois as an antislavery Whig and, like most of his neighbors, Addams followed Abraham Lincoln into the new Republican party in 1854. Indeed, John Addams was elected to the Illinois Senate as a Republican in 1854 and served in that office until 1870, when he chose to retire and focus all of his attention on his family and business ventures.[4]

---

[4]The two most reliable biographies of Jane Addams currently available are by Allen F. Davis, who wrote *American Heroine: The Life and Legend of Jane Addams* (New York: Oxford University Press, 1973), and James Weber Linn, Addams's nephew, who wrote *Jane Addams: A Biography* (New York: D. Appleton-Century Company, 1935). Additional biographical information in this introduction is taken from the research I have conducted in preparation for writing a new biography of Addams.

In the privileged world Jane Addams inhabited as a child, there was little conflict between doing well and doing good. Her father's investment in capitalist endeavors benefited the whole community by providing a reliable mill, a railroad, a bank, and an insurance company. As a child, Jane could see that her father was respected by his neighbors, not resented; his wealth was not built on exploitation, pollution, or rapacious dealings. Moreover, his years of service to the state Senate and his civic attention to Cedarville's school, library, and churches demonstrated his interest in turning his own fortunes toward the well-being of the community. His retirement from the Illinois State Senate in 1870, just when that state's politics were becoming notoriously corrupt, suggests that Senator Addams recoiled from the post–Civil War rush to profit from public service. He was the sort of man who gave elite "stewardship" a good name in the decades before the Civil War, and in that capacity he was an important mentor to his youngest daughter, Jane.

In *Twenty Years at Hull-House,* Addams spoke with understanding about those "self-made men" for whom state regulation of industry was "counter to the instinct and tradition" (pp. 125–26). By the time she wrote those words, Addams had confronted an economic and political world very different from Cedarville's and knew that her father's era of harmonious, unregulated stewardship had passed. But her tolerant tone in discussing wealthy, powerful businessmen serves as a reminder of the affection she bore toward her father and the respect she had for his ethic of responsible stewardship. Addams chose to write, in chapter 2 of *Twenty Years at Hull-House,* that she would "always tend to associate Lincoln with the tenderest thoughts of my father." She also chose to accompany that claim with a story about walking in Lincoln Park for solace at a time when she was in fierce conflict with the tyrannical industrialist, George Pullman. These narrative choices suggest that Addams did not see her father as an overbearing capitalist dictator from the Gilded Age but as a self-made steward from an era when leaders put the community's interest alongside their own.

When Addams left Cedarville to attend Rockford Female Seminary in 1877, she was most definitely her father's daughter. The seminary, led by the imperious and evangelical Anna Peck Sill, was a hothouse of feminine religiosity bent on turning out Christian wives, mothers, and missionaries. John Addams's youngest daughter resisted all of these agendas. Like her father, she subscribed to Christian values but never experienced a religious conversion. Like her father, her diligent work habits and strong intelligence brought her esteem and rewards. And, like her father, she enjoyed the role of "steward," serving as class president at Rockford all four years and serving, as well, as president of the debate society, editor of the campus magazine, and valedictorian of her class in 1881.

As a student at Rockford, Jane Addams did not share her classmates' dreams of marriage or missionary work or a career as a teacher. She was ambitious for a public role, for a life of stewardship, and she drew inspiration for that ambition from her father's example and from the writings of Victorian idealists like John Ruskin and Thomas Carlyle. These British writers from the 1840s and 1850s were very popular among intellectuals in America in the 1870s. While Ruskin and Carlyle felt a strong sense of responsibility to address the problems of the poor and working classes, they were not at all democratic in their proposed solutions. Their solutions involved bold leadership by heroic individuals from the elite classes, individuals "destined" to guide the ignorant masses toward productive lives. As the ambitious, adolescent daughter of the richest man in Stephenson County, Jane Addams particularly resonated to the romantic heroism she encountered in Carlyle's writings; his dramatic language allowed her to dream of a public life of heroic individualism, overcoming all obstacles, even that of gender, because she was somehow destined for greatness.

It may seem surprising to learn that Jane Addams, whose career was entwined with democratic values and a distinctly female political culture, started out in life with such a strong identification with paternalistic, individualistic, and heroic notions. But this was not such an unusual path for ambitious women of Addams's generation. In a society that offered few encouragements and even fewer role models to ambitious young women who lacked a religious or domestic bent, it appears that a number of female leaders spent their youths dreaming dreams of heroic action. As the young Jane Addams once wrote to her friend Ellen Gates Starr, she felt "perfectly enthusiastic" about the "splendid" prospect of throwing "ourselves into the tide of affairs, feeling ourselves swamped by the great flood of human action."[5]

Contributing to Addams's identification with male models of heroism was her lack of familial experience with the female culture of reform and

---

[5]Jane Addams to Ellen Gates Starr, 11 August 1879. Ellen Gates Starr Papers, Smith College Archives. See also Barbara Sicherman, "Reading and Ambition: M. Carey Thomas and Female Heroism," *American Quarterly* 45 (March 1993): 73–103; Helen Lefkowitz Horowitz, "'Nous Autres: Reading, Passion, and the Creation of M. Carey Thomas," *The Journal of American History* 79 (June 1992): 68–95; Martha Vicinus, "What Makes a Heroine? Nineteenth-Century Girls' Biographies," *Genre* 20 (summer 1987): 171–80.

social activism that is so closely associated with nineteenth-century American life. Addams's mother had died when Jane was two years old. Jane was lovingly cared for by her older sister, Mary, until the age of eight when Senator Addams married Anna Haldeman, a widow from Freeport. This turn of events gave Jane Addams a volatile stepmother with aristocratic pretensions who could teach Jane about fashion, deportment, music, poetry, and parlor games but could not teach her about the female culture of community service. Anna Haldeman Addams was not one of the nineteenth-century's club women; she preferred home decorating to visiting the poor and was not liked well enough in the town of Cedarville to join the village's church women in any social reform activity.

When the ambitious young Jane Addams looked around for examples of female achievement, she saw her stepmother and Miss Sill of Rockford, both strong, assertive women who incongruously preached female submissiveness. She also saw her cowed and cloistered teachers at Rockford, who enjoyed a religious faith and scholarly devotion that Jane could not share. It is little wonder that she turned for inspiration to the apparent freedom and excitement offered by the male model of heroic stewardship. Her plan, upon graduating from Rockford Female Seminary in 1881, was to go on for a bachelor's degree from Smith College in Massachusetts and to proceed from there to medical school, undoubtedly hoping that formal status as a physician would guarantee her a position of influence and respect in her community.

Jane Addams did not pursue these post-seminary plans because her father died, very suddenly, just six weeks after Jane delivered her valedictory address at Rockford. This cataclysmic event had two, related, results in Addams's life: first, she had lost the one adult to whom she looked for guidance and support; second, she was now expected to be the "companion" to her needy stepmother, Anna. It is quite possible that, had John Addams lived, he and his youngest daughter would have run into conflict over her ambition for a nontraditional, nondomestic life. Letters written at the time do not indicate, however, that such conflict had yet arisen. For example, Jane's brother-in-law, the Reverend John Linn, commiserated with the great loss Jane felt precisely because "your life aims were high enough and your plans broad enough so that he could take an interest in them, and it was his great delight to prepare you for your mission."[6] Just how that very loving but paternalistic father and his

---

[6]The Rev. John Linn to Jane Addams, 26 August 1881. Swarthmore College Peace Collection.

ambitious daughter would have designed her "mission" together can never be known.

What is known is that Jane Addams spent the eight years following her father's death traveling with her stepmother through Europe, spending winters in Baltimore with her stepmother and stepbrother, George, attending to a series of family crises in her siblings' households, and coping with a recurrent back ailment and the various stress-induced illnesses that typically accompany boredom and self-doubt. As Addams herself admitted at the end of chapter 3 of *Twenty Years at Hull-House,* "During most of that time I was absolutely at sea so far as any moral purpose was concerned, clinging only to the desire to live in a really living world and refusing to be content with a shadowy intellectual or aesthetic reflection of it" (p. 68). A brief attempt at medical school in Philadelphia failed, in part because Addams's heart was not in it, in part because her responsibilities as Anna's companion divided her attention and loyalties. Addams enjoyed her few forays into charity work during these years, noticing that she felt less tired at the end of a day working with the poor than at the end of a day touring art galleries or making social calls. But obligations to what Addams would later call "the family claim" prevented her from making any commitment to what she would also later call "the social claim," and Carlyle's theories of heroic individualism provided no guidance on how a young woman could resolve the conflict.

The story might have ended there and Jane Addams might have disappeared from history as just another maiden dutifully sacrificing herself to her widowed mother and demanding siblings. That it did not end there is a testament to Addams's drive and intelligence as well as to the importance of her friendship with Ellen Gates Starr. During the eight difficult years between 1881, when her father died, and 1889, when she and Starr opened Hull-House, Addams slowly revised her identity and her ideology and gradually moved toward a life plan. Through observation, thought, reading, and experience Addams confronted the inequities of class and gender and concluded that individuals' destinies are constructed as much by social roles and expectations as by personal heroism. She began to replace Ruskin and Carlyle with authors like John Stuart Mill and Count Leo Tolstoy, both of whom advocated democratic methods in social action and opposed elite stewardship. Gradually, Addams came to see a connection between the poor in London's East End and privileged, educated young women like herself; both were prevented from realizing their potential by laws and customs that no heroic individual could overcome all on her own. Ultimately, she sought to resolve the conflicts in her life by imagining harmony and mutuality in the larger scheme of things. Addams postulated that idle, overeducated daughters like herself could escape the strictures of sexism and elitism by devoting themselves to the needs of the poor. Both parties would benefit, she surmised, and their daily, practical efforts would demonstrate that mutuality and cooperation were more effective than heroic individualism in reforming social life.

That Addams could feel excited, even original, in pondering this solution for herself and other young women indicates just how far removed she had been from contemporary female culture. It was hardly original to propose, in the late 1880s, that privileged, educated daughters engage in philanthropic work. What was original in Addams's thinking — and what proved to be most notable — was the assertion that such work had mutual benefits, that in joint ventures the poor were helping the rich as much as the rich were helping the poor. What was also original, at least in the United States, and certainly for females, was the notion that such mutual benefits could be realized best by actually moving into the neighborhoods of the poor and working classes. This was not an undertaking that a young woman, even one as determined as Jane Addams, could manage on her own.

Throughout the difficult years following her father's death, Addams was blessed with the friendship of Ellen Gates Starr. Starr had attended Rockford Female Seminary, but family finances had forced her to leave long before graduation and start work as a teacher in Chicago. She was Addams's primary confidante in these years, and the person who most encouraged Addams not to abandon her dreams of satisfying work outside the family. Indeed, it was Starr who first imagined that the two women might devise work they could do together. And because Starr was a Christian and came from a family that encouraged democratic involvement in the "social claim," she was well positioned to applaud Addams's progress toward a more communitarian and democratic philosophy. Addams matter-of-factly reported to her relatives about observing poor workers in Europe, engaging in charity work in Baltimore, and attending a bullfight in Madrid. But it was with Starr that Addams explored the significance of these experiences and came to the conclusion, in 1887, that it was not as a heroic individual presuming to study or lead others, but as an equal member of a community of workers, that Addams felt most a part of real life and most physically and emotionally vigorous.

On her second tour of Europe, a trip she made with Starr, Addams encountered Samuel and Henrietta Barnett and their Toynbee Hall Settlement House in London. That meeting in June of 1888 helped to focus her developing ideas about mutuality in work with the poor. Samuel Barnett was an Anglican clergyman, but Toynbee Hall was not an evangelical mission. Instead, it brought college-educated men from Oxford and

Cambridge into London's East End to live as settlement house "residents" and engage in direct, practical ways with poor and working-class neighbors. These residents were every bit as sheltered and overeducated as Addams then imagined herself to be. They, too, were being humbled through direct experience and made to see that individualism alone would not solve society's problems, that collective efforts were needed. When Addams visited Toynbee Hall, her ideas had so evolved that she could be responsive to what she saw there, and her imagination was so active that she could adapt the Barnetts' rather elitist British style to America's (and, by then, her own) democratic leanings.

A full year elapsed between the time Jane Addams and Ellen Gates Starr, travelling together in Europe, hatched the "scheme" to open a settlement house in Chicago and their actual move to a real house in the city. During that year, Addams joined the Presbyterian Church. As she noted in *Twenty Years at Hull-House,* this act was not occasioned by a conversion experience but by a new philosophical affinity for the democratic and communitarian aspects of Jesus' preaching; she identified herself by then with "the many" against the "privileged few." Also during this year, Addams extricated herself from her family and announced her intention to move with Ellen Starr to Chicago. Because her "autobiographical notes" are silent on this point, readers are left to imagine how Addams faced down her family's disdainful opposition to her Chicago scheme. There was no patriarch to forbid this undertaking, and her paternal inheritance of nearly $60,000 gave her the financial independence to launch it, if not sustain it, on her own. But later letters between family members make clear that when Jane Addams proposed moving to Chicago to live among the poor (and take Mary Keyser, the family housekeeper, with her), Addams's stepmother and stepbrothers scoffed at the whole idea. They felt at once betrayed, insulted, and threatened by this bold act of independence by the family's twenty-nine-year-old spinster. Ellen Gates Starr was of inestimable importance in fortifying Addams's courage to wrench herself away from what she later called the "family claim" during this difficult year of leave-taking. Starr's faith in their "scheme" to open a settlement inspired Addams to declare that, together, they would "work out a salvation."[7]

---

[7] Jane Addams to Ellen Gates Starr, 24 January 1889. Ellen Gates Starr Papers, Smith College Archives. For indications of familial disdain for Jane Addams's work in Chicago, see Harry Haldeman to Anna Haldeman Addams and George Haldeman, 26 June 1893; Harry Haldeman to Anna Haldeman Addams, 20 May 1894; Anna Haldeman Addams to Harry Haldeman, 10 September 1895. Haldeman-Julius Collection, Lilly Library, Indiana University.

THE NATURE AND PURPOSE OF MEMOIR

Readers of *Twenty Years at Hull-House* are often disconcerted to learn that the "autobiographical notes" Jane Addams provides do not fit precisely with the life record her biographers have been able to reconstruct. On some points, the difference is technical: Addams suggests her father was a Quaker when, in fact, he was not; she says she wanted to attend Smith College in 1877 when, in fact, she did not plan for that until 1880; she claims that the idea of having Rockford Female Seminary grant bachelor's degrees originated with the students, but it had been Miss Sill's goal for many years and was actually an idea Addams initially resisted because she hoped for a bachelor's degree from Smith; she says she joined the Presbyterian Church when she was 25 years old but actually joined when she was 28; and, finally, Addams reports on trying opium while at the seminary and, as a student, debating William Jennings Bryan. The unsubstantiated opium story is highly doubtful given the overwhelming evidence that Addams was, as she herself says, "a girl of serious not to say priggish tendency" and far more likely to lecture her classmates on strict study habits than to engage in dormitory parties (p. 61). And the debate story is, at the very least, challenged by newspaper reports at the time showing that Addams attended the debate tournament at Illinois College strictly as an observer — and a tardy one at that — while Bryan served solely as the chair of local arrangements.[8]

On other points of difference between Addams's autobiographical notes and the biographical record, her omissions and silences are intriguing. Though her stepmother, Anna Haldeman Addams, was a very important person in her life, Jane Addams mentioned only her father's

---

[8] The judgment that Addams did not experiment with opium while at Rockford is based, in part, on the fact that she typically wrote to Ellen Gates Starr about meaningful, interesting experiences on campus, and there is no mention of an opium experience in the surviving correspondence. There are, however, indications that Addams set herself a bit apart from dorm room parties, and every aspect of her seminary writings and correspondence shows her to be a young woman who fancied herself too sensible to engage in youthful escapades.

For tangible confirmation that Jane Addams attended the debate competition in Jacksonville as an observer, not a debater, and that William Jennings Bryan also did not participate in the debate, see Jane Addams to John Huy Addams, 8 May 1881, in which she explains to her father why Miss Sill allowed her to attend. Jane Addams Memorial Collection, University of Illinois, Chicago. See, too, "Home Items," *Rockford Seminary Magazine* 9 (June 1881): 173; "Inter-State Extra," *The College Rambler,* Illinois College student newspaper, Jacksonville, Illinois, 7 May 1881. According to the *College Rambler* report, "Rockford Seminary was represented at the Inter-State by Miss Addams and Miss Wells, both members of the staff of the Rockford Seminary Magazine. They arrived Wednesday evening at 9:00 — in time to hear only part of the [debate] contest."

"second marriage" in her "autobiographical notes," never providing Anna's name or details of her character or their relationship. Similarly, she never mentioned Anna Peck Sill in her chapter on Rockford Female Seminary. And though she referred to her "stepbrother" in chapter 1, she never explained her relationship to George Haldeman, Anna's youngest son, and gave no indication of the existence of her older stepbrother, Harry Haldeman. Readers of *Twenty Years at Hull-House* do not learn that at the time of the book's publication Addams was estranged from her stepmother, that Anna was then grieving over George's recent death, or that Anna blamed George's depressed life as a recluse and his demise at age 49 on Jane's youthful refusal to marry him. They do not learn that Jane's older sister, Alice, had married George's older brother, Harry, or that it was actually Harry who was the "agent" who so "horrified" Addams in chapter 4 by investing her inheritance in mortgages on "wretched" hog farms, or that Harry had drunk himself into an early grave in 1905. Nor do readers learn that Jane's older brother, Weber, spent portions of his delusional adult life in a mental institution, or that the death of Jane's beloved sister, Mary, in 1894 meant that Addams herself, the unmarried head resident of America's leading settlement house, assumed a good bit of maternal responsibility for four children. Finally, Addams made only the most cursory references to Ellen Gates Starr, the woman who had intended to be Jane Addams's partner for life, and was equally brief and casual in her references to Mary Rozet Smith, the woman who actually was Addams's life partner.

Beyond these fascinating omissions of important individuals in her life, there is Addams's equally fascinating depiction of herself in *Twenty Years at Hull-House* as a lifelong democrat. Rather than show her readers her gradual, at times difficult, evolution from an ideology of elite stewardship to one of democratic partnership, Addams painted herself as a person committed from childhood to egalitarian, communitarian relations. She did reveal her self-doubts as a young woman and her confusion about a life course, and did trace her postseminary shift from literary and artistic interests to social and economic ones, a shift that was an important part of her transformation. But the young woman Addams recalled in the pages of *Twenty Years at Hull-House* is a curious construction. In chapter 3, Addams simultaneously mocked her intense scholarship at Rockford as mere "boarding school ideals" while also depicting herself as more of a campaigner for "women's rights" than she was. And in chapter 4, she used the phrase "snare of preparation" as the title in order to align herself with Leo Tolstoy's disdain for spoiled, selfish snobs who waste their youth studying instead of serving, but then she omitted any record of the very real services she was performing for her family and failed to trace the serious ideological changes she underwent while endeavoring to "learn something of the mystery and complexity of life's purposes" (p. 67).

There are several plausible explanations for the gaps between Addams's autobiographical notes and the biographical record. The act of remembering is in itself a hurdle. All those who engage in writing memoirs find it taxing to recall exactly what they were doing at a particular moment, and even more difficult to remember just what they were thinking or feeling about it. As a result, memories are inevitably constructions; they do not come to us in whole strings like a reel of film; rather, they come to us as pieces of a puzzle that we must fit together, knowing that pieces are missing and that the fit is approximate at best. The act of memory construction is then influenced by emotional and cognitive factors. In Addams's case, we must consider her lifelong tendency to ignore, if not forget, unpleasant aspects of her life. This emotional style became part of her political identity as a positive, generous person who did not attack enemies. Keeping in mind that Addams's conscious purpose in writing *Twenty Years at Hull-House* was to mount a positive, persuasive argument for her progressive ideals and to highlight the settlement house movement's civic achievements, it is not surprising that she chose to glide past family conflicts and avoid negative remarks about her stepmother or her Rockford headmistress, Anna Peck Sill.

Moreover, given the fact that Jane Addams had attained, by 1910, a level of national influence and visibility in American life heretofore unknown for a female, it makes sense to find her legitimizing her nontraditional public work with references to two unassailable and masculine inspirations: her father and Abraham Lincoln. That is not to say that when Addams was writing *Twenty Years at Hull-House* she did not actually feel strong attachments to both of these men. It is to say that she could have chosen to tell her story as a bitter rejection of her stepmother and Miss Sill — or as an ideological rejection of John Ruskin and Thomas Carlyle — but that is not the way she arranged the pieces of the puzzle. Instead, as she wrote on the first page of the memoir, "it is quite impossible to set forth all of one's early impressions," so she consciously chose to "string these first memories on that single cord" of her positive experiences with her father and his leader, Abraham Lincoln (p. 43). It is possible that Addams fabricated her fond memories of her father in order to provide herself a legitimizing male mentor; it is possible that she saw her father when she looked at industrial tyrants like George Pullman. But nothing in her correspondence suggests such feelings.

The absence of negative remarks about her father combined with her adult claim in an unpublished letter that "the predominate elements" of her character had come from her father suggest that Addams's choice to focus on her father in the "autobiographical notes" for *Twenty Years at Hull-House* reflects a sincere desire to pay tribute to a man who took her adolescent ambitions and ideas seriously — and who died before conflict over her adult plans could emerge.[9]

But why did Addams not go into more detail about her transformation from elitism to egalitarianism? It is possible that she went into as much detail as she remembered. It is possible that her self-mockery in chapters 3 and 4 represents the important pieces of her memory of herself as a silly, snobbish girl who knew little of real life. It is also possible that Jane Addams was revealing a very important fact about herself as a story-teller when she wrote on the first page of this memoir that it was "simpler" to tell the story as she did. Perhaps she trimmed many of the messy details because trimming made a better, clearer story. It is equally possible that, in her memory, she endowed both herself and her father with a more democratic outlook than they likely shared in the 1870s. Psychologists tell us that people tend to remember their past in ways that are consistent with their current self-image. In her late forties, when she was writing *Twenty Years at Hull-House,* Jane Addams had a firm identity as a democratic communitarian. This meant that she lived her daily life in the conviction that service to the community was the highest purpose and the greatest joy to be derived from the freedom and individuality afforded by democracy. Further, she believed that community service that empowered the participants was vital to a democracy and more appropriate than philanthropic efforts in which some participants overpowered others. Since her conscious motive in writing *Twenty Years at Hull-House* was to inspire these beliefs in others and write a simple, clear story in the process, and since her unconscious inclination was to see her past as consistent with her present, Addams quite understandably crafted a memoir of her childhood and youth that suggested that she had been a democratic communitarian all her life. As soon as the book moves beyond the personal stories of her development before moving to Chicago, however, and begins to discuss her life in the Hull-House Settlement, it becomes clear that Addams knew how fragile her early grasp of democratic methods and egalitarian approaches was. It was in the liv-

---

[9] In 1925, Jane Addams received an inquiry from a James W. Fawcett about her "heredity." She responded with a rather terse reply written on the letter sent to her. James W. Fawcett to Jane Addams, 9 November 1925. University of Virginia Library, James Waldo Fawcett Collection, Item No. 9831.

ing of her life in Chicago that Addams fully and finally became the Progressive she liked to think her father had raised.

TWENTY YEARS AT HULL-HOUSE IN PLACE AND TIME

The Chicago that Jane Addams and Ellen Gates Starr moved to in August of 1889 was a booming, brawling windbag of a city. "The city of the big shoulders," the poet Carl Sandburg called it. The city "first in violence, deepest in dirt; loud, lawless, unlovely, ill-smelling, irreverent . . . the 'tough' among cities," was the rather less poetic image conjured by the journalist Lincoln Steffens.[10] Chicago's explosion in size after the Civil War was unmatched in the United States. In the three decades before Addams's arrival, it had grown from 100,000 people to more than a million, and in the two decades covered in her memoir, Chicago would grow again — to more than two million — becoming the second largest city in the nation. Easterners loved to scoff at the raw, upstart town on Lake Michigan, but in the same month that Addams opened Hull-House, Chicago's civic leaders launched their successful campaign to win the national competition as the site for the World's Columbian Exposition, celebrating the 400th anniversary of Columbus' voyage to the Americas. Chicago's victory in that contest, shocking though it was to New Yorkers, marked the midwest city's "arrival" as an economic, cultural, and political entity.

The contrast between the extravagant Great White City that the Columbian Exposition Committee constructed on 800 acres of lakefront between 1890 and 1893 and the dirty, neglected streets that Jane Addams confronted in the Nineteenth Ward, just ten miles to the northwest, neatly captures the span of conditions that grew up with Chicago. On the one hand, the Chicago Addams experienced between 1890 and 1910 was a city of tremendous wealth, industrial and civic energy, economic and political opportunity, and even cultural and artistic pride. On the other hand, her Chicago, like all major U.S. cities of the time, was a place where industrial and commercial growth had far outpaced any sort of city planning, where the prosperity of a few rested on the poverty of many, and where access to the city's opportunities was denied to hundreds of thousands.[11]

---

[10] Carl Sandburg, "Chicago," in *Chicago Poems* (New York: Henry Holt, 1916), 3–4; Lincoln Steffans, *The Shame of the Cities* (1904. Reprint, New York: Hill & Wang, 1967), 163.

[11] For descriptions of Chicago in this era, see Donald L. Miller, *City of the Century: The Epic of Chicago and the Making of America* (New York: Touchstone Books, Simon & Schus-

The need for civic action in Chicago between 1890 and 1910 was considerable. As was true of every other American city at this time, the expansion of Chicago's population and industrial base had not been matched by a commensurate expansion in city services. Wealth in the city had expanded, but there persisted among the elite a very narrow image of who had created that wealth and who should benefit from it. The city's business titans had made Chicago the hub of an unprecedented railway system that spanned the continent, as well as making it the meat-packing center of the world and the financial capital of the Midwest. Still, many of Chicago's residents lacked sanitation services, their water supply spawned regular outbreaks of typhoid fever, their streets often resembled sewers — or rivers — and their housing, though more dispersed than New York's, was just as likely to be dilapidated and overcrowded. More than 600 people a year were killed or maimed by the railcars crisscrossing the city, and conditions in the meat-packing industry were so bad that after Upton Sinclair exposed them in his 1905 novel *The Jungle,* the federal government passed its first Meat Inspection Act.

Alongside concerns for the general welfare of citizens and consumers were the very particular concerns of workers. Like workers elsewhere in the United States in 1890, workers in Chicago were not protected by regulations controlling factory conditions, wages, or hours of work. Between the time Jane Addams was a child in Cedarville in 1870 and her arrival in Chicago at the end of 1889, the percentage of the world's manufactured goods coming from U.S. industry had increased from less than one-quarter to nearly one-third. The wealth accompanying this increased production was maldistributed, however. Statistics from the era are not precise, but estimates available on the 1890s indicate that the top 10 percent of the people owned 73 percent of the nation's wealth. At the same time, only about 45 percent of U.S. industrial workers earned an annual income above the poverty line of $500 per year for a family of four. The majority of Addams's neighbors around Hull-House earned well below $500 in a year because family members were ill or disabled, and those who could work often took jobs that were seasonal, unstable, or temporary.[12]

---

ter, Inc., 1997); Carl Smith, *Urban Disorder and the Shape of Belief* (Chicago: The University of Chicago Press, 1995); Melvin G. Holli and Peter d'A. Jones, *Ethnic Chicago: A Multicultural Portrait* (Grand Rapids, Mich.: William B. Eerdmans Publishing Company, 1995); Harold M. Mayer and Richard C. Wade (Chicago: University of Chicago Press, 1969); Carl Smith, *Chicago and the American Literary Imagination, 1880–1920* (Chicago: University of Chicago Press, 1984).

[12] For general descriptions of wealth and income distribution in the United States in these years, see Paul Boyer, et. al., *The Enduring Vision: A History of the American People.* vol. 2, 3rd ed. (Lexington, Mass., 1996): 582, 592.

Despite the vagaries of work in America's late nineteenth-century industrial cities, people swarmed to them, especially to Chicago, because there were jobs — in the meat-packing industry, the garment industry, and the sweatshops; at the groceries, the bakeries, the delicatessens, and the restaurants; with the Montgomery Ward or Sears Roebuck mail-order warehouses; at Illinois Steel or the McCormick Reaper Works (later International Harvester); on the railroads and in the machine shops. A newcomer to the city might even get a job in one of the fancy department stores or banks or corporate offices — if he had a high school degree or her accent was muted and her clothing "smart."

Jane Addams arrived in Chicago at a time of extraordinary movement, all over the map and all up, and down, the economic ladder. The Chicago she encountered was a city in flux. Not only was the population growing rapidly, it was also moving around and expanding the city's borders. Chicago's extensive network of railroads, cable cars, and electric railway cars made it possible for people, even those of modest means, to live in the "suburbs" being developed beyond the downtown, thereby leaving the inner city to business, industry, and those without the means to move out. The reason Addams was initially able to rent the Hull family's large house for so little money was that the fashionable set had moved from the West Side to Lakeshore Drive, abandoning Halsted Street to struggling newcomers from midwestern farms and Europe. Between 1880 and 1920, more than twenty-three million Europeans came to the United States as part of a global migration trend; by the time Jane Addams settled in Chicago in 1890, more than three-quarters of its residents were foreign-born or children of the foreign-born.

As Addams was quick to learn, the largely ethnic neighborhood around Hull-House represented a far more complex picture of poverty than her relatively privileged experience had led her to expect. Neither a stagnant site for the permanently poor nor a cheerful village for the upwardly mobile, the community Addams chose for her settlement combined genuine paupers — those so broken by illness, alcohol, or bad luck that they would never escape — with the working poor — those newcomers to the city who came with enough education, skills, or experience to find a way up and out. No one was getting rich in the Hull-House neighborhood, except Johnny Powers, the ward boss. Hull-House residents reported in 1895 that "the theory that 'every man supports his own family' is as idle in a district like this as the fiction that 'every one can get work if he wants it.'" [13] Still, if all the members of a family worked

---

[13] Agnes Sinclair Holbrook, "Map Notes and Comments," *Hull-House Maps and Papers* (Boston: Thomas Y. Crowell & Co., 1895) p. 21.

(and in these years, almost 20 percent of children between 10 and 15 were employed), if the father did not drink or gamble, if the mother could manage a few boarders and then bargain and trade and scavenge and save, and if no one got terribly sick, the family could eventually move out of the neighborhood and on to better quarters in one of the new working-class suburbs — and many of Jane Addams's neighbors did just that. As a result, the Hull-House neighborhood was an ever-changing kaleidoscope of the working poor, most of whom were foreign-born.

In *Twenty Years at Hull-House,* Addams mentions the social survey conducted of the neighborhood in 1895. That survey, published as *Hull-House Maps and Papers,* found that twenty-six ethnic groups lived in the thirty blocks nearest to Hull-House, and that only one-quarter of the area's residents had access to a bathroom with running water. The greatest benefit of this social survey was its elaborate, color-coded, pull-out maps showing in one glance that there were concentrations of Italians or Russian Jews or Irish or Germans on certain blocks, but there was also considerable residential integration, with Bohemian families living alongside Polish, English living next to Irish, Dutch living behind French. So multicultural was the Hull-House neighborhood that the survey's publisher, Thomas Y. Crowell, balked at the expense of printing maps whose colors changed from one house to the next and refused to print a second edition. (Indeed, the discerning reader of *Twenty Years at Hull-House* can still pick up Addams's anger over this slight.) In the years following the survey's publication, the neighborhood's dominant ethnic mix would shift from Italian with German, Irish, and Russian to Italian with Greek and Slavic, to Greek with Slavic and Mexican. But the pattern of mobility persisted, and as the neighbors changed, Hull-House changed.

INSIDE HULL-HOUSE

Jane Addams opened Hull-House with the guiding thought that "the social and industrial problems which are engendered by the modern conditions of life in a great city . . . are not confined to any one portion of a city" (p. 95). She defined these problems as "the overaccumulation at one end of society and the destitution at the other" (p. 95). In that one stroke, Addams reconceptualized reform activity as a way of saving the lives of both the rich and the poor. After her eight years "at sea," Addams believed that extreme material inequality was corrosive to every member of a society, especially a society claiming to be a "democracy." At the core of this assertion were her assumptions that a democracy requires participation by all citizens, that dialogue between a variety of citizens is vital to the process, and that all citizens benefit from that dialogue. Toward that end, Addams was convinced that privileged citizens needed to live as "residents" in "settlement houses" in industrial areas in order to engage in daily efforts with their neighbors.

Hull-House was not the first settlement house in the United States. That honor belonged to the Neighborhood Guild of New York City, which a young man named Stanton Coit opened in 1887 after visiting Toynbee Hall in London. But the Neighborhood Guild floundered, later becoming the University Settlement under different leadership. In the meantime, Addams and Starr opened Hull-House in Chicago; shortly thereafter a group of Smith College graduates opened the College Settlement on Rivington Street in New York and a group of male seminarians opened Andover House in Boston. In the subsequent decade of the 1890s, when more and more privileged young people were choosing to devote a few of their post-college years to social service, settlement houses sprouted up in all major and many smaller U.S. cities. The majority of residents in settlement houses were educated women, but a healthy minority were educated men. Most residents stayed two or three years before moving on to a career or marriage; some stayed as long as a decade; others, like Addams and Starr, lived in a settlement house their whole adult lives. Some settlement houses were quite religious, others were determinedly secular; some served only African Americans, others served primarily the foreign born; some provided direct service by way of food, clothing, and health care, others focused on education and recreation, while still others engaged in local political organizing and union activity. Hull-House, it appears, engaged in all of these activities and more. Of the 400 settlement houses in existence in 1910, Hull-House was universally acknowledged as the most prominent and most successful. This says a great deal about Jane Addams's ability to gain respectability for herself and her work in Chicago because Hull-House was actually less tied to religion and more involved in working-class politics, unionizing, and legislative lobbying than the average settlement of the day.[14]

[14]For an enlarged understanding of the settlement house movement and the atmosphere inside settlement houses, see Mina Carson, *Settlement Folk: Social Thought and the American Settlement Movement, 1885–1930* (Chicago: University of Chicago Press, 1990); Kathryn Kish Sklar, *Florence Kelley and the Nation's Work: The Rise of Women's Political Culture, 1830–1900* (New Haven: Yale University Press, 1995); Allen F. Davis, *Spearheads for Reform: The Social Settlements and the Progressive Movement, 1890–1914* (New York: Oxford University Press, 1967); Allen F. Davis and Mary Lynn McCree Bryan, eds., *100 Years at Hull-House* (Bloomington: Indiana University Press, 1990); Mary Jo Deegan, *Jane Addams and the Men of the Chicago School, 1892–1918* (New Brunswick: Transaction Pub-

Like many aspiring settlement house residents, Addams and Starr
had opened Hull-House in the fall of 1889 with the initial intent of sharing their literary and artistic education with the people in the neighborhood. As young women with little experience beyond the classroom, library, and art gallery, they felt ill-prepared for any other sort of service;
however, they wanted to serve and they had seen the success of cultural
classes at Toynbee Hall in London. Fortunately for them, these early offerings in European "high" culture were well received in the neighborhood; the Hull-House classes, readings, and lectures on literature and
art were consistently well attended and were permanent features of the
settlement's regular activities. From that cultural base, the settlement
branched out in two directions. It made some of its courses in literature,
history, social science, and science more sophisticated by offering them
through University of Chicago Extension, bringing professors to the settlement to teach them, and giving college credit to those who enrolled.
At the same time, Hull-House began to offer more basic, practical classes
in English, American government, crafts, cooking, and sewing. This
dual educational program served neighbors who had already received
basic schooling and aspired to higher learning while also serving those
neighbors, especially the foreign born, who actively sought classes that
would prepare them to become U.S. citizens and would enhance their opportunities in the workforce.

In her discussions of cultural classes at Hull-House, as well as in her
discussions of the settlement's clubs, art gallery, and Labor Museum,
Addams spoke to the skeptical reader of 1910, the person who doubted
that ill-paid, ill-clothed foreigners would attend classes on Shakespeare

lisher, 1990); Ruth Hutchinson Crocker, *Social Work and Social Order: The Settlement Movement in Two Industrial Cities, 1889–1930* (Chicago: University of Illinois Press, 1992); Barbara Sicherman, ed., *Alice Hamilton: A Life in Letters* (Cambridge, Mass.: Harvard University Press, 1984). See also Kathryn Kish Sklar, "Hull-House in the 1890s: A Community of Women Reformers," *Signs* 10 (summer 1985): 658–77; Helen Lefkowitz Horowitz, "Varieties of Cultural Experience in Jane Addams's Chicago," *History of Education Quarterly* 14 (spring 1974): 69–86; Helen Lefkowitz Horowitz, "Hull-House as Women's Sphere," *Chicago History* 12 (winter 1983–84): 40–55; Louise C. Wade, "The Social Gospel Impulse and Chicago Settlement-House Founders," *The Chicago Theological Seminary Register* 55 (April 1965): 1–12; Mary Lynn McCree Bryan, "The First Year of Hull-House, 1889–1890, in Letters by Jane Addams and Ellen Gates Starr," *Chicago History* 1 (fall 1970): 101–14.

For contemporary accounts of life in a settlement house, see May Brown Loomis, "The Inner Life of the Settlement," *Arena* 24 (August 1900): 193–97; Jane E. Robbins, "The First Year at the College Settlement," *The Survey* 27 (24 Feb. 1912): 1800–2; Mary B. Sayles, "Settlement Workers and Their Work," *The Outlook* 78 (1 Oct. 1904): 304–11; Dorothea Moore, "A Day at Hull House," *American Journal of Sociology* 2 (March 1897): 629–42; Florence Kelley, "Hull House," *New England Magazine* 18 (July 1898): 550–66.

or opera or American government. Without directly arguing with such skeptics, Addams designed stories to make three strong points. First, that poverty and a lack of education did not render people impervious to artistic beauty; second, that European immigrants, even of peasant background, had had more exposure to European culture than nativist Americans liked to presume — or than America itself provided for its citizens; and, third, that not everyone in Addams's neighborhood was uncultured. In sharp contrast to those who regarded poverty as a permanent character flaw, Addams reminded her readers that even educated people can fall on temporary hard times and the quality of a person's intellect cannot be measured by the size of that person's purse.

Addams used language throughout her book that revealed her unreconstructed affection for people of "the better sort," meaning those of refinement and intellectual attainment. But at the same time she managed to tweak elitist prejudices by telling stories in which the settlement's student neighbors were wiser than the teachers. Indeed, some of her most barbed remarks in *Twenty Years at Hull-House* were pointed at stuffy college professors who did not know how to make their knowledge accessible and interesting to real people. She derived as much pleasure from seeing intellectuals loosen up in the Hull-House parlor as from watching Italian immigrant men recite passages from Homer. In all of these matters related to "high culture" at Hull-House, Addams drew from her postseminary years of self-doubt. During those years she resented her education because it was unrelated to real life, and she feared that it rendered her useless. From that experience, she concluded that people who knew only about art and literature were as limited in their social effectiveness as people who knew only about daily survival. In her mind a democratic, industrial society required that all participants have a working knowledge of both bread and roses; they had to know what material struggle was really like in order to devise realistic solutions to urban problems, and they had to appreciate human artistry in order to imagine solutions that allowed spiritual growth. It was this philosophy that guided the programming of cultural classes at the Hull-House settlement.

The argument for mutual benefits to be derived from cross-class relations was first set forth in chapter 6, "The Subjective Necessity for Social Settlements," which originally appeared in 1893. But Addams did not confine the argument to those early remarks. Laced throughout the pages of *Twenty Years at Hull-House,* tucked between the folds of each little anecdote, hidden behind the self-deprecating remarks, stirred into the little lectures on tolerance for differing ideas was Jane Addams's attempt to convince her largely middle-class readership that there was much to learn from the poor, the foreign-born, and the working class, and that any formally educated person who wished to teach the uneducated had better approach that activity with a readiness to learn as well. She announced in her preface that she meant for her book to challenge those narratives that made "life in a Settlement all too smooth and charming." Addams used two highly effective narrative strategies to achieve this goal: she told numerous stories about her own and other reformers' naive blunders, and she delineated the logic motivating the conduct of the poor.

It is worth noting that in describing herself and her co-residents in *Twenty Years at Hull-House*, Addams often used the word *fatuous,* meaning complacent, foolish, even silly. She wrote that "we fatuously believed" that if boys were interested in explorers they would become interested in statesmen, she said that the residents "fatuously hoped" that a "consciousness of common destiny" would heal the pain of poverty and inspire cooperation, and she remarked that the residents had "felt fatuously secure" that civil service laws protected them from their alderman's corruption. In these passages and numerous others, Addams was mocking her own middle-class naivete and tracing her own continuing education under the tutelage of her immigrant neighbors. It was a disarming tactic, of course, designed to encourage readers to defend her before she had to defend herself, but there was a tough-minded message in the method as well. Implicit in her litany of errors was Addams's rebuke of reformers and philanthropists who fancied that formal education was more valuable than experience when it came to community organizing. The stories in *Twenty Years at Hull-House* about the failure of the cooperative kitchen and of the Coal Association Cooperative, about the death of the shipping clerk Addams had set to work digging the drainage canal, or about the settlement's electoral defeats in city council elections were all meant to tell middle-class readers that they had much to learn about the complexity of lives lived in poverty before they started preaching to the poor. Addams was speaking more than common sense when she wrote, "I learned that life cannot be administered by definite rules and regulations; that wisdom to deal with a man's difficulties comes only through some knowledge of his life and habits as a whole; and that to treat an isolated episode is almost sure to invite blundering" (p. 109). She was delivering a stinging attack on the then-powerful Charity Organization Society and other philanthropic efforts of the day, all of which claimed that scientific methods and business principles should be strictly applied to each and every poverty "case" managed by a charity "visitor."

So, too, when Addams detailed the logic behind an old woman picking plaster off the walls, another old woman clinging to a chest of drawers, a teenage girl committing theft, two boys' clubs at Hull-House getting into a territorial dispute, or a woman taking in the drunken spouse who had abandoned her and her children, she was elbowing aside those who viewed all such behavior among the industrial classes as immoral or irrational. There was little romance in these stories. Addams was perfectly willing to tell about "ugly human traits" and "untoward experiences." But there was also no moralizing and no racializing. She regretted illicit sex and drug use because the consequences were dire. She shook her head over controlling patriarchs — from George Pullman to the Italian father of a child laborer — because they hardened family relations and damaged children. She disdained war toys because they perpetuated militarism. But she never attributed people's unfortunate behavior to inferior racial traits, innate sex differences, or morally depraved natures. At every turn, she showed how such behavior was actually a logical adaptation to a damaging social environment or a desperate attempt to retrieve some measure of humanity from that environment. It was no small thing to make this argument in a society where the rich had, for decades, dismissed the poor as unfit beasts.

In arguing that reformers were ever in need of reform and that the people in her neighborhood were utterly human and utterly logical in their conduct, Addams made the progressive argument that environment, not heredity, was the cause of social problems, and she made the democratic argument that every citizen had not only the right but the capacity to participate in making social policy.

When Addams wrote *Twenty Years at Hull-House,* the United States was just completing a historic decade in which it received almost nine million immigrants, the largest number that has ever been recorded for any one decade in the nation's history. Much of Jane Addams's daily life was absorbed with serving the immigrant population in her neighborhood; she talked at length about immigrants in her description of life in the settlement. It is, therefore, worth noting that *Twenty Years at Hull-House* did not discuss ways to "Americanize" immigrants. There was quite a lively debate in the country at this time over whether immigrants had to abandon their homeland cultures in order to become good Americans. In that debate, Addams aligned herself with those who believed, as she said at the end of chapter 11, "that our American citizenship might be built without disturbing these [cultural] foundations which were laid of old time" (p. 147). In fact, that particular chapter on "Immigrants and Their Children" focused on ways to preserve immigrant cultures and develop American children's appreciation for the skills and experiences their parents and grandparents brought with them from their homelands.[15]

In Addams's experience in Chicago's Nineteenth Ward, Americanization was not something to be imposed on immigrants; rather, it was something they actively sought. She did not have to bribe her immigrant neighbors to take English classes or citizenship classes; she had to scurry around to find teachers and meeting places to meet the demand. The romantic intellectual in Addams worried much more about immigrants being corrupted by American commercialism and the city's nickelodeon culture than about foreign attitudes challenging America's democratic values. When she wrote in chapter 5 and again in chapter 14 about the ward's problems with corrupt politics, Addams did not blame immigrants. She blamed the city's failure to provide adequate public services to all its citizens, regardless of economic class, and saw the opening that failure created for politicians to "sell" votes in exchange for services their constituents should have been receiving in the first place.

Almost 70,000 people lived in the six-block radius of Hull-House around the turn of the century. Of those 70,000, approximately nine thousand neighbors chose to walk through the settlement's doors each week. After twenty years of living in the neighborhood, Addams understood that the programs she and her residents offered would logically attract the more educated, more artistic, more assimilationist, more ambitious, or more politically active members of the adult community. Although the settlement made an honest effort to be responsive to traditional cultural loyalties by giving up on evening clubs that mixed men and women or combined ethnic groups, the Hull-House clubs for specific nationalities of men and women never replaced other ethnic associations in the neighborhood. Traditional loyalties were as strong in the Nineteenth Ward as in other parts of the city and many members of this predominantly Catholic area chose to center their social lives and charitable requests on their parish church and priest. Others turned to the Chicago Hebrew Institute. Still others in the area preferred the fellowship of their labor union, mutual benefit society, or ethnic saloon. Over the years, Addams grew to respect these institutions and to recognize that they provided the various sub-communities with more social orga-

[15] Addams's assumption that immigrants actively and creatively combine their homeland cultures with American culture is echoed in contemporary scholarship on American immigration history. See John Bodnar, *The Transplanted* (Bloomington: Indiana University Press, 1985); Roger Daniels, *Coming to America: A History of Immigration and Ethnicity in American Life* (New York: HarperCollins, 1990). For more on the ethnic groups Jane Addams worked with, see Melvin G. Holli and Peter d'A. Jones, *Ethnic Chicago: A Multicultural Portrait,* 4th ed. (Grand Rapids, Mich.: Wm. B. Eerdmans Publishing Company, 1995).

nization than she had understood when she first settled there and bemoaned the breakdown of "self-government in such a ward." Indeed, within seven years of opening the settlement, one of the Hull-House residents published a study in the *American Journal of Sociology* on "The Social Value of the Saloon," an indication of the ways in which settlement experience could be used to educate elite Americans about the coherence of working-class culture.[16]

Without competing against other vital institutions in the neighborhood, Hull-House met some very particular needs. It was, for one, more responsive to women and children than other local institutions. In her chapter on her "First Days at Hull-House," Addams was anxious to insist that "the Settlement should not be primarily for the children," and an overview of Hull-House programs makes clear that she adhered to this principle. But the children of the neighborhood played an important role in expanding the settlement's agenda beyond cultural offerings and in bringing adults through its doors. It was one thing, for example, to provide a morning kindergarten program, but many of the neighborhood children needed all-day child care; Hull-House quickly provided it. That engendered the trust of many working mothers who might have been skeptical of a "house" run by unmarried Protestant women. In later years, that trust would be rewarded when Hull-House built a beautiful outdoor camp north of Chicago to which it brought groups of children, along with their mothers, for a week of "country club" rest in the steamy midwest summer.

The children's needs and their openness pushed the settlement to expand its site and its programs. The children inspired Addams to build Chicago's first public playground, to hire gymnastics teachers and coaches for sports teams, to provide dances and clubs and music lessons and pageants and lots and lots of theater because, as Addams said, they "would have been dull indeed" if they had not recognized the value of dramatics as a way of involving young people in the settlement. The big band leader Benny Goodman was a boy in the Hull-House neighborhood and took his first clarinet lessons there; so, too, the actor Paul Muni fell in love with drama as a boy at Hull-House. One former Hull-House youngster who became a screenwriter recalled decades later that, even after his family moved out of the neighborhood, his mother put him and his sisters on the streetcar every Saturday morning to go for

---

[16] Jane Addams, "The Objective Value of a Social Settlement," in *Philanthropy and Social Progress,* ed. Henry C. Adams (New York: Thomas Y. Crowell & Co., 1893), 29. Addams reprinted a small portion of this public address as chapter 5 of *Twenty Years at Hull-House.* Ernest C. Moore, "The Social Value of the Saloon," *American Journal of Sociology* 3 (July 1897): 1–12.

their drama and music lessons at the settlement. Another former member of a tough, teenage Italian gang — gazing out the window of his comfortable lakefront apartment in the early 1990s — recalled that it was the basketball coach at Hull-House who in the 1920s turned his life around.

Hull-House won the loyalty of many neighborhood mothers because of the opportunities it gave their children — and because Miss Addams (as she was always called) shared the mothers' concern about the corruption lurking in dance halls, movie theaters, and pool halls. Civil libertarian though she was, Addams made no apologies for wanting to limit young people's access to such head-turning amusements. Nor did she apologize for offending public sensibilities by openly discussing the sexual exploitation of working girls or the cocaine habits of street urchins. In these campaigns, Addams was perceived by local mothers as their champion. So while the women of the neighborhood utterly rejected the settlement's effort to replace home cooking with a "public kitchen," they happily embraced the provision of public baths and regarded domestic science classes as a valuable opportunity to learn about the dangers of contaminated urban foods, how to buy and prepare American cuts of meat, and how to cook on American-style stoves.

The weekly schedules Hull-House published in its first decades make clear the daily pace that had been established within just a few years of the settlement's opening. Mornings and early afternoons were given over to kindergarten, child care, a few club meetings for women in the neighborhood, perhaps a residents' meeting in the coffeehouse, an English class for newcomers, a labor bureau for those seeking jobs, and time in the Labor Museum for older practitioners of folk crafts. Between the time school let out and dinners were served around the neighborhood, children crowded into the settlement, playing on the playground, taking classes, participating in various club meetings. Teenagers stayed around into the evening for dance and theater and club meetings. They were then joined by workers who went to Hull-House for union meetings, English classes, American naturalization classes, ethnic club meetings, their own theatrical and musical rehearsals, or University Extension classes.

If the neighborhood's immigrants, women, and children pressed Hull-House to provide livelier and more practical programs, the economic depression of 1893–94 pushed it to offer more politicized ones. Ironically, the full impact of the depression (which had begun in 1892) did not hit Chicago until after the summer of 1893 and the closing of the Columbian Exposition. Once again, the city was reminded of the stark contrast between prosperity and poverty. By the winter of that year, the city was home to 200 millionaires and 200,000 unemployed workers. Across America, there was a 20 percent unemployment rate, banks and businesses were failing, hunger and homelessness were common. One Chicago reporter wrote that he had "seen more misery this week than I ever saw in my life before."[17] Although the chapters on settlement experiences in *Twenty Years at Hull-House* were not written as a chronological narrative, it is possible to trace the effect of the depression on Addams in "The Problems of Poverty," "A Decade of Economic Discussion," "Pioneer Labor Legislation," and "Tolstoyism." Laid down between the lines of these chapters is the saga of Jane Addams's struggle to decide whether, in the face of "desperate hunger and need," her settlement programs were anything but "futile" and "superficial."

Addams had never intended Hull-House to provide direct services; she believed that it was better to teach a man to fish than to give him a fish. But the stark contrast between her economic security and her neighbors' desperation in the winter of 1893–94 shook that belief. In those months, the residents at Hull-House did feed the hungry and house the homeless and nurse the sick and bury the dead. Residents like Florence Kelley argued against this use of residents' time and energy; she believed the settlement should concentrate on organizing workers and voters to change the nation's social and economic policies. But residents like Julia Lathrop insisted that the settlement would have no credibility with its neighbors (and, hence, no one to organize) if residents did not provide direct aid in a crisis. Characteristically, Addams agreed with both of her colleagues. But in chapter 12 of *Twenty Years at Hull-House,* Addams explained why, in the aftermath of the depression of 1893–94, she followed Florence Kelley's desire to organize, unionize, lobby, and legislate. That chapter presented a gently damning description of Tolstoy as a self-important purist more interested in saving his own soul than meeting "the demand of actual and pressing human wants" (p. 152). In thus critiquing a man who had been instrumental in democratizing her own thinking in the 1880s, Addams claimed her own authority to argue that collective political action was ultimately more responsive to "human wants" than virtuously baking one's own bread.

As a result of the economic exigencies in the early 1890s, Hull-House opened its doors to groups who could find no other place to meet: women's labor unions, men's socialist and anarchist debate clubs, and local political activists wishing to challenge the ward boss. This political

---

[17] John Mack Faragher, et. al., *Out of Many: A History of the American People,* vol. 2, 2nd ed. (Upper Saddle River, N.J.: Prentice-Hall, 1997), 628. See also Miller, *City of the Century,* chap. 15, "After the Fair."

activity scared off some of the more cautious, conservative members of the immediate community, but served at the same time to bring in Chicagoans from around the city who were attracted by the settlement's growing reputation as a center of political and social innovation. In this context, Addams's description of the settlement house as an "information and interpretation bureau" (p. 110) can be read two ways: Hull-House was certainly a vehicle through which its neighbors learned about the city beyond the Nineteenth Ward, but it was more vital as a medium for explaining the people of the ward to the wider community and rallying that community to action.

At the heart of much of the creative social policy associated with Hull-House lay the settlement's residents and volunteers. At various points in time, the settlement housed between twenty and fifty "residents." These individuals — about three-quarters of whom were women — had attended college and then moved into the settlement and set about to find or create productive pursuits in the community. Some worked for pay during the day and taught classes or ran clubs at the settlement after work; others were able to devote full time to organizing the Hull-House labor bureau or the Immigrants' Protective Association or to meeting with influential members of the community to set up the nation's first Juvenile Court. Some, like Florence Kelley, parlayed investigative work on the lives of Chicago factory workers into a government job as a factory inspector. Others, like Julia Lathrop and Grace Abbott, used their base at the settlement to lobby the state for better services for immigrants, orphans, the handicapped, and the insane. In all of these endeavors, the residents were assisted greatly by the efforts and the community contacts provided by Hull-House "volunteers." These tended to be wealthy women from the best neighborhoods of Chicago who traveled to Hull-House in private carriages or automobiles to teach classes, run meetings, supervise children's play, or gather data on housing and sanitation in the neighborhood.

Jane Addams herself taught virtually none of the classes at the settlement, only popped in on club gatherings from time to time, and probably participated most regularly in the union and political meetings. Her very long days were filled with correspondence and, later, phone calls, as well as meetings at the settlement and in the city, and private conferences with residents about their separate undertakings in the neighborhood. By 1910, when *Twenty Years at Hull-House* was published, her job as "head resident" of Hull-House meant that it was up to Addams to oversee expansion of the operation, to maintain ties with influential supporters in the city and around the country, to "lobby" on behalf of individuals and programs in the offices of various officials, and to coordinate her efforts with those of Chicago's thirty-four other settlement houses and other progressive organizations. It also fell to Addams, because she was so supremely good at it, to ensure Hull-House's visibility in public life by writing speeches and magazine articles and attending luncheons and dinners and going on speaking tours.

Visibility had two purposes: to persuade people to subscribe to her progressive philosophy and to ensure the settlement a reliable base of financial donors. Addams noted in *Twenty Years at Hull-House* that the settlement was "often bitterly pressed for money," and it was certainly the case that Addams's own inheritance quickly disappeared into early expenditures on the enterprise. She made clear, as well, that she was vigilant about accepting money which might compromise her independence or her ethics. What Addams did not make clear was the extent to which financial backing for Hull-House buildings and programs was provided by a handful of very wealthy, very devoted, very progressive women in Chicago. As Hull-House expanded from one rundown private home to thirteen substantial brick buildings, the bulk of its growth was funded by two of Addams's closest friends: Louise deKoven Bowen and Mary Rozet Smith. Other important donors were Helen Culver, the original owner of the Hull mansion, and Anita McCormick Blaine, the most progressive member of the McCormick Reaper family. It is clear from the record of donations to Hull-House that Jane Addams stood at the center of the interests and activities of the city's elite, reform-minded women.[18]

As head resident, Addams's position was similarly central within Hull-House which, according to one former resident, "was not an institution over which Miss Addams presided; it was Miss Addams around whom an institution insisted on clustering."[19] She was a charismatic leader who, according to one settlement scholar, used "the power of personality to impart internal coherence" to Hull-House.[20] All residents were obliged to attend house meetings and share basic duties, including housework, playground supervision, and receiving all visitors who came through the front door. Beyond that, however, Addams allowed residents to find or invent their own activities in the neighborhood and to

[18] Kathryn Kish Sklar, "Who Funded Hull-House?" in Kathleen McCarthy, ed., *Women and Philanthropy: Three Strategies in Historical Perspective* (New York: Graduate School and University Center, CUNY, 1994).

[19] Francis Hackett, "Hull-House—A Souvenir," *The Survey* 54 (1 June 1925): 275–80.

[20] Mina Carson, *Settlement Folk: Social Thought and the American Settlement Movement, 1885–1930* (Chicago: University of Chicago Press, 1990), 88.

pursue those activities on their own unless or until they ran into trouble. Ironically, this style made Addams the least formally directive of the head residents in U.S. settlement houses, but it also meant that those who would "survive" their probationary period at Hull-House had to be the "fittest." If new residents were independent, energetic, and innovative, the veteran residents would vote to have them stay on. If new residents proved to be timid or unimaginative or sanctimonious, they would be asked to leave. At no point during Addams's tenure as head resident did the settlement bring working-class, foreign-born neighbors on to the staff as residents, a fact which delineates the limits to Addams's democratic zeal. Instead, there evolved a settlement house made up of vigorous, middle-class, educated social activists who were enthusiastic about their reform mission and utterly dedicated to Miss Addams.

Over time, power in the settlement emerged in a pattern of concentric circles; there were certain women — notably Julia Lathrop, Florence Kelley, Alice Hamilton, and Grace Abbott — who were closest to Miss Addams and, as part of the inner circle, most influential in deciding the direction of the settlement's activities. Beyond the inner circle were the younger or less aggressive residents who lobbied for their pet projects by gaining the ear of a resident from the inner circle. Ellen Gates Starr, Addams's partner in starting Hull-House, remained a resident for most of her life but functioned very independently after personal and political differences cooled relations between the two women. At all times, Jane Addams was at the center of Hull-House, probably imagining that she presided over a democratic collective and probably denying the personal power she wielded.[21]

Addams took obvious pride in *Twenty Years at Hull-House* in the "companionship of mutual interests" which grew up among residents and the way in which they became "solidly united through our mutual experience" (pp. 105, 121). Addams created this climate of mutuality by never flatly asserting the authority she so clearly possessed. Her style throughout the day seems to have been reflected in her style at dinner: Every evening she was in Chicago, Addams sat at the head of one of the several long tables in the Hull-House dining hall and encouraged con-

[21] Robyn Muncy, *Creating a Female Dominion in American Reform 1890–1935* (New York: Oxford University Press, 1991); Louise W. Knight, "Jane Addams and Hull House: Historical Lessons on Nonprofit Leadership," *Nonprofit Management and Leadership* 2 (winter 1991), 125–41. See also Carson, *Settlement Folk*, chap. 5, "Leaders and Followers," and Sklar, *Florence Kelley: The Rise and Fall of Women's Political Culture, 1830–1900* (New Haven: Yale University Press, 1995), chap. 8, "'A Colony of Efficient and Intelligent Women.'"

versation among the variety of individuals who might, on any given evening, be arrayed there. The philosopher John Dewey, from the University of Chicago, might be seated next to an aspiring young ballerina just in from Kansas and across from a visiting dignitary from Russia and down the table from a labor organizer from Chicago's north side. In that setting, as in all her dealings around the settlement, Addams's voice would not be the loudest nor her laugh the most boisterous nor her opinions the most extreme. But her patient, encouraging, bemused manner would endow her with such authority that she could enjoy all the power and control she wanted without ever having to assert her position or create formal hierarchies. In her personal conduct as in her writing, Addams managed to project such a charming, self-effacing style that she gained an almost unassailable position of influence in the Progressive Era.

JANE ADDAMS AND THE PROGRESSIVE ERA

Jane Addams stands alongside Teddy Roosevelt and Woodrow Wilson as one of the pillars of the American Progressive Era. Her position in that triumvirate is a useful reminder of two things: First, it reminds us of just how big the "progressive" tent was; a wide variety of people and positions crowded under that political identity in the early twentieth century. Second, Addams's leadership role in the era reflected widespread support for the particular variant of progressivism that she represented; this was a variant that spoke for, not to, those who were excluded from power in the democracy: women, workers, immigrants, blacks, children, and the poor.

Despite the variations in progressives' policies, it is possible to discern basic commonalities in their ideological stances. At its core, Progressivism was a rejection of the Gilded Age belief that human affairs are determined by natural law. Progressives denied that the Darwinian principle of survival of the fittest could be used as a guide to economic, social, or political relationships, and they rejected the Gilded Age's enthusiasm for using profit as the final measure of social and moral worth. Progressives argued, instead, that Darwinian theory actually proved that human beings were so evolved that their lives were not determined by genetics but rather by culture and environment. One's social status, therefore, had as much to do with social opportunity as it did with genetic "fitness." In addition, said the Progressives, the lesson of evolution was not that human beings were governed by fixed natural laws; rather, they were capable of shaping their destinies. Through collective action, humans could consciously construct a social environment that emphasized opportunity, not survival of the fittest, and balanced individual wealth and community health.[22]

In making this argument, progressives drew on two streams of contemporary thought: the Social Gospel and social science. The Social Gospel was a religious movement that tried to shift Christians' focus away from individual salvation and toward social salvation. Advocates of the Social Gospel argued that the best way to serve the individual soul was to reform social, economic, and political practices according to values of love, mercy, and charity. At the same time, enthusiasts for the social science disciplines emerging at this time — especially economics, political science, and sociology — held out the hope that "data" on social life, scientifically collected and analyzed by trained experts, could point the way to the most rational, democratic, and Christian solution to a given social problem. These Progressive beliefs constituted a sharp and powerful retort to the assumptions of laissez-faire capitalism and Social Darwinism. They represented a new generation's refusal to accept the poverty and exploitation resulting from unregulated capitalism and represented, as well, that new generation's optimistic embrace of the possibility of social change through human agency.

Jane Addams was not a convert to the Christian faith, but she did endorse the values of the Social Gospel and aligned herself with the more open-minded leaders of that movement. Neither was she a trained social scientist but she placed great faith in the power of social investigation to enlighten people on social conditions and to mobilize for change in public policy. Hull-House residents were encouraged to engage in sociological studies in the neighborhood, and even though Addams rejected a proposal to become a "sociological laboratory" for the University of Chicago, she worked closely with a number of that institution's leading

---

[22]There is a vast literature on the Progressive Era. This discussion was most informed by Richard L. McCormick, *The Party Period and Public Policy* (New York: Oxford University Press, 1986); Arthur S. Link and Richard L. McCormick, *Progressivism* (Arlington Heights, Ill.: Harlan Davidson, Inc., 1983); Nell Irvin Painter, *Standing at Armageddon: The United States, 1877–1919* (New York: W. W. Norton, 1987); James C. Kloppenberg, *Uncertain Victory: Social Democracy and Progressivism in European and American Thought, 1870–1920* (New York: Oxford University Press, 1986); Stephen Skowronek, *Building a New American State: The Expansion of National Administrative Capacities, 1877–1920* (Cambridge: Cambridge University Press, 1982); Robert C. Wiebe, *The Search for Order, 1877–1920* (New York: Hill & Wang, 1967); David B. Danbom, *"The World of Hope": Progressives and the Struggle for an Ethical Public Life* (Philadelphia: Temple University Press, 1987); Daniel Rodgers, "In Search of Progressivism," *Reviews in American History* 10 (Dec. 1982): 113–32; Peter G. Filene, "An Obituary for 'The Progressive Movement,'" *American Quarterly* 22 (spring 1970): 20–34.

social scientists. The sources of Jane Addams's particular Progressive philosophy stretched beyond the Social Gospel and social science, however. Her thinking was shaped significantly by the political culture that women had developed in American life and shaped, too, by the views of labor activists and socialists.

As a student at Rockford Female Seminary, Addams had recoiled from the feminized charity work extolled by the school's evangelical headmistress. It is quite likely that Addams's stepmother influenced her disdain for do-gooding church women, and just as likely that her beloved father, though on record in support of women's suffrage, expressed a low opinion of women who campaigned too assertively for "rights." During her twenties, Addams had a few positive experiences with female social service; she admired her professors at Woman's Medical College of Pennsylvania and enjoyed her charity work in Baltimore. But the fact of the matter is that Jane Addams — who was to become a central figure in women's political culture in the twentieth century — arrived in Chicago in 1889 with relatively little background in that culture. In Chicago she encountered what was, for her, a whole new breed of female activists. These women represented a political amalgam of the antebellum female moral reformers and women's rights activists; like the former, they believed that citizens in a democracy should consider the common good in all their individual actions and, like the latter, they believed that women should be given a voice in determining the common good. The women Addams met when she first arrived in Chicago were, from her perspective, an impressive lot: educated, married to wealthy men or professionals in their own right, articulate, well-organized, and adept at lobbying for civic improvements. They did not believe that poverty could be eliminated through the salvation of individual souls, nor did they believe that women should win political rights by adopting men's opinions. They did not claim innate female moral superiority, but they did assert without apology that women's domestic responsibilities and practical experiences gave them valuable insight on the social problems plaguing urban, industrial communities. Chicago's particular urban history had created unique opportunities for the city's women to play significant public roles and, especially after the great Chicago fire of 1871, they took full advantage of those opportunities.[23]

[23]There is an extensive body of literature on women's political culture in the Progressive Era. See, for example, Paula Baker, "The Domestication of Politics: Women and American Political Society, 1780–1920," *American Historical Review* 89 (June 1984): 620–47; Sklar, *Florence Kelley and the Nation's Work;* Maureen Flanagan, "Gender and Urban Political Reform: The City Club and the Woman's City Club of Chicago in the Progressive Era," *The American Historical Review* 95 (Oct. 1990): 1032–50; Seth Koven and Sonya Michel,

Jane Addams was invited to become a member of the prestigious Chicago Woman's Club within weeks of her arrival in the city in 1889. This signaled not only her social status but also the club members' interest in Addams's publicly announced intention to open a settlement house in one of the city's "industrial" neighborhoods. The members of the Chicago Woman's Club resonated to Addams's insistence that her efforts would not be "philanthropic"; she was not going into the ghetto to save souls or uplift the downtrodden. Addams was interested in improving civic relations across classes and so were the members of the Chicago Woman's Club. They had been engaged in efforts to improve the educational and sanitary conditions of the city's poor for years before Addams came on the scene, but in Addams the members of the Woman's Club found the perfect vehicle for realizing their civic ambitions.

It would be impossible to separate the story of Jane Addams's role in the Progressive Era from the story of her immersion in the female political culture of her day. From the moment she began her work in Chicago through her founding of the Women's International League for Peace and Freedom in 1919 and until her death in 1935, Addams drew her political energy from associating with women and from women's outsider perspective as critics of the world men had wrought. Jane Addams and her female colleagues at Hull-House and in the Chicago Woman's Club looked on the urban degradation and social inequity caused by industrial capitalism and Gilded Age politics and concluded that the leadership of male elites was inadequate. Their response was to link the health of the democracy and the health of the economy to the literal health of the people and to insist that politicians place on the public agenda those very issues that had traditionally been dismissed as "women's" issues or as private, domestic issues. Addams was hardly alone in demanding that issues like housing, sanitation, child labor, public nursing, environmental pollution, factory conditions, and compulsory education be taken as seriously as the tariff, the gold standard, and civil service reform. At every step of the way, her efforts were buttressed by the political activism of women in Chicago and across the nation; just as Addams's efforts were carried along in the stream of the Social Gospel and social science, so, too, was she strengthened and supported by the Progressive Era's vibrant female political culture.

In their collective critique of unregulated capitalism, a whole spectrum of Progressives shared the view that America's tradition of limited

eds., *Mothers of the New World: Maternalist Politics and the Origins of Welfare States* (New York: Routledge, 1993); Robyn Muncy, *Creating a Female Dominion in American Reform, 1890–1935* (New York: Oxford University Press, 1991).

government was inadequate to the challenges posed by urban, corporate industrialization. Progressives then differed on just where and how government should be more activist. Addams allied with those who sought legislation on issues like factory conditions, maximum hours, the minimum wage, child labor, and the right of workers to unionize. To those who argued that such regulations interfered with the rights of the individual employer, Addams responded that the American enterprise was about democratic process and not the individual accumulation of great wealth. For that reason, said Addams, "the very existence of the state depends upon the character of its citizens" (p. 135), and "if we would have our democracy endure" (p. 206) then citizens must be equipped, materially and spiritually, for participation in the democratic dialogue. From this she drew what she called her "standard of life argument": it is appropriate for the state to regulate private enterprise if "certain industrial conditions are forcing the workers below the standard of decency" (p. 135). That is to say, in a conflict between the rights of private property and the needs of participatory democracy, the needs of democracy should take priority.

In making this argument, Addams found herself in great sympathy with the thousands of Americans who identified with either the labor union movement or the socialist movement at the turn of the century. Addams rather bravely aligned herself with the labor movement at a time when unionists were regarded as enemies of the state. But to the socialists' regret, and even rage, Addams did not define herself as a socialist. In *Twenty Years at Hull-House,* Addams claimed that she "longed for the comfort of a definite social creed" (p. 118) like socialism, but felt as temperamentally and intellectually incapable of becoming a believer in socialism as she was of becoming a believer in foreordination. In her opinion, both belief systems assumed a cosmic rigidity which her devotion to constant change and human complexity could not admit. Most American socialists in these years looked to gradual legislative change rather than violent revolution as the route to a socialist future, so it was not her pacifism that held Addams back. Rather, it appears from her comments in *Twenty Years at Hull-House* and in other writings, that Addams preferred her friends in the labor movement to her socialist friends because she found her socialist colleagues to be more rigidly ideological, more bitterly partisan, and more uncompromising toward capitalism than she could ever be.[24]

---

[24]Treatments of American socialism in this era include Nick Salvatore, *Eugene V. Debs: Citizen and Socialist* (Urbana: University of Illinois Press, 1982); Daniel Bell, *Marxian*

Addams's resistance to affiliation with socialists highlights an important distinction in her political stance. While she shared common ground with devotees of the Social Gospel, social science, women's political culture, and working-class radicalism, she often stood alone in her insistence that all political initiatives should seek compromise rather than victory. Whatever influence she gained with the general public for her democratic demeanor and quiet charm, Addams gave up some influence with her natural allies because she could not share their passion for partisanship. This commitment to mediation above all else was a strong philosophical position for Addams but was also an expression of her temperamental discomfort with hostility and divisiveness. So great was Addams's need to believe that people could overcome differences through rational discourse and negotiation that she was not always as patient or as effective in the messy trenches of angry politics as she was within the walls of Hull-House or on the pages of her writing. She could comprehend the daily passions driving her neighbors but was puzzled by the political passions driving Chicago schoolteachers or striking workers. For example, at the height of the tensions between Chicago's teachers' union and Board of Education, Addams wrote to another member of the school board, "I cannot understand where all the emotion comes from."[25] This was not elitism on Addams's part, but a philosophical and emotional inability to understand why others could not privilege compromise over a clear victory. Like many others in her political world, Addams's old friend and colleague, Ellen Gates Starr, came to see Addams's nonpartisan posture as irritating. Starr, who became a Christian Socialist in the late 1890s, scoffed at Addams's devotion to mediation during a bitter garment strike in Chicago, claiming exasperatedly, "Jane, if the devil himself came riding down Halsted Street with his tail waving out behind him, you'd say, 'what a beautiful curve he has in his tail.'"[26] Others, however, admired Addams's insistence on recognizing validity in others' positions. Charlotte Perkins Gilman, an unabashedly partisan feminist-socialist philosopher of the era, recognized this mediating quality in Addams as a great strength when she wrote that the head resident of Hull-

---

Socialism in the United States (Princeton, N.J.: Princeton University Press, 1967); Ira Kipnis, *The American Socialist Movement, 1897–1912* (New York: Columbia University Press, 1972); L. Glen Seretan, *Daniel DeLeon: The Odyssey of an American Marxist* (Cambridge, Mass.: Harvard University Press, 1979); Oakley C. Johnson, *Marxism in United States History before the Russian Revolution, 1876–1917* (New York: Humanities Press, 1974).

[25] Jane Addams to Anita McCormick Blaine, 27 December 1906. Jane Addams Memorial Collection, University of Illinois, Chicago.

[26] Jane Addams to Mary Rozet Smith, 8 November 1910. Jane Addams Memorial Collection, University of Illinois, Chicago.

House was possessed of a mind "with more 'floor space' in it than any other I have known. She could set a subject down, unprejudiced, and walk all around it, allowing fairly for every one's point of view."[27]

Consistent with her commitment to mediation, Addams stated in *Twenty Years at Hull-House* that the settlement "can stand for no political or social propaganda" (p. 95), that it must welcome all points of view. This sincere conviction conflicted with Addams's equally firm commitment to concrete social action. Indeed, her memoir provides abundant evidence that while Hull-House did foster active debate and brought a wide variety of viewpoints under one roof, it also affiliated itself with very specific political positions. And once Addams aligned herself with labor unions or legislation regulating factory conditions or municipal housing regulations, she could no longer claim the nonpartisan high ground she so cherished. No matter how much Addams liked to think of herself as bearing "independent witness to social righteousness" (p. 117) the fact of the matter was that she had positioned herself in clear opposition to both laissez-faire capitalists and socialists. As she acknowledged in *Twenty Years at Hull-House,* this nonaligned alignment meant that Addams and her settlement colleagues often felt that "we were destined to alienate everybody" (p. 117).

Complicating her ostensibly patient, nonpartisan stance was Addams's growing impatience with the social and economic problems of the era. The longer she lived in the Nineteenth Ward, the more determined she was to stop the abuses and corruptions she witnessed every day. The intellectual in Addams delighted in the endless philosophical debates at Hull-House and throughout the city, but the activist in her grew tired of all the talk. The logical result of this frustration is not played out in the pages of *Twenty Years at Hull-House.* But understanding it can help to explain the ironic fact that Progressives like Addams, who were genuinely devoted to expanding democracy, often wound up supporting public policies that gave more power to trained experts in government than to the people. The respect for social science and the urgent desire to get something done encouraged Addams and her Progressive colleagues to support the creation of state mechanisms that often imposed the same sorts of rigid rules that Addams had opposed for the very reason that those rules eliminated the messy, inefficient, but very democratic voice of the people.

---

[27] Charlotte Perkins Gilman, *The Living of Charlotte Perkins Gilman: An Autobiography* (New York: Appleton-Century, 1935), 184. Gilman's observation is quoted in Sklar, *Florence Kelley,* 305.

When Jane Addams was writing *Twenty Years at Hull-House* in 1909 and 1910, she took the view that the era of social reform of which she was a part was just beginning. She could not know then that America's entry into World War I in the spring of 1917 would bring a halt to Americans' zeal for social action. By the time that zeal returned, in the New Deal of the 1930s, Jane Addams was in her seventies. In the twenty-five years between publication of *Twenty Years at Hull-House* and her death at age 75 in 1935, Addams risked her reputation and the public's adulation by steadfastly opposing U.S. participation in World War I because she believed that hostility and violence never produced the desired end, however noble. She withstood being labeled "public enemy number one" in the repressive 1920s and stubbornly organized the Women's International League for Peace and Freedom in that postwar decade. Her base of operations continued to be Hull-House and she maintained her interest in domestic reform efforts, but her focus shifted away from the Nineteenth Ward and toward international women's efforts to create a peaceful climate in which democratic reforms could flourish. For this effort she was awarded the Nobel Peace Prize in 1931, and with the return of reform zeal in the thirties, she enjoyed renewed public approval in her last years. Throughout these decades of activism, in fair weather and foul, Addams never wavered from her belief in bringing all members of society to the table of democracy to speak and listen, debate and deliberate, and reach a harmonious compromise that respected the rights of the individual and the needs of the collective. It was this belief that Addams sought to popularize in writing *Twenty Years at Hull-House.*

PART TWO

The Document

Twenty Years
at Hull-House
with Autobiographical Notes

PREFACE

Every preface is, I imagine, written after the book has been completed, and now that I have finished this volume I will state several difficulties which may put the reader upon his guard unless he too postpones the preface to the very last.

Many times during the writing of these reminiscences, I have become convinced that the task was undertaken all too soon. One's fiftieth year is indeed an impressive milestone at which one may well pause to take an accounting, but the people with whom I have so long journeyed have become so intimate a part of my lot that they cannot be written of either in praise or blame; the public movements and causes with which I am still identified have become so endeared, some of them through their very struggles and failures, that it is difficult to discuss them.

It has also been hard to determine what incidents and experiences should be selected for recital, and I have found that I might give an accurate report of each isolated event and yet give a totally misleading impression of the whole, solely by the selection of the incidents. For these reasons and many others I have found it difficult to make a faithful record of the years since the autumn of 1889 when without any preconceived social theories or economic views, I came to live in an industrial district of Chicago.

If the reader should inquire why the book was ever undertaken in the face of so many difficulties, in reply I could instance two purposes, only one of which in the language of organized charity, is "worthy." Because Settlements have multiplied so easily in the United States I hoped that a simple statement of an earlier effort, including the stress and storm, might be of value in their interpretation and possibly clear them of a certain charge of superficiality. The unworthy motive was a desire to start a "backfire," as it were, to extinguish two biographies of myself, one of which had been submitted to me in outline, that made life in a Settlement all too smooth and charming.

The earlier chapters present influences and personal motives with a detail which will be quite unpardonable if they fail to make clear the personality upon whom various social and industrial movements in Chicago reacted during a period of twenty years. No effort is made in the recital to separate my own history from that of Hull-House during the years when I was "launched deep into the stormy intercourse of human life" for, so far as a mind is pliant under the pressure of events and experiences, it becomes hard to detach it.

It has unfortunately been necessary to abandon the chronological order in favor of the topical, for during the early years at Hull-House, time seemed to afford a mere framework for certain lines of activity and I have found in writing this book, that after these activities have been recorded, I can scarcely recall the scaffolding.

More than a third of the material in the book has appeared in *The American Magazine,* one chapter of it in *McClure's Magazine,* and earlier statements of the Settlement motive, published years ago, have been utilized in chronological order because it seemed impossible to reproduce their enthusiasm.

If the conclusions of the whole matter are similar to those I have already published at intervals during the twenty years at Hull-House, I can only make the defense that each of the earlier books was an attempt to set forth a thesis supported by experience, whereas this volume endeavors to trace the experiences through which various conclusions were forced upon me.

CHAPTER 1
EARLIEST IMPRESSIONS

On the theory that our genuine impulses may be connected with our childish experiences, that one's bent may be tracked back to that "No-Man's Land" where character is formless but nevertheless settling into definite lines of future development, I begin this record with some impressions of my childhood.

All of these are directly connected with my father, although of course I recall many experiences apart from him. I was one of the younger members of a large family and an eager participant in the village life, but because my father was so distinctly the dominant influence and because it is quite impossible to set forth all of one's early impressions, it has seemed simpler to string these first memories on that single cord. Moreover, it was this cord which not only held fast my supreme affection, but also first drew me into the moral concerns of life, and later afforded a clew there to which I somewhat wistfully clung in the intricacy of its mazes.

It must have been from a very early period that I recall "horrid nights" when I tossed about in my bed because I had told a lie. I was held in the grip of a miserable dread of death, a double fear, first, that I myself should die in my sins and go straight to that fiery Hell which was never mentioned at home, but which I had heard all about from other children, and, second, that my father — representing the entire adult world which I had basely deceived — should himself die before I had time to tell him. My only method of obtaining relief was to go downstairs to my father's room and make full confession. The high resolve to do this would push me out of bed and carry me down the stairs without a touch of fear. But at the foot of the stairs I would be faced by the awful necessity of passing the front door — which my father, because of his Quaker tendencies, did not lock — and of crossing the wide and black expanse of the living room in order to reach his door. I would invariably cling to the newel post while I contemplated the perils of the situation, complicated by the fact that the literal first step meant putting my bare foot upon a piece of oilcloth in front of the door, only a few inches wide, but lying straight in my path. I would finally reach my father's bedside perfectly breathless and, having panted out the history of my sin, invariably received the same assurance that if he "had a little girl who told lies," he was very glad that she "felt too bad to go to sleep afterwards." No absolution was asked for nor received, but apparently the sense that the knowledge of my wickedness was shared, or an obscure understanding of the affection which underlay the grave statement, was sufficient, for I always went back to bed as bold as a lion, and slept, if not the sleep of the just, at least that of the comforted. . . .

That curious sense of responsibility for carrying on the world's affairs which little children often exhibit . . . I remember in myself in a very absurd manifestation. I dreamed night after night that every one in the world was dead excepting myself, and that upon me rested the responsibility of making a wagon wheel. The village street remained as usual, the village blacksmith shop was "all there," even a glowing fire upon the forge and the anvil in its customary place near the door, but no human being was within sight. They had all gone around the edge of the hill to the village cemetery, and I alone remained alive in the deserted world. I always stood in the same spot in the blacksmith shop, darkly pondering as to how to begin, and never once did I know how, although I fully realized that the affairs of the world could not be resumed until at least one wheel should be made and something started. Every victim of nightmare is, I imagine, overwhelmed by an excessive sense of responsibility and the consciousness of a fearful handicap in the effort to perform what is required; but perhaps never were the odds more heavily against "a warder of the world" than in these reiterated dreams of mine, doubtless compounded in equal parts of a childish version of Robinson Crusoe and of the end-of-the-world predictions of the Second Adventists, a few of whom were found in the village. The next morning would often find me, a delicate little girl of six, with the further disability of a curved spine, standing in the doorway of the village blacksmith shop, anxiously watching the burly, red-shirted figure at work. I would store my mind with such details of the process of making wheels as I could observe, and sometimes I plucked up courage to ask for more. "Do you always have to sizzle the iron in water?" I would ask, thinking how horrid it would be to do. "Sure!" the good-natured blacksmith would reply, "that makes the iron hard." I would sigh heavily and walk away, bearing my responsibility as best I could, and this of course I confided to no one, for there is something too mysterious in the burden of "the winds that come from the fields of sleep" to be communicated, although it is at the same time too heavy a burden to be borne alone. . . .

My great veneration and pride in my father manifested itself in curious ways. On several Sundays, doubtless occurring in two or three different years, the Union Sunday School of the village was visited by strangers, some of those "strange people" who live outside a child's realm, yet constantly thrill it by their close approach. My father taught the large Bible class in the left-hand corner of the church next to the pulpit, and to my eyes at least, was a most imposing figure in his Sunday frock coat, his fine head rising high above all the others. I imagined that the strangers were filled with admiration for this dignified person, and I prayed with all my heart that the ugly, pigeon-toed little girl, whose crooked back obliged her to walk with her head held very much upon one side, would never be pointed out to these visitors as the daughter of this fine man. In order to lessen the possibility of a connection being made, on these particular Sundays I did not walk beside my father, although this walk was the great event of the week, but attached myself firmly to the side of my Uncle James Addams, in the hope that I should be mistaken for his child, or at least that I should not remain so conspicuously unattached that troublesome questions might identify an Ugly Duckling with her imposing parent. . . . He fortunately never explored my motives, nor do I remember that my father ever did, so that in all probability my machinations have been safe from public knowledge until this hour.

It is hard to account for the manifestations of a child's adoring affection, so emotional, so irrational, so tangled with the affairs of the imagination. I simply could not endure the thought that "strange people" should know that my handsome father owned this homely little girl. . . . Happily, however, this specter was laid before it had time to grow into a morbid familiar by a very trifling incident. One day I met my father coming out of his bank on the main street of the neighboring city which seemed to me a veritable whirlpool of society and commerce. With a playful touch of exaggeration, he lifted his high and shining silk hat and made me an imposing bow. This distinguished public recognition, this totally unnecessary identification among a mass of "strange people" who couldn't possibly know unless he himself made the sign, suddenly filled me with a sense of the absurdity of the entire feeling. It may not even then have seemed as absurd as it really was, but at least it seemed enough so to collapse or to pass into the limbo of forgotten specters.

I made still other almost equally grotesque attempts to express this doglike affection. The house at the end of the village in which I was born, and which was my home until I moved to Hull-House, in my earliest childhood had opposite to it — only across the road and then across a little stretch of greensward — two mills belonging to my father; one flour mill, to which the various grains were brought by the neighboring farmers, and one sawmill, in which the logs of the native timber were sawed into lumber. The latter offered the great excitement of sitting on a log while it slowly approached the buzzing saw which was cutting it into slabs, and of getting off just in time to escape a sudden and gory death. But the flouring mill was much more beloved. It was full of dusky, floury places which we adored, of empty bins in which we might play house; it had a basement with piles of bran and shorts which were almost as good as sand to play in, whenever the miller let us wet the edges of the pile with water brought in his sprinkling pot from the mill-race.

In addition to these fascinations was the association of the mill with my father's activities, for doubtless at that time I centered upon him all that careful imitation which a little girl ordinarily gives to her mother's ways and habits. My mother had died when I was a baby and my father's second marriage did not occur until my eighth year.

I had a consuming ambition to possess a miller's thumb, and would sit contentedly for a long time rubbing between my thumb and fingers the ground wheat as it fell from between the millstones, before it was taken up on an endless chain of mysterious little buckets to be bolted into flour. I believe I have never since wanted anything more desperately than I wanted my right thumb to be flattened, as my father's had become, during his earlier years of a miller's life. . . .

This sincere tribute of imitation, which affection offers to its adored object, had later, I hope, subtler manifestations, but certainly these first ones were altogether genuine. In this case, too, I doubtless contributed my share to that stream of admiration which our generation so generously poured forth for the self-made man. I was consumed by a wistful desire to apprehend the hardships of my father's earlier life in that faraway time when he had been a miller's apprentice. I knew that he still woke up punctually at three o'clock because for so many years he had taken his turn at the mill in the early morning, and if by chance I awoke at the same hour, as curiously enough I often did, I imagined him in the early dawn in my uncle's old mill reading through the entire village library, book after book, beginning with the lives of the signers of the Declaration of Independence. Copies of the same books, mostly bound in calfskin, were to be found in the library below, and I courageously resolved that I too would read them all and try to understand life as he did. I did in fact later begin a course of reading in the early morning hours, but I was caught by some fantastic notion of chronological order and early legendary form. Pope's translation of the "Iliad," even followed by Dryden's "Virgil," did not leave behind the residuum of wisdom for which I longed, and I finally gave them up for a thick book entitled "The History of the World" as affording a shorter and an easier path.

Although I constantly confided my sins and perplexities to my father, there are only a few occasions on which I remember having received direct advice or admonition; it may easily be true, however, that I have forgotten the latter, in the manner of many seekers after advice who enjoyably set forth their situation but do not really listen to the advice itself. I can remember an admonition on one occasion, however, when, as a little girl of eight years, arrayed in a new cloak, gorgeous beyond anything I had ever worn before, I stood before my father for his approval. I was much chagrined by his remark that it was a very pretty cloak — in fact so much prettier than any cloak the other little girls in the Sunday school had, that he would advise me to wear my old cloak, which would keep me quite as warm, with the added advantage of not making the other little girls feel badly. I complied with the request but I fear without inner consent, and I certainly was quite without the joy of self-sacrifice as I walked soberly through the village street by the side of my counselor. My mind was busy, however, with the old question eternally suggested by the inequalities of the human lot. Only as we neared the church door did I venture to ask what could be done about it, receiving the reply that it might never be righted so far as clothes went, but that people might be equal in things that mattered much more than clothes, the affairs of education and religion, for instance, which we attended to when we went to school and church, and that it was very stupid to wear the sort of clothes that made it harder to have equality even there.

It must have been a little later when I held a conversation with my father upon the doctrine of foreordination,[1] which at one time very much perplexed my childish mind. After setting the difficulty before him and complaining that I could not make it out, although my best friend "understood it perfectly," I settled down to hear his argument, having no doubt that he could make it quite clear. To my delighted surprise, for any intimation that our minds were on an equality lifted me high indeed, he said that he feared that he and I did not have the kind of mind that would ever understand foreordination very well and advised me not to give too much time to it; but he then proceeded to say other things of which the final impression left upon my mind was, that it did not matter much whether one understood foreordination or not, but that it was very important not to pretend to understand what you didn't understand and that you must always be honest with yourself inside, whatever happened. Perhaps on the whole as valuable a lesson as the shorter catechism itself contains.

My memory merges this early conversation on religious doctrine into one which took place years later when I put before my father the situation in which I found myself at boarding school when under great evangelical pressure, and once again I heard his testimony in favor of "mental integrity above everything else."

At the time we were driving through a piece of timber in which the wood choppers had been at work during the winter, and so earnestly were we talking that he suddenly drew up the horses to find that he did

---

[1] The theological belief that God predetermines those individuals who will achieve eternal salvation and those who will experience eternal damnation.

not know where he was. We were both entertained by the incident, I that my father had been "lost in his own timber" so that various cords of wood must have escaped his practiced eye, and he on his side that he should have become so absorbed in this maze of youthful speculation. We were in high spirits as we emerged from the tender green of the spring woods into the clear light of day, and as we came back into the main road I categorically asked him:—

"What are you? What do you say when people ask you?"

His eyes twinkled a little as he soberly replied:

"I am a Quaker."

"But that isn't enough to say," I urged.

"Very well," he added, "to people who insist upon details, as some one is doing now, I add that I am a Hicksite Quaker"; and not another word on the weighty subject could I induce him to utter.

These early recollections are set in a scene of rural beauty, unusual at least for Illinois. The prairie round the village was broken into hills, one of them crowned by pine woods, grown up from a bag full of Norway pine seeds sown by my father in 1844, the very year he came to Illinois, a testimony perhaps that the most vigorous pioneers gave at least an occasional thought to beauty. The banks of the mill stream rose into high bluffs too perpendicular to be climbed without skill, and containing caves of which one at least was so black that it could not be explored without the aid of a candle; ... My stepbrother and I carried on games and crusades which lasted week after week, and even summer after summer, as only free-ranging country children can do. It may be in contrast to this that one of the most piteous aspects in the life of city children, as I have seen it in the neighborhood of Hull-House, is the constant interruption to their play which is inevitable on the streets, so that it can never have any continuity,—the most elaborate "plan or chart" or "fragment from their dream of human life" is sure to be rudely destroyed by the passing traffic. Although they start over and over again, even the most vivacious become worn out at last and take to that passive "standing 'round" varied by rude horse-play, which in time becomes so characteristic of city children. ...

Long before we had begun the study of Latin at the village school, my brother and I had learned the Lord's Prayer in Latin out of an old copy of the Vulgate, and gravely repeated it every night in an execrable pronunciation because it seemed to us more religious than "plain English."

When, however, I really prayed, what I saw before my eyes was a most outrageous picture which adorned a song-book used in Sunday school, portraying the Lord upon His throne surrounded by tiers and tiers of saints and angels all in a blur of yellow. I am ashamed to tell how old I was when that picture ceased to appear before my eyes, especially when moments of terror compelled me to ask protection from the Heavenly powers.

I recall with great distinctness my first direct contact with death when I was fifteen years old: Polly was an old nurse who had taken care of my mother and had followed her to frontier Illinois to help rear a second generation of children. She had always lived in our house, but made annual visits to her cousins on a farm a few miles north of the village. During one of these visits, word came to us one Sunday evening that Polly was dying, and for a number of reasons I was the only person able to go to her. I left the lamp-lit, warm house to be driven four miles through a blinding storm which every minute added more snow to the already high drifts, with a sense of starting upon a fateful errand. An hour after my arrival all of the cousins' family went downstairs to supper, and I was left alone to watch with Polly. The square, old-fashioned chamber in the lonely farmhouse was very cold and still, with nothing to be heard but the storm outside. Suddenly the great change came. I heard a feeble call of "Sarah," my mother's name, as the dying eyes were turned upon me, followed by a curious breathing and in place of the face familiar from my earliest childhood and associated with homely household cares, there lay upon the pillow strange, august features, stern and withdrawn from all the small affairs of life. That sense of solitude, of being unsheltered in a wide world of relentless and elemental forces which is at the basis of childhood's timidity and which is far from outgrown at fifteen, seized me irresistibly before I could reach the narrow stairs and summon the family from below.

As I was driven home in the winter storm, the wind through the trees seemed laden with a passing soul and the riddle of life and death pressed hard; once to be young, to grow old, and to die, everything came to that, and then a mysterious journey out into the Unknown. Did she mind faring forth alone? Would the journey perhaps end in something as familiar and natural to the aged and dying as life is to the young and living? Through all the drive and indeed throughout the night these thoughts were pierced by sharp worry, a sense of faithlessness because I had forgotten the text Polly had confided to me long before as the one from which she wished her funeral sermon to be preached. My comfort as usual finally came from my father, who pointed out what was essential and what was of little avail even in such a moment as this, and while he was much too wise to grow dogmatic upon the great theme of death, I felt a new fellowship with him because we had discussed it together.

Perhaps I may record here my protest against the efforts, so often made, to shield children and young people from all that has to do with death and sorrow, to give them a good time at all hazards on the assumption that the ills of life will come soon enough. Young people themselves often resent this attitude on the part of their elders; they feel set aside and belittled as if they were denied the common human experiences. They too wish to climb steep stairs and to eat their bread with tears, and they imagine that the problems of existence which so press upon them in pensive moments would be less insoluble in the light of these great happenings.

An incident which stands out clearly in my mind as an exciting suggestion of the great world of moral enterprise and serious undertakings must have occurred earlier than this, for in 1872, when I was not yet twelve years old, I came into my father's room one morning to find him sitting beside the fire with a newspaper in his hand, looking very solemn; and upon my eager inquiry what had happened, he told me that Joseph Mazzini[2] was dead. I had never even heard Mazzini's name, and after being told about him I was inclined to grow argumentative, asserting that my father did not know him, that he was not an American, and that I could not understand why we should be expected to feel badly about him. It is impossible to recall the conversation with the complete breakdown of my cheap arguments, but in the end I obtained that which I have ever regarded as a valuable possession, a sense of the genuine relationship which may exist between men who share large hopes and like desires, even though they differ in nationality, language, and creed; that those things count for absolutely nothing between groups of men who are trying to abolish slavery in America or to throw off Hapsburg oppression in Italy. At any rate, I was heartily ashamed of my meager notion of patriotism, and I came out of the room exhilarated with the consciousness that impersonal and international relations are actual facts and not mere phrases. I was filled with pride that I knew a man who held converse with great minds and who really sorrowed and rejoiced over happenings across the sea. I never recall those early conversations with

---

[2]Italian patriot and republican leader (1805–72) who founded the Young Italy Society in 1832 and worked with Giuseppe Garibaldi toward unifying Italy. Unification came in 1861 in the form of a restored monarchy; Mazzini led a republican revolt in Sicily in 1870. He died two years after the revolt failed.

my father, nor a score of others like them, but there comes into my mind a line from Mrs. Browning in which a daughter describes her relations with her father:—

> He wrapt me in his large
> Man's doublet, careless did it fit or no.

CHAPTER 2
INFLUENCE OF LINCOLN

I suppose all the children who were born about the time of the Civil War have recollections quite unlike those of the children who are living now. Although I was but four and a half years old when Lincoln died, I distinctly remember the day when I found on our two white gate posts American flags companioned with black. I tumbled down on the harsh gravel walk in my eager rush into the house to inquire what they were "there for." To my amazement I found my father in tears, something that I had never seen before, having assumed, as all children do, that grown-up people never cried. The two flags, my father's tears, and his impressive statement that the greatest man in the world had died, constituted my initiation, my baptism, as it were, into the thrilling and solemn interests of a world lying quite outside the two white gate posts. The great war touched children in many ways. . . .

However much we were given to talk of war heroes, we always fell silent as we approached an isolated farmhouse in which two old people lived alone. Five of their sons had enlisted in the Civil War, and only the youngest had returned alive in the spring of 1865. In the autumn of the same year, when he was hunting for wild ducks in a swamp on the rough little farm itself, he was accidentally shot and killed, and the old people were left alone to struggle with the half-cleared land as best they might. When we were driven past this forlorn little farm our childish voices always dropped into speculative whisperings as to how the accident could have happened to this remaining son out of all the men in the world, to him who had escaped so many chances of death! Our young hearts swelled in first rebellion against that which Walter Pater[3] calls "the inexplicable shortcoming or misadventure on the part of life itself"; we

---

[3]British essayist and critic (1839–94) associated with aestheticism, the belief in beauty as the most enduring and meaningful feature of life. This quote is taken from chapter 25 of Pater's best-known novel, *Marius the Epicurean*.

were overwhelmingly oppressed by that grief of things as they are, so much more mysterious and intolerable than those griefs which we think dimly to trace to man's own wrongdoing.

It was well perhaps that life thus early gave me a hint of one of her most obstinate and insoluble riddles, for I have sorely needed the sense of universality thus imparted to that mysterious injustice, the burden of which we are all forced to bear and with which I have become only too familiar.

My childish admiration for Lincoln is closely associated with a visit made to the war eagle, Old Abe, who, as we children well knew, lived in the state capitol of Wisconsin, only sixty-five miles north of our house, really no farther than an eagle could easily fly! He had been carried by the Eighth Wisconsin Regiment through the entire war, and now dwelt an honored pensioner in the state building itself. . . .

The entire journey to the veteran war eagle had itself symbolized that search for the heroic and perfect which so persistently haunts the young; and as I stood under the great white dome of Old Abe's stately home, for one brief moment the search was rewarded. I dimly caught a hint of what men have tried to say in their world-old effort to imprison a space in so divine a line that it shall hold only yearning devotion and high-hearted hopes. Certainly the utmost rim of my first dome was filled with the tumultuous impression of soldiers marching to death for freedom's sake, of pioneers streaming westward to establish self-government in yet another sovereign state. . . .

Through all my vivid sensations there persisted the image of the eagle in the corridor below and Lincoln himself as an epitome of all that was great and good. I dimly caught the notion of the martyred President as the standard bearer to the conscience of his countrymen, as the eagle had been the ensign of courage to the soldiers of the Wisconsin regiment.

Thirty-five years later, as I stood on the hill campus of the University of Wisconsin with a commanding view of the capitol building a mile directly across the city, I saw again the dome which had so uplifted my childish spirit. The university, which was celebrating its fiftieth anniversary, had honored me with a doctor's degree, and in the midst of the academic pomp and the rejoicing, the dome again appeared to me as a fitting symbol of a state's aspiration even in its high mission of universal education.

Thousands of children in the sixties and seventies, in the simplicity which is given to the understanding of a child, caught a notion of imperishable heroism when they were told that brave men had lost their lives that the slaves might be free. . . .

My father always spoke of the martyred President as Mr. Lincoln, and I never heard the great name without a thrill. I remember the day — it must have been one of comparative leisure, perhaps a Sunday — when at my request my father took out of his desk a thin packet marked "Mr. Lincoln's Letters," the shortest one of which bore unmistakable traces of that remarkable personality. These letters began, "My dear Double-D'ed Addams," and to the inquiry as to how the person thus addressed was about to vote on a certain measure then before the Legislature, was added the assurance that he knew that this Addams "would vote according to his conscience," but he begged to know in which direction the same conscience "was pointing." As my father folded up the bits of paper I fairly held my breath in my desire that he should go on with the reminiscence of this wonderful man, whom he had known in his comparative obscurity, or better still, that he should be moved to tell some of the exciting incidents of the Lincoln-Douglas debates. There were at least two pictures of Lincoln that always hung in my father's room, and one in our old-fashioned upstairs parlor, of Lincoln with little Tad. For one or all of these reasons I always tend to associate Lincoln with the tenderest thoughts of my father.

I recall a time of great perplexity in the summer of 1894, when Chicago was filled with federal troops sent there by the President of the United States, and their presence was resented by the governor of the state, that I walked the wearisome way from Hull-House to Lincoln Park — for no cars were running regularly at that moment of sympathetic strikes — in order to look at and gain magnanimous counsel, if I might, from the marvelous St. Gaudens statue which had been but recently placed at the entrance of the park. Some of Lincoln's immortal words were cut into the stone at his feet, and never did a distracted town more solely need the healing of "with charity towards all" than did Chicago at that moment, and the tolerance of the man who had won charity for those on both sides of "an irrepressible conflict."

Of the many things written of my father in that sad August in 1881, when he died, the one I cared for most was written by an old political friend of his who was then editor of a great Chicago daily. He wrote that while there were doubtless many members of the Illinois Legislature who during the great contracts of the war time and the demoralizing reconstruction days that followed, had never accepted a bribe, he wished to bear testimony that he personally had known but this one man who had never been offered a bribe because bad men were instinctively afraid of him.

I feel now the hot chagrin with which I recalled this statement during those early efforts of Illinois in which Hull-House joined, to secure the passage of the first factory legislation. I was told by the representatives of an informal association of manufacturers that if the residents of Hull-House would drop this nonsense about a sweatshop bill, of which they knew nothing, certain business men would agree to give fifty thousand dollars within two years to be used for any of the philanthropic activities of the Settlement. As the fact broke upon me that I was being offered a bribe, the shame was enormously increased by the memory of this statement. What had befallen the daughter of my father that such a thing could happen to her? The salutary reflection that it could not have occurred unless a weakness in myself had permitted it, withheld me at least from an heroic display of indignation before the two men making the offer, and I explained as gently as I could that we had no ambition to make Hull-House "the largest institution on the West Side," but that we were much concerned that our neighbors should be protected from untoward conditions of work, and — so much heroics, youth must permit itself — if to accomplish this the destruction of Hull-House was necessary, that we would cheerfully sing a Te Deum on its ruins. The good friend who had invited me to lunch at the Union League Club to meet two of his friends who wanted to talk over the sweatshop bill here kindly intervened, and we all hastened to cover over the awkward situation by that scurrying away from ugly morality which seems to be an obligation of social intercourse. . . .

There was something in the admiration of Lincoln's contemporaries, or at least of those men who had known him personally, which was quite unlike even the best of the devotion and reverent understanding which has developed since. In the first place, they had so large a fund of common experience; they too had pioneered in a western country, and had urged the development of canals and railroads in order that the raw prairie crops might be transported to market; they too had realized that if this last tremendous experiment in self-government failed here, it would be the disappointment of the centuries, and that upon their ability to organize self-government in state, county, and town depended the verdict of history. These men also knew, as Lincoln himself did, that if this tremendous experiment was to come to fruition, it must be brought about by the people themselves; that there was no other capital fund upon which to draw. I remember an incident occurring when I was about fifteen years old, in which the conviction was driven into my mind that the people themselves were the great resource of the country. My father had made a little address of reminiscence at a meeting of "the old settlers of Stephenson County," which was held every summer in the grove beside the mill, relating his experiences in inducing the farmers of the county to subscribe for stock in the Northwestern Railroad,[4] which was the first to penetrate the county and to make a connection with the Great Lakes at Chicago. Many of the Pennsylvania German farmers doubted the value of "the whole new-fangled business," and had no use for any railroad, much less for one in which they were asked to risk their hard-earned savings. My father told of his despair in one farmers' community dominated by such prejudice which did not in the least give way under his argument, but finally melted under the enthusiasm of a high-spirited German matron who took a share to be paid for "out of butter and egg money." As he related his admiration of her, an old woman's piping voice in the audience called out: "I'm here to-day, Mr. Addams, and I'd do it again if you asked me." The old woman, bent and broken by her seventy years of toilsome life, was brought to the platform and I was much impressed by my father's grave presentation of her as "one of the public-spirited pioneers to whose heroic fortitude we are indebted for the development of this country." I remember that I was at that time reading with great enthusiasm Carlyle's[5] "Heroes and Hero Worship," but on the evening of "Old Settlers' Day," to my surprise, I found it difficult to go on. Its sonorous sentences and exaltation of the man who "can" suddenly ceased to be convincing. I had already written down in my commonplace book a resolution to give at least twenty-five copies of this book each year to noble young people of my acquaintance. It is perhaps fitting to record in this chapter that the very first Christmas we spent at Hull-House, in spite of exigent demands upon my slender purse for candy and shoes, I gave to a club of boys twenty-five copies of the then new Carl Schurz's[6] "Appreciation of Abraham Lincoln."

[4]The interstate company that bought the original Galena and Chicago Railroad in 1864. John Addams had been instrumental in raising funds for the Galena and Chicago Railroad between 1846 and 1853.

[5]Thomas Carlyle (1795–1881) was the most famous and popular British social philosopher in the United States when Jane Addams was growing up. In *On Heroes, Hero-Worship, and the Heroic in History* (London: Chapman and Hall, 1840), Carlyle argued that social progress is caused by strong, heroic leaders.

[6]German immigrant (1829–1906) who had fought in Germany's failed democratic revolution of 1848; was active in the antislavery movement in the United States and an ally of Abraham Lincoln in the Republican Party.

In our early effort at Hull-House to hand on to our neighbors whatever of help we had found for ourselves, we made much of Lincoln. We were often distressed by the children of immigrant parents who were ashamed of the pit whence they were digged, who repudiated the language and customs of their elders, and counted themselves successful as they were able to ignore the past. Whenever I held up Lincoln for their admiration as the greatest American, I invariably pointed out his marvelous power to retain and utilize past experiences; that he never forgot how the plain people in Sangamon County thought and felt when he himself had moved to town; that this habit was the foundation for his marvelous capacity for growth; that during those distracting years in Washington it enabled him to make clear beyond denial to the American people themselves, the goal towards which they were moving. I was sometimes bold enough to add that proficiency in the art of recognition and comprehension did not come without effort, and that certainly its attainment was necessary for any successful career in our conglomerate America.

An instance of the invigorating and clarifying power of Lincoln's influence came to me many years ago in England. I had spent two days in Oxford under the guidance of Arnold Toynbee's[7] old friend Sidney Ball of St. John's College, who was closely associated with that group of scholars we all identify with the beginnings of the Settlement movement. It was easy to claim the philosophy of Thomas Hill Green, the roadbuilding episode of Ruskin, the experimental living in the East End by Frederick Maurice, the London Workingmen's College of Edward Dennison, as foundations laid by university men for the establishment of Toynbee Hall.[8] I was naturally much interested in the beginnings of a movement whose slogan was "Back to the People," and which could doubtless claim the Settlement as one of its manifestations. Nevertheless the processes by which so simple a conclusion as residence among the poor in East London was reached, seemed to me very involved and roundabout. However inevitable these processes might be for class-conscious Englishmen, they could not but seem artificial to a western American who had been born in a rural community where the early

[7] Political economist (1852–83) at Balliol College, Oxford University; argued for mutual aid and understanding across social classes but died before he could implement his ideas. London's Toynbee Hall Settlement House was named in his honor.

[8] British intellectuals and social reformers who sought to improve relations across social classes through educational and service projects. Their social policies were rooted in the "idealist" philosophical belief in the spiritual connectedness of all beings.

pioneer life had made social distinctions impossible. Always on the alert lest American Settlements should become mere echoes and imitations of the English movement, I found myself assenting to what was shown me only with that part of my consciousness which had been formed by reading of English social movements, while at the same time the rustic American inside looked on in detached comment.

Why should an American be lost in admiration of a group of Oxford students because they went out to mend a disused road, inspired thereto by Ruskin's teaching for the bettering of the common life, when all the country roads in America were mended each spring by self-respecting citizens, who were thus carrying out the simple method devised by a democratic government for providing highways. No humor penetrated my high mood even as I somewhat uneasily recalled certain spring thaws when I had been mired in roads provided by the American citizen. I continued to fumble for a synthesis which I was unable to make until I developed that uncomfortable sense of playing two rôles at once. It was therefore almost with a dual consciousness that I was ushered, during the last afternoon of my Oxford stay, into the drawing-room of the Master of Balliol. Edward Caird's[9] "Evolution of Religion," which I had read but a year or two before, had been of unspeakable comfort to me in the labyrinth of differing ethical teachings and religious creeds which the many immigrant colonies of our neighborhood presented. I remember that I wanted very much to ask the author himself, how far it was reasonable to expect the same quality of virtue and a similar standard of conduct from these divers people. I was timidly trying to apply his method of study to those groups of homesick immigrants huddled together in strange tenement houses, among whom I seemed to detect the beginnings of a secular religion or at least of a wide humanitarianism evolved out of the various exigencies of the situation; somewhat as a household of children, whose mother is dead, out of their sudden necessity perform unaccustomed offices for each other and awkwardly exchange consolations, as children in happier households never dream of doing. Perhaps Mr. Caird could tell me whether there was any religious content in this

> Faith to each other; this fidelity
> Of fellow wanderers in a desert place.

[9]British philosopher (1835–1908) and part of the Oxford University movement toward an ethical and spiritual, if not strictly religious, embrace of human connectedness and community. His *Evolution of Religion* was published in 1893.

But when tea was over and my opportunity came for a talk with my host, I suddenly remembered, to the exclusion of all other associations, only Mr. Caird's fine analysis of Abraham Lincoln, delivered in a lecture two years before.

The memory of Lincoln, the mention of his name, came like a refreshing breeze from off the prairie, blowing aside all the scholarly implications in which I had become so reluctantly involved, and as the philosopher spoke of the great American "who was content merely to dig the channels through which the moral life of his countrymen might flow," I was gradually able to make a natural connection between this intellectual penetration at Oxford and the moral perception which is always necessary for the discovery of new methods by which to minister to human needs. In the unceasing ebb and flow of justice and oppression we must all dig channels as best we may, that at the propitious moment somewhat of the swelling tide may be conducted to the barren places of life.

Gradually a healing sense of well-being enveloped me and a quick remorse for my blindness, as I realized that no one among his own countrymen had been able to interpret Lincoln's greatness more nobly than this Oxford scholar had done, and that vision and wisdom as well as high motives must lie behind every effective stroke in the continuous labor for human equality; I remembered that another Master of Balliol, Jowett[10] himself, had said that it was fortunate for society that every age possessed at least a few minds which, like Arnold Toynbee's, were "perpetually disturbed over the apparent inequalities of mankind." Certainly both the English and American Settlements could unite in confessing to that disturbance of mind.

Traces of this Oxford visit are curiously reflected in a paper I wrote soon after my return at the request of the American Academy of Political and Social Science.[11] It begins as follows:—

> The word "settlement" which we have borrowed from London, is apt to grate a little upon American ears. It is not, after all, so long ago that Americans who settled were those who had adventured into a new

---

[10]Benjamin Jowett (1817–93) was the beloved head of Balliol College, Oxford University. A distinguished classicist and renowned teacher, Jowett linked Balliol College men to social reform efforts like Toynbee Hall in the late nineteenth century.

[11]The *Annals of the American Academy of Political and Social Science* article to which Addams referred was "A Function of the Social Settlement," 13 (May 1899): 323–45. Her phrase "two nations" in the quoted selection refers to the novel *Sybil* in which Benjamin Disraeli, British prime minister from 1874 to 1880 under Queen Victoria, wrote that England was composed of two nations, the rich and the poor.

country, where they were pioneers in the midst of difficult surroundings. The word still implies migrating from one condition of life to another totally unlike it, and against this implication the resident of an American settlement takes alarm.

We do not like to acknowledge that Americans are divided into two nations, as her Prime Minister once admitted of England. We are not willing, openly and professedly, to assume that American citizens are broken up into classes, even if we make that assumption the preface to a plea that the superior class has duties to the inferior. Our democracy is still our most precious possession, and we do well to resent any inroads upon it, even though they may be made in the name of philanthropy.

Is it not Abraham Lincoln who has cleared the title to our democracy? He made plain, once for all, that democratic government, associated as it is with all the mistakes and shortcomings of the common people, still remains the most valuable contribution America has made to the moral life of the world.

CHAPTER 3
BOARDING-SCHOOL IDEALS

As my three older sisters had already attended the seminary at Rockford, of which my father was trustee, without any question I entered there at seventeen, with such meager preparation in Latin and algebra as the village school had afforded. I was very ambitious to go to Smith College, although I well knew that my father's theory in regard to the education of his daughters implied a school as near at home as possible, to be followed by travel abroad in lieu of the wider advantages which an eastern college is supposed to afford. I was much impressed by the recent return of my sister from a year in Europe, yet I was greatly disappointed at the moment of starting to humdrum Rockford. After the first weeks of homesickness were over, however, I became very much absorbed in the little world which the boarding school in any form always offers to its students.

The school at Rockford in 1877 had not changed its name from seminary to college, although it numbered, on its faculty and among its alumnae, college women who were most eager that this should be done, and who really accomplished it during the next five years. The school was one of the earliest efforts for women's higher education in the Mississippi Valley, and from the beginning was called "the Mount Holyoke of the West." It reflected much of the missionary spirit of that pioneer institution, and the proportion of missionaries among its early graduates was almost as large as Mount Holyoke's own. In addition there had been thrown about the founders of the early western school the glamour of frontier privations, and the first students, conscious of the heroic self-sacrifice made in their behalf, felt that each minute of the time thus dearly bought must be conscientiously used. This inevitably fostered an atmosphere of intensity, a fever of preparation which continued long after the direct making of it had ceased, and which the later girls accepted, as they did the campus and the buildings, without knowing that it could have been otherwise. . . .

As I attempt to reconstruct the spirit of my contemporary group by looking over many documents, I find nothing more amusing than a plaint registered against life's indistinctness, which I imagine more or less reflected the sentiments of all of us. At any rate here it is for the entertainment of the reader if not for his edification: "So much of our time is spent in preparation, so much in routine, and so much in sleep, we find it difficult to have any experience at all." We did not, however, tamely accept such a state of affairs, for we made various and restless attempts to break through this dull obtuseness.

At one time five of us tried to understand De Quincey's [12] marvelous "Dreams" more sympathetically, by drugging ourselves with opium. We solemnly consumed small white powders at intervals during an entire long holiday, but no mental reorientation took place, and the suspense and excitement did not even permit us to grow sleepy. About four o'clock on the weird afternoon, the young teacher whom we had been obliged to take into our confidence, grew alarmed over the whole performance, took away our De Quincey and all the remaining powders, administered an emetic to each of the five aspirants for sympathetic understanding of all human experience, and sent us to our separate rooms with a stern command to appear at family worship after supper "whether we were able to or not."

Whenever we had chances to write, we took, of course, large themes, usually from the Greek because they were the most stirring to the imagination. The Greek oration I gave at our Junior Exhibition was written with infinite pains and taken to the Greek professor in Beloit College that there might be no mistakes, even after the Rockford College teacher

---

[12] Thomas De Quincey (1785–1859) was closely associated with Wordsworth and Coleridge and the romance of England's Lake District. His *Confessions of an Opium-Eater* (1821, 1856) was a self-report on his opium-induced dream life and a guided tour of London's underworld.

and the most scholarly clergyman in town had both passed upon it. The oration upon Bellerophon and his successful fight with the Minotaur, contended that social evils could only be overcome by him who soared above them into idealism, as Bellerophon mounted upon the winged horse Pegasus, had slain the earthy dragon.

There were practically no Economics taught in women's colleges — at least in the fresh-water ones — thirty years ago, although we painstakingly studied "Mental" and "Moral" Philosophy, which, though far from dry in the classroom, became the subject of more spirited discussion outside, and gave us a clew for animated rummaging in the little college library. Of course we read a great deal of Ruskin and Browning, and liked the most abstruse parts the best; but like the famous gentleman who talked prose without knowing it, we never dreamed of connecting them with our philosophy. My genuine interest was history, partly because of a superior teacher, and partly because my father had always insisted upon a certain amount of historic reading ever since he had paid me, as a little girl, five cents a "Life" for each Plutarch hero I could intelligently report to him, and twenty-five cents for every volume of Irving's "Life of Washington."

When we started for the long vacations, a little group of five would vow that during the summer we would read all of Motley's "Dutch Republic" or, more ambitious still, all of Gibbon's "Decline and Fall of the Roman Empire." When we returned at the opening of school and three of us announced we had finished the latter, each became skeptical of the other two. We fell upon each other with a sort of rough-and-tumble examination, in which no quarter was given or received; but the suspicion was finally removed that any one had skipped. We took for a class motto the early Saxon word for "lady," translated into "breadgiver,"[13] and we took for our class color the poppy, because poppies grew among the wheat, as if Nature knew that wherever there was hunger that needed food there would be pain that needed relief. We must have found the sentiment in a book somewhere, but we used it so much that it finally seemed like an idea of our own, although of course none of us had ever seen a European field, the only page upon which Nature has written this particular message. . . .

Of course in such an atmosphere a girl like myself, of serious not to say priggish tendency, did not escape a concerted pressure to push her into the "missionary field." During the four years it was inevitable that

[13] A term for female service coined by John Ruskin in "Lilies: of Queen's Gardens," *Sesame and Lilies: Two Lectures Delivered at Manchester in 1864* (New York: John Wiley and Son, 1866), 74–119.

every sort of evangelical appeal should have been made to reach the comparatively few "unconverted" girls in the school. We were the subject of prayer at the daily chapel exercise and the weekly prayer meeting, attendance upon which was obligatory.

I was singularly unresponsive to all these forms of emotional appeal, although I became unspeakably embarrassed when they were presented to me at close range by a teacher during the "silent hour," which we were all required to observe every evening and which was never broken into, even by a member of the faculty, unless the errand was one of grave import. I found these occasional interviews on the part of one of the more serious young teachers, of whom I was extremely fond, hard to endure, as was a long series of conversations in my senior year conducted by one of the most enthusiastic members of the faculty, in which the desirability of Turkey as a field for missionary labor was enticingly put before me. I suppose I held myself aloof from all these influences, partly owing to the fact that my father was not a communicant of any church, and I tremendously admired his scrupulous morality and sense of honor in all matters of personal and public conduct, and also because the little group to which I have referred was much given to a sort of rationalism, doubtless founded upon an early reading of Emerson. . . .

But I think in my case there were other factors as well that contributed to my unresponsiveness to the evangelical appeal. A curious course of reading I had marked out for myself in medieval history, seems to have left me fascinated by an ideal of mingled learning, piety, and physical labor, more nearly exemplified by the Port Royalists than by any others.

The only moments in which I seem to have approximated in my own experience to a faint realization of the "beauty of holiness," as I conceived it, was each Sunday morning between the hours of nine and ten, when I went into the exquisitely neat room of the teacher of Greek and read with her from a Greek testament. We did this every Sunday morning for two years. It was not exactly a lesson, for I never prepared for it, and while I was held within reasonable bounds of syntax, I was allowed much more freedom in translation than was permitted the next morning when I read Homer; neither did we discuss doctrines, for although it was with this same teacher that in our junior year we studied Paul's Epistle to the Hebrews, committing all of it to memory and analyzing and reducing it to doctrines within an inch of our lives, we never allowed an echo of this exercise to appear at these blessed Sunday morning readings. It was as if the disputatious Paul had not yet been, for we always read from the Gospels. The régime of Rockford Seminary was still very simple in the seventies. Each student made her own fire and kept her own room in order. Sunday morning was a great clearing up day, and the sense of having made immaculate my own immediate surroundings, the consciousness of clean linen, said to be close to the consciousness of a clean conscience, always mingles in my mind with these early readings. I certainly bore away with me a lifelong enthusiasm for reading the Gospels in bulk, a whole one at a time, and an insurmountable distaste for having them cut up into chapter and verse, or for hearing the incidents in that wonderful Life thus referred to as if it were merely a record.

My copy of the Greek testament had been presented to me by the brother of our Greek teacher, Professor Blaisdell of Beloit College, a true scholar in "Christian Ethics," as his department was called. I recall that one day in the summer after I left college — one of the black days which followed the death of my father — this kindly scholar came to see me in order to bring such comfort as he might and to inquire how far I had found solace in the little book he had given me so long before. When I suddenly recall the village in which I was born, its steeples and roofs look as they did that day from the hilltop where we talked together, the familiar details smoothed out and merging, as it were, into that wide conception of the universe, which for the moment swallowed up my personal grief or at least assuaged it with a realization that it was but a drop in that "torrent of sorrow and anguish and terror which flows under all the footsteps of man." This realization of sorrow as the common lot, of death as the universal experience, was the first comfort which my bruised spirit had received. In reply to my impatience with the Christian doctrine of "resignation," that it implied that you thought of your sorrow only in its effect upon you and were disloyal to the affection itself, I remember how quietly the Christian scholar changed his phraseology, saying that sometimes consolation came to us better in the words of Plato, and, as nearly as I can remember, that was the first time I had ever heard Plato's sonorous argument for the permanence of the excellent. . . .

Throughout our school years we were always keenly conscious of the growing development of Rockford Seminary into a college. The opportunity for our Alma Mater to take her place in the new movement of full college education for women filled us with enthusiasm, and it became a driving ambition with the undergraduates to share in this new and glorious undertaking. We gravely decided that it was important that some of the students should be ready to receive the bachelor's degree the very first moment that the charter of the school should secure the right to confer it. Two of us, therefore, took a course in mathematics, advanced beyond anything previously given in the school, from one of those early young women working for a Ph.D., who was temporarily teaching in Rockford that she might study more mathematics in Leipsic.

My companion in all these arduous labors has since accomplished more than any of us in the effort to procure the franchise for women, for even then we all took for granted the righteousness of that cause into which I at least had merely followed my father's conviction. In the old-fashioned spirit of that cause I might cite the career of this companion as an illustration of the efficacy of higher mathematics for women, for she possesses singular ability to convince even the densest legislators of their legal right to define their own electorate, even when they quote against her the dustiest of State Constitutions or City Charters.

In line with this policy of placing a woman's college on an equality with the other colleges of the state, we applied for an opportunity to compete in the intercollegiate oratorical contest of Illinois, and we succeeded in having Rockford admitted as the first woman's college. When I was finally selected as the orator, I was somewhat dismayed to find that, representing not only one school but college women in general, I could not resent the brutal frankness with which my oratorical possibilities were discussed by the enthusiastic group who would allow no personal feelings to stand in the way of progress, especially the progress of Woman's Cause. I was told among other things that I had an intolerable habit of dropping my voice at the end of a sentence in the most feminine, apologetic, and even deprecatory manner which would probably lose Woman the first place.

Woman certainly did lose the first place and stood fifth, exactly in the dreary middle, but the ignominious position may not have been solely due to bad mannerisms, for a prior place was easily accorded to William Jennings Bryan,[14] who not only thrilled his auditors with an almost prophetic anticipation of the cross of gold, but with a moral earnestness which we had mistakenly assumed would be the unique possession of the feminine orator.

I so heartily concurred with the decision of the judges of the contest that it was with a care-free mind that I induced my colleague and alternate to remain long enough in "the Athens of Illinois," in which the successful college was situated, to visit the state institutions, one for the

---

[14]Bryan (1860–1925) was an unsuccessful nominee for president of the United States on the Democratic ticket in 1896, 1900, and 1908. Bryan was renowned for his oratorical skills. He delivered his most famous speech, "The Cross of Gold," at the Democratic Party convention in 1896. He was born in Salem, Illinois, and in 1881 he was a senior at Illinois College in Jacksonville, "the Athens of Illinois."

blind and one for the deaf and dumb. Doctor Gillette was at that time head of the latter institution; his scholarly explanation of the method of teaching, his concern for his charges, this sudden demonstration of the care the state bestowed upon its most unfortunate children, filled me with grave speculations in which the first, the fifth, or the ninth place in an oratorical contest seemed of little moment.

However, this brief delay between our field of Waterloo and our arrival at our aspiring college turned out to be most unfortunate, for we found the ardent group not only exhausted by the premature preparations for the return of a successful orator, but naturally much irritated as they contemplated their garlands drooping disconsolately in tubs and bowls of water. They did not fail to make me realize that I had dealt the cause of woman's advancement a staggering blow, and all my explanations of the fifth place were haughtily considered insufficient before that golden Bar of Youth, so absurdly inflexible!

To return to my last year at school, it was inevitable that the pressure toward religious profession should increase as graduating day approached. So curious, however, are the paths of moral development that several times during subsequent experiences have I felt that this passive resistance of mine, this clinging to an individual conviction, was the best moral training I received at Rockford College. During the first decade of Hull-House, it was felt by propagandists of divers social theories that the new Settlement would be a fine coign of vantage from which to propagate social faiths, and that a mere preliminary step would be the conversion of the founders; hence I have been reasoned with hours at a time, and I recall at least three occasions when this was followed by actual prayer. In the first instance, the honest exhorter who fell upon his knees before my astonished eyes, was an advocate of single tax upon land values. He begged, in that indirect phraseology which is deemed appropriate for prayer, that "the sister might see the beneficent results it would bring to the poor who live in the awful congested districts around this very house."

The early socialists used every method of attack, — a favorite one being the statement, doubtless sometimes honestly made, that I really was a socialist, but "too much of a coward to say so." I remember one socialist who habitually opened a very telling address he was in the habit of giving upon the street corners, by holding me up as an awful example to his fellow-socialists, as one of their number "who had been caught in the toils of capitalism." He always added as a final clinching of the statement, that he knew what he was talking about because he was a member of the Hull-House Men's Club. When I ventured to say to him that not all of the thousands of people who belong to a class or club at Hull-House could possibly know my personal opinions, and to mildly inquire upon what he founded his assertions, he triumphantly replied that I had once admitted to him that I had read Sombart and Loria,[15] and that any one of sound mind must see the inevitable conclusions of such master reasonings.

I could multiply these two instances a hundred-fold, and possibly nothing aided me to stand on my own feet and to select what seemed reasonable from this wilderness of dogma, so much as my early encounter with genuine zeal and affectionate solicitude, associated with what I could not accept as the whole truth. . . .

Towards the end of our four years' course we debated much as to what we were to be, and long before the end of my school days it was quite settled in my mind that I should study medicine and "live with the poor." This conclusion of course was the result of many things, perhaps epitomized in my graduating essay on "Cassandra"[16] and her tragic fate "always to be in the right, and always to be disbelieved and rejected."

This state of affairs, it may readily be guessed, the essay held to be an example of the feminine trait of mind called intuition, "an accurate perception of Truth and Justice, which rests contented in itself and will make no effort to confirm itself or to organize through existing knowledge." The essay then proceeds — I am forced to admit, with overmuch conviction — with the statement that woman can only "grow accurate and intelligible by the thorough study of at least one branch of physical science, for only with eyes thus accustomed to the search for truth can she detect all self-deceit and fancy in herself and learn to express herself without dogmatism." So much for the first part of the thesis. Having thus "gained accuracy, would woman bring this force to bear throughout morals and justice, then she must find in active labor the promptings and inspirations that come from growing insight." I was quite certain that by following these directions carefully, in the end the contemporary woman would find "her faculties clear and acute from the study of science, and her hand upon the magnetic chain of humanity."

This veneration for science portrayed in my final essay was doubtless the result of the statements the textbooks were then making of what was

---

[15] Werner Sombart (1863–1941) was a German economist whose masterwork *Modern Capitalism* (1902) presented a Marxist interpretation of economic history. Achille Loria (1857–1943) was an Italian economist whose theories emphasized the relationship of land and people.

[16] The Trojan princess of mythology whose prophecy of a Greek victory over the walled city of Troy was mocked and dismissed by her father's warriors. Euripides told of her fate in "The Trojan Women."

called the theory of evolution, the acceptance of which even thirty years after the publication of Darwin's "Origin of Species" had about it a touch of intellectual adventure. We knew, for instance, that our science teacher had accepted this theory, but we had a strong suspicion that the teacher of Butler's "Analogy" had not. We chafed at the meagerness of the college library in this direction, and I used to bring back in my handbag books belonging to an advanced brother-in-law[17] who had studied medicine in Germany and who therefore was quite emancipated. The first gift I made when I came into possession of my small estate the year after I left school, was a thousand dollars to the library of Rockford College, with the stipulation that it be spent for scientific books. In the long vacations I pressed plants, stuffed birds, and pounded rocks in some vague belief that I was approximating the new method, and yet when my stepbrother who was becoming a real scientist,[18] tried to carry me along with him into the merest outskirts of the methods of research, it at once became evident that I had no aptitude and was unable to follow intelligently Darwin's careful observations on the earthworm. I made an heroic effort, although candor compels me to state that I never would have finished if I had not been pulled and pushed by my really ardent companion, who in addition to a multitude of earthworms and a fine microscope, possessed untiring tact with one of flagging zeal.

As our boarding-school days neared the end, in the consciousness of approaching separation we vowed eternal allegiance to our "early ideals," and promised each other we would "never abandon them without conscious justification," and we often warned each other of "the perils of self-tradition."

We believed, in our sublime self-conceit, that the difficulty of life would lie solely in the direction of losing these precious ideals of ours, of failing to follow the way to martyrdom and high purpose we had marked out for ourselves, and we had no notion of the obscure paths of tolerance, just allowance, and self-blame wherein, if we held our minds open, we might learn something of the mystery and complexity of life's purposes.

The year after I had left college I came back, with a classmate, to receive the degree we had so eagerly anticipated. Two of the graduating

[17]A reference to Harry Haldeman (1848–1905), the elder son of Jane Addams's stepmother, Anna Haldeman Addams, and the husband of Jane Addams's sister, Alice Addams Haldeman.

[18]A reference to George Haldeman (1861–1909), the younger son of Jane Addams's stepmother, who was close in age to Jane. George's psychological problems prevented him from completing his Ph.D. in biology at Johns Hopkins University and prevented him from ever working as a scientist.

class were also ready and four of us were dubbed B.A. on the very day that Rockford Seminary was declared a college in the midst of tumultuous anticipations. Having had a year outside of college walls in that trying land between vague hope and definite attainment, I had become very much sobered in my desire for a degree, and was already beginning to emerge from that rose-colored mist with which the dream of youth so readily envelops the future.

Whatever may have been the perils of self-tradition, I certainly did not escape them, for it required eight years — from the time I left Rockford in the summer of 1881 until Hull-House was opened in the autumn of 1889 — to formulate my convictions even in the least satisfactory manner, much less to reduce them to a plan for action. During most of that time I was absolutely at sea so far as any moral purpose was concerned, clinging only to the desire to live in a really living world and refusing to be content with a shadowy intellectual or aesthetic reflection of it.

CHAPTER 4
THE SNARE OF PREPARATION

The winter after I left school was spent in the Woman's Medical College of Philadelphia, but the development of the spinal difficulty which had shadowed me from childhood forced me into Dr. Weir Mitchell's hospital for the late spring, and the next winter I was literally bound to a bed in my sister's house for six months. In spite of its tedium, the long winter had its mitigations, for after the first few weeks I was able to read with a luxurious consciousness of leisure, and I remember opening the first volume of Carlyle's "Frederick the Great" with a lively sense of gratitude that it was not Gray's "Anatomy," having found, like many another, that general culture is a much easier undertaking than professional study. The long illness inevitably put aside the immediate prosecution of a medical course, and although I had passed my examinations creditably enough in the required subjects for the first year, I was very glad to have a physician's sanction for giving up clinics and dissecting rooms and to follow his prescription of spending the next two years in Europe.

Before I returned to America I had discovered that there were other genuine reasons for living among the poor than that of practicing medicine upon them, and my brief foray into the profession was never resumed.

The long illness left me in a state of nervous exhaustion with which I struggled for years, traces of it remaining long after Hull-House was opened in 1889. At the best it allowed me but a limited amount of energy, so that doubtless there was much nervous depression at the foundation of the spiritual struggles which this chapter is forced to record. However, it could not have been all due to my health, for as my wise little notebook sententiously remarked, "In his own way each man must struggle, lest the moral law become a far-off abstraction utterly separated from his active life."

It would, of course, be impossible to remember that some of these struggles ever took place at all, were it not for these selfsame notebooks, in which, however, I no longer wrote in moments of high resolve, but judging from the internal evidence afforded by the books themselves, only in moments of deep depression when overwhelmed by a sense of failure.

One of the most poignant of these experiences, which occurred during the first few months after our landing upon the other side of the Atlantic, was on a Saturday night, when I received an ineradicable impression of the wretchedness of East London, and also saw for the first time the overcrowded quarters of a great city at midnight. A small party of tourists were taken to the East End by a city missionary to witness the Saturday night sale of decaying vegetables and fruit, which, owing to the Sunday laws in London, could not be sold until Monday, and, as they were beyond safe keeping, were disposed of at auction as late as possible on Saturday night. On Mile End Road, from the top of an omnibus which paused at the end of a dingy street lighted by only occasional flares of gas, we saw two huge masses of ill-clad people clamoring around two hucksters' carts. They were bidding their farthings and ha'pennies for a vegetable held up by the auctioneer, which he at last scornfully flung, with a gibe for its cheapness, to the successful bidder. In the momentary pause only one man detached himself from the groups. He had bidden in a cabbage, and when it struck his hand, he instantly sat down on the curb, tore it with his teeth, and hastily devoured it, unwashed and uncooked as it was. He and his fellows were types of the "submerged tenth," as our missionary guide told us, with some little satisfaction in the then new phrase, and he further added that so many of them could scarcely be seen in one spot save at this Saturday night auction, the desire for cheap food being apparently the one thing which could move them simultaneously. They were huddled into ill-fitting, cast-off clothing, the ragged finery which one sees only in East London. Their pale faces were dominated by that most unlovely of human expressions, the cunning and shrewdness of the bargain-hunter who starves if he cannot make a successful trade, and yet the final impression was not of ragged, tawdry clothing nor of pinched and sallow faces, but of myriads of hands, empty, pathetic, nerveless, and workworn, showing white in the uncertain light of the street, and clutching forward for food which was already unfit to eat.

Perhaps nothing is so fraught with significance as the human hand, this oldest tool with which man has dug his way from savagery, and with which he is constantly groping forward. I have never since been able to see a number of hands held upward, even when they are moving rhythmically in a calisthenic exercise, or when they belong to a class of chubby children who wave them in eager response to a teacher's query, without a certain revival of this memory, a clutching at the heart reminiscent of the despair and resentment which seized me then.

For the following weeks I went about London almost furtively, afraid to look down narrow streets and alleys lest they disclose again this hideous human need and suffering. I carried with me for days at a time that curious surprise we experience when we first come back into the streets after days given over to sorrow and death; we are bewildered that the world should be going on as usual and unable to determine which is real, the inner pang or the outward seeming. In time all huge London came to seem unreal save the poverty in its East End. During the following two years on the continent, while I was irresistibly drawn to the poorer quarters of each city, nothing among the beggars of south Italy nor among the salt miners of Austria carried with it the same conviction of human wretchedness which was conveyed by this momentary glimpse of an East London street. It was, of course, a most fragmentary and lurid view of the poverty of East London, and quite unfair. I should have been shown either less or more, for I went away with no notion of the hundreds of men and women who had gallantly identified their fortunes with these empty-handed people, and who, in church and chapel, "relief works," and charities, were at least making an effort towards its mitigation.

Our visit was made in November, 1883, the very year when the *Pall Mall Gazette* exposure started "The Bitter Cry of Outcast London," and the conscience of England was stirred as never before over this joyless city in the East End of its capital. Even then, vigorous and drastic plans were being discussed, and a splendid program of municipal reforms was already dimly outlined. Of all these, however, I had heard nothing but the vaguest rumor.

No comfort came to me then from any source, and the painful impression was increased because at the very moment of looking down the

East London street from the top of the omnibus, I had been sharply and painfully reminded of "The Vision of Sudden Death" which had confronted De Quincey one summer's night as he was being driven through rural England on a high mail coach. Two absorbed lovers suddenly appear between the narrow, blossoming hedgerows in the direct path of the huge vehicle which is sure to crush them to their death. De Quincey tries to send them a warning shout, but finds himself unable to make a sound because his mind is hopelessly entangled in an endeavor to recall the exact lines from the "Iliad" which describe the great cry with which Achilles alarmed all Asia militant. Only after his memory responds is his will released from its momentary paralysis, and he rides on through the fragrant night with the horror of the escaped calamity thick upon him, but he also bears with him the consciousness that he had given himself over so many years to classic learning — that when suddenly called upon for a quick decision in the world of life and death, he had been able to act only through a literary suggestion.

This is what we were all doing, lumbering our minds with literature that only served to cloud the really vital situation spread before our eyes. It seemed to me too preposterous that in my first view of the horror of East London I should have recalled De Quincey's literary description of the literary suggestion which had once paralyzed him. In my disgust it all appeared a hateful, vicious circle which even the apostles of culture themselves admitted, for had not one of the greatest among the moderns [19] plainly said that "conduct, and not culture, is three fourths of human life."

For two years in the midst of my distress over the poverty which, thus suddenly driven into my consciousness, had become to me the *Weltschmerz,* there was mingled a sense of futility, of misdirected energy, the belief that the pursuit of cultivation would not in the end bring either solace or relief. I gradually reached a conviction that the first generation of college women had taken their learning too quickly, had departed too suddenly from the active, emotional life led by their grandmothers and great-grandmothers; that the contemporary education of young women had developed too exclusively the power of acquiring knowledge and of merely receiving impressions; that somewhere in the process of "being educated" they had lost that simple and almost automatic response to the human appeal, that old healthful reaction resulting in activity

---

[19] A reference to Matthew Arnold (1822–88), a poet and literary leader in Victorian England who subscribed to the belief that members of the elite have obligations to society.

from the mere presence of suffering or of helplessness; that they are so sheltered and pampered they have no chance even to make "the great refusal."

In the German and French *pensions,* which twenty-five years ago were crowded with American mothers and their daughters who had crossed the seas in search of culture, one often found the mother making real connection with the life about her, using her inadequate German with great fluency, gayly measuring the enormous sheets or exchanging recipes with the German Hausfrau, visiting impartially the nearest kindergarten and market, making an atmosphere of her own, hearty and genuine as far as it went, in the house and on the street. On the other hand, her daughter was critical and uncertain of her linguistic acquirements, and only at ease when in the familiar receptive attitude afforded by the art gallery and the opera house. In the latter she was swayed and moved, appreciative of the power and charm of the music, intelligent as to the legend and poetry of the plot, finding use for her trained and developed powers as she sat "being cultivated" in the familiar atmosphere of the classroom which had, as it were, become sublimated and romanticized.

I remember a happy busy mother who, complacent with the knowledge that her daughter daily devoted four hours to her music, looked up from her knitting to say, "If I had had your opportunities when I was young, my dear, I should have been a very happy girl. I always had musical talent, but such training as I had, foolish little songs and waltzes and not time for half an hour's practice a day."

The mother did not dream of the sting her words left and that the sensitive girl appreciated only too well that her opportunities were fine and unusual, but she also knew that in spite of some facility and much good teaching she had no genuine talent and never would fulfill the expectations of her friends. She looked back upon her mother's girlhood with positive envy because it was so full of happy industry and extenuating obstacles, with undisturbed opportunity to believe that her talents were unusual. The girl looked wistfully at her mother, but had not the courage to cry out what was in her heart: "I might believe I had unusual talent if I did not know what good music was; I might enjoy half an hour's practice a day if I were busy and happy the rest of the time. You do not know what life means when all the difficulties are removed! I am simply smothered and sickened with advantages. It is like eating a sweet dessert the first thing in the morning."

This, then, was the difficulty, this sweet dessert in the morning and the assumption that the sheltered, educated girl has nothing to do with the bitter poverty and the social maladjustment which is all about her, and which, after all, cannot be concealed, for it breaks through poetry and literature in a burning tide which overwhelms her; it peers at her in the form of heavy-laden market women and underpaid street laborers, gibing her with a sense of her uselessness.

I recall one snowy morning in Saxe-Coburg, looking from the window of our little hotel upon the town square, that we saw crossing and re-crossing it a single file of women with semicircular heavy wooden tanks fastened upon their backs. They were carrying in this primitive fashion to a remote cooling room these tanks filled with a hot brew incident to one stage of beer making. The women were bent forward, not only under the weight which they were bearing, but because the tanks were so high that it would have been impossible for them to have lifted their heads. Their faces and hands, reddened in the cold morning air, showed clearly the white scars where they had previously been scalded by the hot stuff which splashed if they stumbled ever so little on their way. Stung into action by one of those sudden indignations against cruel conditions which at times fill the young with unexpected energy, I found myself across the square, in company with mine host, interviewing the phlegmatic owner of the brewery who received us with exasperating indifference, or rather received me, for the innkeeper mysteriously slunk away as soon as the great magnate of the town began to speak. I went back to a breakfast for which I had lost my appetite, as I had for Gray's "Life of Prince Albert"[20] and his wonderful tutor, Baron Stockmar, which I had been reading late the night before. The book had lost its fascination; how could a good man, feeling so keenly his obligation "to make princely the mind of his prince," ignore such conditions of life for the multitude of humble, hard-working folk. We were spending two months in Dresden that winter, given over to much reading of "The History of Art" and to much visiting of its art gallery and opera house, and after such an experience I would invariably suffer a moral revulsion against this feverish search after culture. It was doubtless in such moods that I founded my admiration for Albrecht Dürer, taking his wonderful pictures, however, in the most unorthodox manner, merely as human documents. I was chiefly appealed to by his unwillingness to lend himself to a smooth and cultivated view of life, by his determination to record its frustrations and even the hideous forms which darken the day for our human imagination and to ignore no human complications. . . .

[20] Prince Albert (1819–86) was the husband of Queen Victoria of England. Son of the Duke of Saxe-Coburg, Albert showed some interest in the condition of Britain's working classes.

The wonder and beauty of Italy later brought healing and some relief to the paralyzing sense of the futility of all artistic and intellectual effort when disconnected from the ultimate test of the conduct it inspired. The serene and soothing touch of history also aroused old enthusiasms, although some of their manifestations were such as one smiles over more easily in retrospection than at the moment. I fancy that it was no smiling matter to several people in our party, whom I induced to walk for three miles in the hot sunshine beating down upon the Roman Campagna, that we might enter the Eternal City on foot through the Porta del Popolo, as pilgrims had done for centuries. To be sure, we had really entered Rome the night before, but the railroad station and the hotel might have been anywhere else, and we had been driven beyond the walls after breakfast and stranded at the very spot where the pilgrims always said "Ecco Roma," as they caught the first glimpse of St. Peter's dome. This melodramatic entrance into Rome, or rather pretended entrance, was the prelude to days of enchantment, and I returned to Europe two years later in order to spend a winter there and to carry out a great desire to systematically study the Catacombs. In spite of my distrust of "advantages" I was apparently not yet so cured but that I wanted more of them.

The two years which elapsed before I again found myself in Europe brought their inevitable changes. Family arrangements had so come about that I had spent three or four months of each of the intervening winters in Baltimore, where I seemed to have reached the nadir of my nervous depression and sense of maladjustment. . . .

The summers were spent in the old home in northern Illinois, and one Sunday morning I received the rite of baptism and became a member of the Presbyterian church in the village. At this time there was certainly no outside pressure pushing me towards such a decision, and at twenty-five one does not ordinarily take such a step from a mere desire to conform. While I was not conscious of any emotional "conversion," I took upon myself the outward expressions of the religious life with all humility and sincerity. It was doubtless true that I was

> Weary of myself and sick of asking
> What I am and what I ought to be,

and that various cherished safeguards and claims to self-dependence had been broken into by many piteous failures. But certain I had been brought to the conclusion that "sincerely to give up one's conceit or hope of being good in one's own right is the only door to the Universe's deeper reaches." Perhaps the young clergyman recognized this as the test of the Christian temper, at any rate he required little assent to dogma or miracle, and assured me that while both the ministry and the officers of

his church were obliged to subscribe to doctrines of well-known sever-
ity, the faith required of the laity was almost early Christian in its simplicity. I was conscious of no change from my childish acceptance of
the teachings of the Gospels, but at this moment something persuasive
within made me long for an outward symbol of fellowship, some bond of
peace, some blessed spot where unity of spirit might claim right of way
over all differences. There was also growing within me an almost pas-
sionate devotion to the ideals of democracy, and when in all history had
these ideals been so thrillingly expressed as when the faith of the fisher-
man and the slave had been boldly opposed to the accepted moral belief
that the well-being of a privileged few might justly be built upon the ignorance and sacrifice of the many? Who was I, with my dreams of universal fellowship, that I did not identify myself with the institutional
statement of this belief, as it stood in the little village in which I was born,
and without which testimony in each remote hamlet of Christendom it
would be so easy for the world to slip back into the doctrines of selection
and aristocracy?

In one of the intervening summers between these European journeys
I visited a western state where I had formerly invested a sum of money
in mortgages. I was much horrified by the wretched conditions among
the farmers, which had resulted from a long period of drought, and one
forlorn picture was fairly burned into my mind. A number of starved
hogs — collateral for a promissory note — were huddled into an open
pen. Their backs were humped in a curious, camel-like fashion, and they
were devouring one of their own number, the latest victim of absolute
starvation or possibly merely the one least able to defend himself against
their voracious hunger. The farmer's wife looked on indifferently, a picture of despair as she stood in the door of the bare, crude house, and the
two children behind her, whom she vainly tried to keep out of sight, continually thrust forward their faces almost covered by masses of coarse,
sunburned hair, and their little feet so black, so hard, the great cracks so
filled with dust that they looked like flattened hoofs. The children could
not be compared to anything so joyous as satyrs, although they appeared
but half-human. It seemed to me quite impossible to receive interest
from mortgages placed upon farms which might at any season be reduced to such conditions, and with great inconvenience to my agent and
doubtless with hardship to the farmers, as speedily as possible I withdrew all my investment. But something had to be done with the money,
and in my reaction against unseen horrors I bought a farm near my native village and also a flock of innocent-looking sheep. My partner in the
enterprise had not chosen the shepherd's lot as a permanent occupation,
but hoped to speedily finish his college course upon half the proceeds of

our venture. This pastoral enterprise still seems to me to have been essentially sound, both economically and morally, but perhaps one partner depended too much upon the impeccability of her motives and the other found himself too preoccupied with study to know that it is not a real kindness to bed a sheepfold with straw, for certainly the venture ended in a spectacle scarcely less harrowing than the memory it was designed to obliterate. At least the sight of two hundred sheep with four rotting hoofs each, was not reassuring to one whose conscience craved economic peace. A fortunate series of sales of mutton, wool, and farm enabled the partners to end the enterprise without loss, and they passed on, one to college and the other to Europe, if not wiser, certainly sadder for the experience.

It was during this second journey to Europe that I attended a meeting of the London match girls who were on strike and who met daily under the leadership of well-known labor men of London. The low wages that were reported at the meetings, the phossy jaw which was described and occasionally exhibited, the appearance of the girls themselves I did not, curiously enough, in any wise connect with what was called the labor movement, nor did I understand the efforts of the London trades-unionists, concerning whom I held the vaguest notions. But of course this impression of human misery was added to the others which were already making me so wretched. I think that up to this time I was still filled with the sense which Wells describes in one of his young characters, that somewhere in Church or State are a body of authoritative people who will put things to rights as soon as they really know what is wrong. Such a young person persistently believes that behind all suffering, behind sin and want, must lie redeeming magnanimity. He may imagine the world to be tragic and terrible, but it never for an instant occurs to him that it may be contemptible or squalid or self-seeking. Apparently I looked upon the efforts of the trades-unionists as I did upon those of Frederic Harrison and the Positivists[21] whom I heard the next Sunday in Newton Hall, as a manifestation of "loyalty to humanity" and an attempt to aid in its progress. I was enormously interested in the Positivists during these European years; I imagined that their philosophical conception of man's religious development might include all expressions of that for which so many ages of men have struggled and aspired. . . .

---

[21] A reference to the then-popular theory of August Comte, a French sociologist who traced the evolution of human thought from theology to metaphysics to science. Comte proposed a "positivist" religion centered on humanity, not any diety; Frederic Harrison (1831–1923) founded the Church of Humanity in London in the late nineteenth century to disseminate Comte's ideas.

It is hard to tell just when the very simple plan which afterward developed into the Settlement began to form itself in my mind. It may have been even before I went to Europe for the second time, but I gradually became convinced that it would be a good thing to rent a house in a part of the city where many primitive and actual needs are found, in which young women who had been given over too exclusively to study, might restore a balance of activity along traditional lines and learn of life from life itself; where they might try out some of the things they had been taught and put truth to "the ultimate test of the conduct it dictates or inspires." I do not remember to have mentioned this plan to any one until we reached Madrid in April, 1888.

We had been to see a bull-fight rendered in the most magnificent Spanish style, where greatly to my surprise and horror, I found that I had seen, with comparative indifference, five bulls and many more horses killed. The sense that this was the last survival of all the glories of the amphitheater, the illusion that the riders on the caparisoned horses might have been knights of a tournament, or the matadore a slightly armed gladiator facing his martyrdom, and all the rest of the obscure yet vivid associations of an historic survival, had carried me beyond the endurance of any of the rest of the party. I finally met them in the foyer, stern and pale with disapproval of my brutal endurance, and but partially recovered from the faintness and disgust which the spectacle itself had produced upon them. I had no defense to offer to their reproaches save that I had not thought much about the bloodshed; but in the evening the natural and inevitable reaction came, and in deep chagrin I felt myself tried and condemned, not only by this disgusting experience but by the entire moral situation which it revealed. It was suddenly made quite clear to me that I was lulling my conscience by a dreamer's scheme, that a mere paper reform had become a defense for continued idleness, and that I was making it a *raison d'être* for going on indefinitely with study and travel. It is easy to become the dupe of a deferred purpose, of the promise the future can never keep, and I had fallen into the meanest type of self-deception in making myself believe that all this was in preparation for great things to come. Nothing less than the moral reaction following the experience at a bull-fight had been able to reveal to me that so far from following in the wake of a chariot of philanthropic fire, I had been tied to the tail of the veriest ox-cart of self-seeking.

I had made up my mind that next day, whatever happened, I would begin to carry out the plan, if only by talking about it. I can well recall the stumbling and uncertainty with which I finally set it forth to Miss Starr, my old-time school friend, who was one of our party. I even dared to hope that she might join in carrying out the plan, but nevertheless I told it in the fear of that disheartening experience which is so apt to afflict our most cherished plans when they are at last divulged, when we suddenly feel that there is nothing there to talk about, and as the golden dream slips through our fingers we are left to wonder at our own fatuous belief. But gradually the comfort of Miss Starr's companionship, the vigor and enthusiasm which she brought to bear upon it, told both in the growth of the plan and upon the sense of its validity, so that by the time we had reached the enchantment of the Alhambra, the scheme had become convincing and tangible although still most hazy in detail.

A month later we parted in Paris, Miss Starr to go back to Italy, and I to journey on to London to secure as many suggestions as possible from those wonderful places of which we had heard, Toynbee Hall and the People's Palace.[22] So that it finally came about that in June, 1888, five years after my first visit in East London, I found myself at Toynbee Hall equipped not only with a letter of introduction from Canon Fremantle,[23] but with high expectations and a certain belief that whatever perplexities and discouragement concerning the life of the poor were in store for me, I should at least know something at first hand and have the solace of daily activity. I had confidence that although life itself might contain many difficulties, the period of mere passive receptivity had come to an end, and I had at last finished with the everlasting "preparation for life," however ill-prepared I might be.

It was not until years afterward that I came upon Tolstoy's phrase "the snare of preparation," which he insists we spread before the feet of young people, hopelessly entangling them in a curious inactivity at the very period of life when they are longing to construct the world anew and to conform it to their own ideals.

CHAPTER 5
FIRST DAYS AT HULL-HOUSE

The next January found Miss Starr and myself in Chicago, searching for a neighborhood in which we might put our plans into execution. In our eagerness to win friends for the new undertaking, we utilized every opportunity to set forth the meaning of the Settlement as it had been embodied in Toynbee Hall, although in those days we made no appeal for money, meaning to start with our own slender resources. From the very

---

[22] A center for workers' education and entertainment in London, funded and built by upper-class social reformers in 1887.

[23] A leader in the Anglican Church in London and an important mentor for Samuel Barnett, the founder of the Toynbee Hall Settlement House, which inspired Hull-House.

first the plan received courteous attention, and the discussion, while often skeptical, was always friendly. Professor Swing[24] wrote a commendatory column in the *Evening Journal,* and our early speeches were reported quite out of proportion to their worth. I recall a spirited evening at the home of Mrs. Wilmarth,[25] which was attended by that renowned scholar Thomas Davidson,[26] and by a young Englishman who was a member of the then new Fabian society[27] and to whom a peculiar glamour was attached because he had scoured knives all summer in a camp of high-minded philosophers in the Adirondacks. Our new little plan met with criticism, not to say disapproval, from Mr. Davidson, who, as nearly as I can remember, called it "one of those unnatural attempts to understand life through coöperative living."

It was in vain we asserted that the collective living was not an essential part of the plan, that we would always scrupulously pay our own expenses, and that at any moment we might decide to scatter through the neighborhood and to live in separate tenements; he still contended that the fascination for most of those volunteering residence would lie in the collective living aspect of the Settlement. His contention was, of course, essentially sound; there is a constant tendency for the residents to "lose themselves in the cave of their own companionship," as the Toynbee Hall phrase goes, but on the other hand, it is doubtless true that the very companionship, the give and take of colleagues, is what tends to keep the Settlement normal and in touch with "the world of things as they are." I am happy to say that we never resented this nor any other difference of opinion. . . .

I think that time has also justified our early contention that the mere foothold of a house, easily accessible, ample in space, hospitable, and tolerant in spirit, situated in the midst of the large foreign colonies which so easily isolate themselves in American cities, would be in itself a serviceable thing for Chicago. I am not so sure that we succeeded in our endeavors "to make social intercourse express the growing sense of the

[24] David Swing was a popular, iconoclastic preacher in Chicago who had fought his way back from a heresy trial before the Chicago Presbytery in the 1870s and established an independent congregation in the city.

[25] Mrs. Mary Hawes Wilmarth (1837–1919) was a wealthy matron in Chicago and a leading figure in the Chicago Woman's Club who served on the board of the Hull-House Association from 1895 until 1907. She also taught classes, including French, at Hull-House.

[26] Davidson (1848–1903) was a leader of the Anglican Church in Britain and became the archbishop of Canterbury in 1903.

[27] The Fabian Society was a socialist society founded by elite British intellectuals in 1884. Named for Quintus Fabius Maximus, a Roman general who refused to engage Hannibal in battle and thereby avoided defeat, the Fabian Society took the position that socialism could be introduced gradually, through legislation, rather than through violent revolution.

economic unity of society and to add the social function to democracy." But Hull-House was soberly opened on the theory that the dependence of classes on each other is reciprocal; and that as the social relation is essentially a reciprocal relation, it gives a form of expression that has peculiar value.

In our search for a vicinity in which to settle we went about with the officers of the compulsory education department, with city missionaries, and with the newspaper reporters. . . .

One Sunday afternoon in the late winter a reporter took me to visit a so-called anarchist Sunday school, several of which were to be found on the Northwest Side of the city. The young man in charge was of the German student type, and his face flushed with enthusiasm as he led the children singing one of Koerner's poems. The newspaper man, who did not understand German, asked me what abominable stuff they were singing, but he seemed dissatisfied with my translation of the simple words and darkly intimated that they were "deep ones," and had probably "fooled" me. When I replied that Koerner was an ardent German poet whose songs inspired his countrymen to resist the aggressions of Napoleon, and that his bound poems were found in the most respectable libraries, he looked at me rather askance and I then and there had my first intimation that to treat a Chicago man who is called an anarchist as you would treat any other citizen, is to lay yourself open to deep suspicion.

Another Sunday afternoon in the early spring, on the way to a Bohemian mission in the carriage of one of its founders, we passed a fine old house standing well back from the street, surrounded on three sides by a broad piazza which was supported by wooden pillars of exceptionally pure Corinthian design and proportion. . . .

Near the junction of Blue Island Avenue, Halsted Street, and Harrison Street . . . the hospitable old house . . . was of course rented, the lower part of it used for offices and storerooms in connection with a factory that stood back of it. However, after some difficulties were overcome, it proved to be possible to sublet the second floor and what had been the large drawing-room on the first floor.

The house had passed through many changes since it had been built in 1856 for the homestead of one of Chicago's pioneer citizens, Mr. Charles J. Hull, and although battered by its vicissitudes, was essentially sound. Before it had been occupied by the factory, it had sheltered a second-hand furniture store, and at one time the Little Sisters of the Poor had used it for a home for the aged. . . .

The fine old house responded kindly to repairs, its wide hall and open fireplaces always insuring it a gracious aspect. Its generous owner, Miss

Helen Culver,[28] in the following spring gave us a free leasehold of the entire house. Her kindness has continued through the years until the group of thirteen buildings, which at present comprises our equipment, is built largely upon land which Miss Culver has put at the service of the Settlement which bears Mr. Hull's name. In those days the house stood between an undertaking establishment and a saloon. "Knight, Death, and the Devil," the three were called by a Chicago wit, and yet any mock heroics which might be implied by comparing the Settlement to a knight quickly dropped away under the genuine kindness and hearty welcome extended to us by the families living up and down the street.

We furnished the house as we would have furnished it were it in another part of the city, with the photographs and other impedimenta we had collected in Europe, and with a few bits of family mahogany. While all the new furniture which was bought was enduring in quality, we were careful to keep it in character with the fine old residence. Probably no young matron ever placed her own things in her own house with more pleasure than that with which we first furnished Hull-House. We believed that the Settlement may logically bring to its aid all those adjuncts which the cultivated man regards as good and suggestive of the best life of the past.

On the 18th of September, 1889, Miss Starr and I moved into it, with Miss Mary Keyser,[29] who began by performing the housework, but who quickly developed into a very important factor in the life of the vicinity as well as in that of the household, and whose death five years later was most sincerely mourned by hundreds of our neighbors. In our enthusiasm over "settling," the first night we forgot not only to lock but to close a side door opening on Polk Street, and were much pleased in the morning to find that we possessed a fine illustration of the honesty and kindliness of our new neighbors.

Our first guest was an interesting young woman who lived in a neighboring tenement, whose widowed mother aided her in the support of the family by scrubbing a downtown theater every night. The mother, of English birth, was well bred and carefully educated, but was in the midst

[28]Helen Culver (1832–1925) was the niece, secretary, and beneficiary of Charles Hull, the real estate developer and philanthropist who built Hull-House. When Mr. Hull died in 1889, he left his estate, worth $4 million, to Miss Culver. She was an important contributor to the Hull-House Settlement. In addition to donating the house rent-free in 1890, she later donated the land on which it stood and adjacent lots, worth over $75,000. In 1920, shortly before her death, Culver bequeathed a $250,000 endowment to Hull-House, the settlement's largest gift.

[29]A native of Cedarville, Illinois, and the housekeeper to Jane Addams's stepmother before she moved to Chicago with the young Miss Addams, leaving the older Mrs. Addams without household help.

of that bitter struggle which awaits so many strangers in American cities who find that their social position tends to be measured solely by the standards of living they are able to maintain. Our guest has long since married the struggling young lawyer to whom she was then engaged, and he is now leading his profession in an eastern city. She recalls that month's experience always with a sense of amusement over the fact that the succession of visitors who came to see the new Settlement invariably questioned her most minutely concerning "these people" without once suspecting that they were talking to one who had been identified with the neighborhood from childhood. I at least was able to draw a lesson from the incident, and I never addressed a Chicago audience on the subject of the Settlement and its vicinity without inviting a neighbor to go with me, that I might curb any hasty generalization by the consciousness that I had an auditor who knew the conditions more intimately than I could hope to do.

Halsted Street has grown so familiar during twenty years of residence, that it is difficult to recall its gradual changes, — the withdrawal of the more prosperous Irish and Germans, and the slow substitution of Russian Jews, Italians, and Greeks. A description of the street [30] such as I gave in those early addresses still stands in my mind as sympathetic and correct.

> Halsted Street is thirty-two miles long, and one of the great thoroughfares of Chicago; Polk Street crosses it midway between the stockyards to the south and the ship-building yards on the north branch of the Chicago River. For the six miles between these two industries the street is lined with shops of butchers and grocers, with dingy and gorgeous saloons, and pretentious establishments for the sale of ready-made clothing. Polk Street, running west from Halsted Street, grows rapidly more prosperous; running a mile east to State Street, it grows steadily worse, and crosses a network of vice on the corners of Clark Street and Fifth Avenue. Hull-House once stood in the suburbs, but the city has steadily grown up around it and its site now has corners on three or four foreign colonies. Between Halsted Street and the river live about ten thousand Italians — Neapolitans, Sicilians, and Calabrians, with an occasional Lombard or Venetian. To the south on Twelfth Street are many Germans, and side streets are given over almost entirely to Polish and Russian Jews. Still farther south, these Jewish

---

[30] Quoted from one of Jane Addams's first public speeches, "The Objective Value of a Social Settlement." She delivered the speech at a conference of the School of Applied Ethics in Plymouth, Massachusetts, in 1892, just two years after founding Hull-House. It was published in *Philanthropy and Social Progress,* ed. Henry C. Adams (New York: Crowell Publishing Company, 1893), 27–56.

colonies merge into a huge Bohemian colony, so vast that Chicago ranks as the third Bohemian city in the world. To the northwest are many Canadian French, clannish in spite of their long residence in America, and to the north are Irish and first-generation Americans. On the streets directly west and farther north are well-to-do English-speaking families, many of whom own their houses and have lived in the neighborhood for years; one man is still living in his old farm-house.

The policy of the public authorities of never taking an initiative, and always waiting to be urged to do their duty, is obviously fatal in a neighborhood where there is little initiative among the citizens. The idea underlying our self-government breaks down in such a ward. The streets are inexpressibly dirty, the number of schools inadequate, sanitary legislation unenforced, the street lighting bad, the paving miserable and altogether lacking in the alleys and smaller streets, and the stables foul beyond description. Hundreds of houses are unconnected with the street sewer. The older and richer inhabitants seem anxious to move away as rapidly as they can afford it. They make room for newly arrived immigrants who are densely ignorant of civic duties. This substitution of the older inhabitants is accomplished industrially also, in the south and east quarters of the ward. The Jews and Italians do the finishing for the great clothing manufacturers, formerly done by Americans, Irish, and Germans, who refused to submit to the extremely low prices to which the sweating system has reduced their successors. As the design of the sweating system is the elimination of rent from the manufacture of clothing, the "outside work" is begun after the clothing leaves the cutter. An unscrupulous contractor regards no basement too dark, no stable loft too foul, no rear shanty too provisional, no tenement room too small for his workroom, as these conditions imply low rental. Hence these shops abound in the worst of the foreign districts where the sweater easily finds his cheap basement and his home finishers.

The houses of the ward, for the most part wooden, were originally built for one family and are now occupied by several. They are after the type of the inconvenient frame cottages found in the poorer suburbs twenty years ago. Many of them were built where they now stand; others were brought thither on rollers, because their previous sites had been taken for factories. The fewer brick tenement buildings which are three or four stories high are comparatively new, and there are few large tenements. The little wooden houses have a temporary aspect, and for this reason, perhaps, the tenement-house legislation in Chicago is totally inadequate. Rear tenements flourish; many houses have no water supply save the faucet in the back yard, there are no fire escapes, the garbage and ashes are placed in wooden boxes which are fastened to the street pavements. One of the most discouraging features about the present system of tenement houses is that many are owned by sordid and ignorant immigrants. The theory that wealth brings responsibility, that possession entails at length education and refinement, in these cases fails utterly. The children of an Italian immigrant owner may "shine" shoes in the street, and his wife may pick rags from the street gutter, laboriously sorting them in a dingy court. Wealth may do something for her self-complacency and feeling of consequence; it certainly does nothing for her comfort or her children's improvement nor for the cleanliness of any one concerned. Another thing that prevents better houses in Chicago is the tentative attitude of the real estate men. Many unsavory conditions are allowed to continue which would be regarded with horror if they were considered permanent. Meanwhile, the wretched conditions persist until at least two generations of children have been born and reared in them.

In every neighborhood where poorer people live, because rents are supposed to be cheaper there, is an element which, although uncertain in the individual, in the aggregate can be counted upon. It is composed of people of former education and opportunity who have cherished ambitions and prospects, but who are caricatures of what they meant to be — "hollow ghosts which blame the living men." There are times in many lives when there is a cessation of energy and loss of power. Men and women of education and refinement come to live in a cheaper neighborhood because they lack the ability to make money, because of ill health, because of an unfortunate marriage, or for other reasons which do not imply criminality or stupidity. Among them are those who, in spite of untoward circumstances, keep up some sort of an intellectual life; those who are "great for books," as their neighbors say. To such the Settlement may be a genuine refuge.

In the very first weeks of our residence Miss Starr started a reading party in George Eliot's "Romola," which was attended by a group of young women who followed the wonderful tale with unflagging interest. The weekly reading was held in our little upstairs dining-room, and two members of the club came to dinner each week, not only that they might be received as guests, but that they might help us wash the dishes afterwards and so make the table ready for the stacks of Florentine photographs. . . .

Volunteers to the new undertaking came quickly; a charming young girl conducted a kindergarten in the drawing-room, coming regularly every morning from her home in a distant part of the North Side of the city. Although a tablet to her memory has stood upon a mantel shelf in Hull-House for five years, we still associate her most vividly with the play of little children, first in her kindergarten and then in her own nursery. . . . Her daily presence for the first two years made it quite impossible for us to become too solemn and self-conscious in our strenuous routine, for her mirth and buoyancy were irresistible and her eager desire to share the life of the neighborhood never failed, although it was often put to a severe test. One day at luncheon she gayly recited her futile attempt to impress temperance principles upon the mind of an Italian mother, to whom she had returned a small daughter of five sent to the kindergarten "in quite a horrid state of intoxication" from the wine-soaked bread upon which she had breakfasted. The mother, with the gentle courtesy of a south Italian, listened politely to her graphic portrayal of the untimely end awaiting so immature a wine bibber; but long before the lecture was finished, quite unconscious of the incongruity, she hospitably set forth her best wines, and when her baffled guest refused one after the other, she disappeared, only to quickly return with a small dark glass of whisky, saying reassuringly, "See, I have brought you the true American drink." The recital ended in seriocomic despair, with the rueful statement that "the impression I probably made upon her darkened mind was, that it is the American custom to breakfast children on bread soaked in whisky instead of light Italian wine."

That first kindergarten was a constant source of education to us. We were much surprised to find social distinctions even among its lambs, although greatly amused with the neat formulation made by the superior little Italian boy who refused to sit beside uncouth little Angelina because "we eat our macaroni this way" — imitating the movement of a fork from a plate to his mouth, — "and she eat her macaroni this way," holding his hand high in the air and throwing back his head, that his wide-open mouth might receive an imaginary cascade. Angelina gravely nodded her little head in approval of this distinction between gentry and peasant. "But isn't it astonishing that merely table manners are made such a test all the way along?" was the comment of their democratic teacher. . . .

We encouraged the younger boys in tournaments and dramatics of all sorts, and we somewhat fatuously believed that boys who were early interested in adventurers or explorers might later want to know the lives of living statesmen and inventors. It is needless to add that the boys quickly responded to such a program, and that the only difficulty lay in finding leaders who were able to carry it out. This difficulty has been with us through all the years of growth and development in the Boys' Club until now, with its five-story building, its splendid equipment of shops, of recreation and study rooms, that group alone is successful which commands the services of a resourceful and devoted leader.

The dozens of younger children who from the first came to Hull-House were organized into groups which were not quite classes and not quite clubs. The value of these groups consisted almost entirely in arousing a higher imagination and in giving the children the opportunity which they could not have in the crowded schools, for initiative and for independent social relationships. The public schools then contained little hand work of any sort, so that naturally any instruction which we provided for the children took the direction of this supplementary work. But it required a constant effort that the pressure of poverty itself should not defeat the educational aim. The Italian girls in the sewing classes would count that day lost when they could not carry home a garment, and the insistence that it should be neatly made seemed a super-refinement to those in dire need of clothing.

As these clubs have been continued during the twenty years, they have developed classes in the many forms of handicraft. . . .

It seems to us important that these children shall find themselves permanently attached to a House that offers them evening clubs and classes with their old companions, that merges as easily as possible the school life into the working life and does what it can to find places for the bewildered young things looking for work. A large proportion of the delinquent boys brought into the Juvenile Court in Chicago are the oldest sons in large families whose wages are needed at home. The grades from which many of them leave school, as the records show, are piteously far from the seventh and eighth where the very first instruction in manual training is given, nor have they been caught by any other abiding interest.

In spite of these flourishing clubs for children early established at Hull-House, and the fact that our first organized undertaking was a kindergarten, we were very insistent that the Settlement should not be primarily for the children, and that it was absurd to suppose that grown people would not respond to opportunities for education and social life. Our enthusiastic kindergartner herself demonstrated this with an old woman of ninety, who, because she was left alone all day while her daughter cooked in a restaurant, had formed such a persistent habit of picking the plaster off the walls that one landlord after another refused to have her for a tenant. It required but a few weeks' time to teach her to make large paper chains, and gradually she was content to do it all day long, and in the end took quite as much pleasure in adorning the walls as she had formerly taken in demolishing them. Fortunately the landlord had never heard the aesthetic principle that the exposure of basic construction is more desirable than gaudy decoration. In course of time it was discovered that the old woman could speak Gaelic, and when one or two grave professors came to see her, the neighborhood was filled with pride that such a wonder lived in their midst. To mitigate life for a woman of ninety was an unfailing refutation of the statement that the Settlement was designed for the young.

On our first New Year's Day at Hull-House we invited the older people in the vicinity, sending a carriage for the most feeble and announcing to all of them that we were going to organize an Old Settlers' Party.

Every New Year's Day since, older people in varying numbers have come together at Hull-House to relate early hardships, and to take for the moment the place in the community to which their pioneer life entitles them. Many people who were formerly residents of the vicinity, but whom prosperity has carried into more desirable neighborhoods, come back to these meetings and often confess to each other that they have never since found such kindness as in early Chicago when all its citizens came together in mutual enterprises. Many of these pioneers, so like the men and women of my earliest childhood that I always felt comforted by their presence in the house, were very much opposed to "foreigners," whom they held responsible for a depreciation of property and a general lowering of the tone of the neighborhood. Sometimes we had a chance for championship; I recall one old man, fiercely American, who had reproached me because we had so many "foreign views" on our walls, to whom I endeavored to set forth our hope that the pictures might afford a familiar island to the immigrants in a sea of new and strange impressions. The old settler guest, taken off his guard, replied, "I see; they feel as we did when we saw a Yankee notion from down East," — thereby formulating the dim kinship between the pioneer and the immigrant, both "buffeting the waves of a new development." The older settlers as well as their children throughout the years have given genuine help to our various enterprises for neighborhood improvement, and from their own memories of earlier hardships have made many shrewd suggestions for alleviating the difficulties of that first sharp struggle with untoward conditions.

In those early days we were often asked why we had come to live on Halsted Street when we could afford to live somewhere else. I remember one man who used to shake his head and say it was "the strangest thing he had met in his experience," but who was finally convinced that it was "not strange but natural." In time it came to seem natural to all of us that the Settlement should be there. If it is natural to feed the hungry and care for the sick, it is certainly natural to give pleasure to the young, comfort to the aged, and to minister to the deep-seated craving for social intercourse that all men feel. Whoever does it is rewarded by something which, if not gratitude, is at least spontaneous and vital and lacks that irksome sense of obligation with which a substantial benefit is too often acknowledged.

In addition to the neighbors who responded to the receptions and classes, we found those who were too battered and oppressed to care for them. To these, however, was left that susceptibility to the bare offices of humanity which raises such offices into a bond of fellowship.

From the first it seemed understood that we were ready to perform the humblest neighborhood services. We were asked to wash the newborn babies, and to prepare the dead for burial, to nurse the sick, and to "mind the children."

Occasionally these neighborly offices unexpectedly uncovered ugly human traits. For six weeks after an operation we kept in one of our three bedrooms a forlorn little baby who, because he was born with a cleft palate, was most unwelcome even to his mother, and we were horrified when he died of neglect a week after he was returned to his home; a little Italian bride of fifteen sought shelter with us one November evening, to escape her husband who had beaten her every night for a week when he returned home from work, because she had lost her wedding ring; two of us officiated quite alone at the birth of an illegitimate child because the doctor was late in arriving, and none of the honest Irish matrons would "touch the likes of her"; we ministered at the deathbed of a young man, who during a long illness of tuberculosis had received so many bottles of whisky through the mistaken kindness of his friends, that the cumulative effect produced wild periods of exultation, in one of which he died.

We were also early impressed with the curious isolation of many of the immigrants; an Italian woman once expressed her pleasure in the red roses that she saw at one of our receptions in surprise that they had been "brought so fresh all the way from Italy." She would not believe for an instant that they had been grown in America. She said that she had lived in Chicago for six years and had never seen any roses, whereas in Italy she had seen them every summer in great profusion. During all that time, of course, the woman had lived within ten blocks of a florist's window; she had not been more than a five-cent car ride away from the public parks; but she had never dreamed of faring forth for herself, and no one had taken her. Her conception of America had been the untidy street in which she lived and had made her long struggle to adapt herself to American ways.

But in spite of some untoward experiences, we were constantly impressed with the uniform kindness and courtesy we received. Perhaps these first days laid the simple human foundations which are certainly essential for continuous living among the poor: first, genuine preference for residence in an industrial quarter to any other part of the city, because it is interesting and makes the human appeal; and second, the conviction, in the words of Canon Barnett,[31] that the things which make men alike are finer and better than the things that keep them apart, and that these basic likenesses, if they are properly accentuated, easily transcend the less essential differences of race, language, creed, and tradition.

Perhaps even in those first days we made a beginning toward that object which was afterwards stated in our charter: "To provide a center for a higher civic and social life; to institute and maintain educational and philanthropic enterprises; and to investigate and improve the conditions in the industrial districts of Chicago."

CHAPTER 6
THE SUBJECTIVE NECESSITY
FOR SOCIAL SETTLEMENTS

The ethical culture societies held a summer school at Plymouth, Massachusetts, in 1892, to which they invited several people representing the then new Settlement movement, that they might discuss with others the general theme of Philanthropy and Social Progress.

I venture to produce here parts of a lecture I delivered in Plymouth, both because I have found it impossible to formulate with the same freshness those early motives and strivings, and because, when published with other papers given that summer, it was received by the Settlement people themselves as a satisfactory statement.

I remember one golden summer afternoon during the sessions of the summer school that several of us met on the shores of a pond in a pine wood a few miles from Plymouth, to discuss our new movement. The natural leader of the group was Robert A. Woods.[32] He had recently returned from a residence in Toynbee Hall, London, to open Andover House in Boston, and had just issued a book, "English Social Movements," in which he had gathered together and focused the many forms

---

[31] An Anglican clergyman (1844–1913) who, with his wife and partner in reform, Henrietta Rowland Barnett, founded the Toynbee Hall Settlement House in the Whitechapel district of London's East End in 1883. His first name was Samuel; "Canon" indicates his position in the Anglican hierarchy.

[32] Woods (1865–1925) was the founder of the Andover House Settlement, later known as South End House, in Boston in the early 1890s. He and Addams worked to create a national network of settlement houses despite the fact that Woods was more politically conservative than Addams.

of social endeavor preceding and contemporaneous with the English Settlements. There were Miss Vida A. Scudder and Miss Helena Dudley[33] from the College Settlement Association, Miss Julia C. Lathrop and myself from Hull-House. Some of us had numbered our years as far as thirty, and we all carefully avoided the extravagance of statement which characterizes youth, and yet I doubt if anywhere on the continent that summer could have been found a group of people more genuinely interested in social development or more sincerely convinced that they had found a clew by which the conditions in crowded cities might be understood and the agencies for social betterment developed.

We were all careful to avoid saying that we had found a "life work," perhaps with an instinctive dread of expending all our energy in vows of constancy, as so often happens; and yet it is interesting to note that all of the people whom I have recalled as the enthusiasts at that little conference, have remained attached to Settlements in actual residence for longer or shorter periods each year during the eighteen years which have elapsed since then, although they have also been closely identified as publicists or governmental officials with movements outside. It is as if they had discovered that the Settlement was too valuable as a method as a way of approach to the social question to be abandoned, although they had long since discovered that it was not a "social movement" in itself. This, however, is anticipating the future, whereas the following paper on "The Subjective Necessity for Social Settlements"[34] should have a chance to speak for itself. It is perhaps too late in the day to express regret for its stilted title.

This paper is an attempt to analyze the motives which underlie a movement based, not only upon conviction, but upon genuine emotion, wherever educated young people are seeking an outlet for that sentiment of universal brotherhood, which the best spirit of our times is forcing from an emotion into a motive. These young people accomplish little toward the solution of this social problem, and bear the brunt of being cultivated into unnourished, oversensitive lives. They have been shut off from the common labor by which they live which is

[33] Scudder (1861–1954) was a professor of English at Wellesley College in Wellesley, Massachusetts, and a Christian Socialist. She and Helena Dudley, both of whom were Smith College graduates, were instrumental in founding the College Settlement in New York City the same year that Hull-House opened. Dudley later served as head resident of Denison House in Boston.

[34] A speech Jane Addams delivered at the School of Applied Ethics conference where she delivered "The Objective Value of a Social Settlement." Of the two, "Subjective Necessity" was more original in its argument. It was published in *Philanthropy and Social Progress,* ed. Henry C. Adams (New York: Crowell Publishing Company, 1893), pp. 27–56.

a great source of moral and physical health. They feel a fatal want of harmony between their theory and their lives, a lack of coördination between thought and action. I think it is hard for us to realize how seriously many of them are taking to the notion of human brotherhood, how eagerly they long to give tangible expression to the democratic ideal. These young men and women, longing to socialize their democracy, are animated by certain hopes which may be thus loosely formulated; that if in a democratic country nothing can be permanently achieved save through the masses of the people, it will be impossible to establish a higher political life than the people themselves crave; that it is difficult to see how the notion of a higher civic life can be fostered save through common intercourse; that the blessings which we associate with a life of refinement and cultivation can be made universal and must be made universal if they are to be permanent; that the good we secure for ourselves is precarious and uncertain, is floating in mid-air, until it is secured for all of us and incorporated into our common life. It is easier to state these hopes than to formulate the line of motives, which I believe to constitute the trend of the subjective pressure toward the Settlement. There is something primordial about these motives, but I am perhaps overbold in designating them as a great desire to share the race life. We all bear traces of the starvation struggle which for so long made up the life of the race. Our very organism holds memories and glimpses of that long life of our ancestors which still goes on among so many of our contemporaries. Nothing so deadens the sympathies and shrivels the power of enjoyment, as the persistent keeping away from the great opportunities for helpfulness and a continual ignoring of the starvation struggle which makes up the life of at least half the race. To shut one's self away from that half of the race life is to shut one's self away from the most vital part of it; it is to live out but half the humanity to which we have been born heir and to use but half our faculties. We have all had longings for a fuller life which should include the use of these faculties. . . .

You may remember the forlorn feeling which occasionally seizes you when you arrive early in the morning a stranger in a great city: the stream of laboring people goes past you as you gaze through the plate-glass window of your hotel; you see hardworking men lifting great burdens; you hear the driving and jostling of huge carts and your heart sinks with a sudden sense of futility. The door opens behind you and you turn to the man who brings you in your breakfast with a quick sense of human fellowship. You find yourself praying that you may never lose your hold on it all. A more poetic prayer would be that the great mother breasts of our common humanity, with its labor and suffering and its homely comforts, may never be withheld from you. You turn helplessly to the waiter and feel that it would be almost grotesque to claim from him the sympathy you crave because civilization has placed you apart, but you resent your position with a sudden sense of snobbery. . . .

"It is true that there is nothing after disease, indigence, and a sense of guilt, so fatal to health and to life itself as the want of a proper outlet for active faculties." I have seen young girls suffer and grow sensibly lowered in vitality in the first years after they leave school. In our attempt then to give a girl pleasure and freedom from care we succeed, for the most part, in making her pitifully miserable. She finds "life" so different from what she expected it to be. She is besotted with innocent little ambitions, and does not understand this apparent waste of herself, this elaborate preparation, if no work is provided for her. There is a heritage of noble obligation which young people accept and long to perpetuate. The desire for action, the wish to right wrong and alleviate suffering haunts them daily. Society smiles at it indulgently instead of making it of value to itself. The wrong to them begins even farther back, when we restrain the first childish desires for "doing good" and tell them that they must wait until they are older and better fitted. We intimate that social obligation begins at a fixed date, forgetting that it begins with birth itself. . . .

Parents are often inconsistent: they deliberately expose their daughters to knowledge of the distress in the world; they send them to hear missionary addresses on famines in India and China; they accompany them to lectures on the suffering in Siberia; they agitate together over the forgotten region of East London. In addition to this, from babyhood the altruistic tendencies of these daughters are persistently cultivated. They are taught to be self-forgetting and self-sacrificing, to consider the good of the whole before the good of the ego. But when all this information and culture show results, when the daughter comes back from college and begins to recognize her social claim to the "submerged tenth," and to evince a disposition to fulfill it, the family claim is strenuously asserted; she is told that she is unjustified, ill-advised in her efforts. If she persists, the family too often are injured and unhappy unless the efforts are called missionary and the religious zeal of the family carry them over their sense of abuse. When this zeal does not exist, the result is perplexing. It is a curious violation of what we would fain believe a fundamental law — that the final return of the deed is upon the head of the doer. The deed is that of exclusiveness and caution, but the return, instead of falling upon the head of the exclusive and cautious, falls upon a young head full of generous and unselfish plans. The girl loses something vital out of her life to which she is entitled. She is restricted and unhappy; her elders, meanwhile, are unconscious of the situation and we have all the elements of a tragedy.

We have in America a fast-growing number of cultivated young people who have no recognized outlet for their active faculties. They hear constantly of the great social maladjustment, but no way is provided for them to change it, and their uselessness hangs about them heavily. Huxley declares that the sense of uselessness is the severest shock which the human system can sustain, and that if persistently sustained, it results in atrophy of function. These young people have had advantages of college, of European travel, and of economic study, but they are sustaining this shock of inaction. They have pet phrases, and they tell you that the things that make us all alike are stronger than the things that make us different. They say that all men are united by needs and sympathies far more permanent and radical than anything that temporarily divides them and sets them in opposition to each other. If they affect art, they say that the decay in artistic expression is due to the decay in ethics, that art when shut away from the human interests and from the great mass of humanity is self-destructive. They tell their elders with all the bitterness of youth that if they expect success from them in business or politics or in whatever lines their ambition for them has run, they must let them consult all of humanity; that they must let them find out what the people want and how they want it. It is only the stronger young people, however, who formulate this. Many of them dissipate their energies in so-called enjoyment. Others not content with that, go on studying and go back to college for their second degrees; not that they are especially fond of study, but because they want something definite to do, and their powers have been trained in the direction of mental accumulation. Many are buried beneath this mental accumulation with lowered vitality and discontent.

This young life, so sincere in its emotion and good phrases and yet so undirected, seems to me as pitiful as the other great mass of destitute lives. One is supplementary to the other, and some method of communication can surely be devised. . . .

Our young people feel nervously the need of putting theory into action, and respond quickly to the Settlement form of activity.

Other motives which I believe make toward the Settlement are the result of a certain renaissance going forward in Christianity. The impulse to share the lives of the poor, the desire to make social service, irrespective of propaganda, express the spirit of Christ, is as old as Christianity itself. . . .

The Christians looked for the continuous revelation, but believed what Jesus said, that this revelation, to be retained and made manifest, must be put into terms of action; that action is the only medium man has for receiving and appropriating truth; that the doctrine must be known through the will.

That Christianity has to be revealed and embodied in the line of social progress is a corollary to the simple proposition that man's action is found in his social relationships in the way in which he connects with his fellows; that his motives for action are the zeal and affection with which he regards his fellows. By this simple process was created a deep enthusiasm for humanity, which regarded man as at once the organ and the object of revelation; and by this process came about the wonderful fellowship, the true democracy of the early Church, that so captivates the imagination. The early Christians were preëminently nonresistant. They believed in love as a cosmic force. There was no iconoclasm during the minor peace of the Church. They did not yet denounce nor tear down temples, nor preach the end of the world. They grew to a mighty number, but it never occurred to them, either in their weakness or in their strength, to regard other men for an instant as their foes or as aliens. The spectacle of the Christians loving all men was the most astounding Rome had ever seen. They were eager to sacrifice themselves for the weak, for children, and for the aged; they identified themselves with slaves and did not avoid the plague; they longed to share the common lot that they might receive the constant revelation. It was a new treasure which the early Christians added to the sum of all treasures, a joy hitherto unknown in the world — the joy of finding the Christ which lieth in each man, but which no man can unfold save in fellowship. A happiness ranging from the heroic to the pastoral enveloped them. They were to possess a revelation as long as life had new meaning to unfold, new action to propose.

I believe that there is a distinct turning among many young men and women toward this simple acceptance of Christ's message. They resent the assumption that Christianity is a set of ideas which belong to the religious consciousness, whatever that may be. They insist that it cannot be proclaimed and instituted apart from the social life of the community and that it must seek a simple and natural expression in the social organism itself. The Settlement movement is only one manifestation of that wider humanitarian movement which throughout Christendom, but preëminently in England, is endeavoring to embody itself, not in a sect, but in society itself.

I believe that this turning, this renaissance of the early Christian humanitarianism, is going on in America, in Chicago, if you please, without leaders who write or philosophize, without much speaking, but with a bent to express in social service and in terms of action the spirit of Christ. Certain it is that spiritual force is found in the Settlement movement, and it is also true that this force must be evoked and must be called into play before the success of any Settlement is assured. There must be the overmastering belief that all that is noblest in life is common to men as men, in order to accentuate the likenesses and ignore the differences which are found among the people whom the Settlement constantly brings into juxtaposition. . . .

It is quite impossible for me to say in what proportion or degree the subjective necessity which led to the opening of Hull-House combined the three trends: first, the desire to interpret democracy in social terms; secondly, the impulse beating at the very source of our lives, urging us to aid in the race progress; and, thirdly, the Christian movement toward humanitarianism. It is difficult to analyze a living thing; the analysis is at best imperfect. Many more motives may blend with the three trends; possibly the desire for a new form of social success due to the nicety of imagination, which refuses worldly pleasures unmixed with the joys of self-sacrifice; possibly a love of approbation, so vast that it is not content with the treble clapping of delicate hands, but wishes also to hear the bass notes from toughened palms, may mingle with these.

The Settlement, then, is an experimental effort to aid in the solution of the social and industrial problems which are engendered by the modern conditions of life in a great city. It insists that these problems are not confined to any one portion of a city. It is an attempt to relieve, at the same time, the overaccumulation at one end of society and the destitution at the other; but it assumes that this overaccumulation and destitution is most sorely felt in the things that pertain to social and educational advantages. From its very nature it can stand for no political or social propaganda. It must, in a sense, give the warm welcome of an inn to all such propaganda, if perchance one of them be found an angel. The one thing to be dreaded in the Settlement is that it lose its flexibility, its power of quick adaptation, its readiness to change its methods as its environment may demand. It must be open to conviction and must have a deep and abiding sense of tolerance. It must be hospitable and ready for experiment. It should demand from its residents a scientific patience in the accumulation of facts and the steady holding of their sympathies as one of the best instruments for that accumulation. It must be grounded in a philosophy whose foundation is on the solidarity of the human race, a philosophy which will not waver when the race happens to be represented by a drunken woman or an idiot boy. Its residents must be emptied of all conceit of opinion and all self-assertion, and ready to arouse and interpret the public opinion of their neighborhood. They must be content to live quietly side by side with their neighbors, until they grow into a sense of relationship and mutual interests. Their neighbors are held apart by differences of race and language which the residents can more easily overcome. They are bound to see the needs of their neighborhood as a whole, to furnish data for legislation, and to use their influence to secure it. In short, residents are pledged to devote themselves to the duties of good citizenship and to the arousing of the social energies which too largely lie dormant in every neighborhood given over to industrialism. They are bound to regard the entire life of their city as organic, to make an effort to unify it, and to protest against its overdifferentiation.

It is always easy to make all philosophy point one particular moral and all history adorn one particular tale; but I may be forgiven the reminder that the best speculative philosophy sets forth the solidarity of the human race; that the highest moralists have taught that without the advance and improvement of the whole, no man can hope for any lasting improvement in his own moral or material individual condition; and that the subjective necessity for Social Settlements is therefore identical with that necessity, which urges us on toward social and individual salvation.

CHAPTER 7
SOME EARLY UNDERTAKINGS AT HULL-HOUSE

If the early American settlements stood for a more exigent standard in philanthropic activities, insisting that each new undertaking should be preceded by carefully ascertained facts, then certainly Hull-House held to this standard in the opening of our new coffee-house first started as a public kitchen. An investigation of the sweatshops had disclosed the fact, that sewing women during the busy season paid little attention to the feeding of their families, for it was only by working steadily through the long day that the scanty pay of five, seven, or nine cents for finishing a dozen pairs of trousers could be made into a day's wage; and they bought from the nearest grocery the canned goods that could be most quickly heated, or gave a few pennies to the children with which they might secure a lunch from a neighboring candy shop.

One of the residents made an investigation, at the instance of the United States Department of Agriculture, into the food values of the dietaries of the various immigrants, and this was followed by an investigation made by another resident, for the United States Department of Labor, into the foods of the Italian colony, on the supposition that the constant use of imported products bore a distinct relation to the cost of living. I recall an Italian who, coming into Hull-House one day as we were sitting at the dinner table, expressed great surprise that Americans ate a variety of food, because he believed that they partook only of potatoes and beer. A little inquiry showed that this conclusion was drawn from the fact that he lived next to an Irish saloon and had never seen anything but potatoes going in and beer coming out.

At that time the New England kitchen was comparatively new in Boston, and Mrs. Richards,[35] who was largely responsible for its foun-

---

[35] Ellen Swallow Richards (1842–1911) was a Vassar graduate and the first woman to attend MIT, where she earned a B.S. in chemistry in 1873. Barred from a traditionally masculine career in science, she applied the principles of chemistry to the home and became a leader of the home economics movement.

dation, hoped that cheaper cuts of meat and simpler vegetables, if they were subjected to slow and thorough processes of cooking, might be made attractive and their nutritive value secured for the people who so sadly needed more nutritious food. It was felt that this could be best accomplished in public kitchens, where the advantage of scientific training and careful supervision could be secured. One of the residents went to Boston for a training under Mrs. Richards, and when the Hull-House kitchen was fitted under her guidance and direction, our hopes ran high for some modification of the food of the neighborhood. We did not reckon, however, with the wide diversity in nationality and inherited tastes, and while we sold a certain amount of the carefully prepared soups and stews in the neighboring factories — a sale which has steadily increased throughout the years — and were also patronized by a few households, perhaps the neighborhood estimate was best summed up by the woman who frankly confessed, that the food was certainly nutritious, but that she didn't like to eat what was nutritious, that she liked to eat "what she'd ruther."

If the dietetics were appreciated but slowly, the social value of the coffee-house and the gymnasium, which were in the same building, were quickly demonstrated. At that time the saloon halls were the only places in the neighborhood where the immigrant could hold his social gatherings, and where he could celebrate such innocent and legitimate occasions as weddings and christenings.

These halls were rented very cheaply with the understanding that various sums of money should be "passed across the bar," and it was considered a mean host or guest who failed to live up to this implied bargain. The consequence was that many a reputable party ended with a certain amount of disorder, due solely to the fact that the social instinct was traded upon and used as a basis for money-making by an adroit host. From the beginning the young people's clubs had asked for dancing, and nothing was more popular than the increased space for parties offered by the gymnasium, with the chance to serve refreshments in the room below. We tried experiments with every known "soft drink," from those extracted from an expensive soda water fountain to slender glasses of grape juice, but so far as drinks were concerned we never became a rival to the saloon, nor indeed did any one imagine that we were trying to do so. I remember one man who looked about the cozy little room and said, "This would be a nice place to sit in all day, if one could only have beer." But the coffee-house gradually performed a mission of its own and became something of a social center to the neighborhood as well as a real convenience. Business men from the adjacent factories and school teachers from the nearest public schools, used it increasingly. The Hull-House students and club members supped together in little groups or held their reunions and social banquets, as, to a certain extent, did organizations from all parts of the town. The experience of the coffee-house taught us not to hold to preconceived ideas of what the neighborhood ought to have, but to keep ourselves in readiness to modify and adapt our undertakings as we discovered those things which the neighborhood was ready to accept.

Better food was doubtless needed, but more attractive and safer places for social gatherings were also needed, and the neighborhood was ready for one and not for the other. . . .

There was in the earliest undertakings at Hull-House a touch of the artist's enthusiasm when he translates his inner vision through his chosen material into outward form. Keenly conscious of the social confusion all about us and the hard economic struggle, we at times believed that the very struggle itself might become a source of strength. The devotion of the mothers to their children, the dread of the men lest they fail to provide for the family dependent upon their daily exertions, at moments seemed to us the secret stores of strength from which society is fed, the invisible array of passion and feeling which are the surest protectors of the world. We fatuously hoped that we might pluck from the human tragedy itself a consciousness of a common destiny which should bring its own healing, that we might extract from life's very misfortunes a power of coöperation which should be effective against them.

Of course there was always present the harrowing consciousness of the difference in economic condition between ourselves and our neighbors. Even if we had gone to live in the most wretched tenement, there would have always been an essential difference between them and ourselves, for we should have had a sense of security in regard to illness and old age and the lack of these two securities are the specters which most persistently haunt the poor. Could we, in spite of this, make their individual efforts more effective through organization and possibly complement them by small efforts of our own?

Opposite: Corruption in Chicago's municipal sanitation services meant that streets and alleys in working-class neighborhoods were piled with refuse. Children played and shoppers marketed amidst flies, maggots, and the stench of rotting garbage. Addams fought for years to reform the system, even serving as garbage inspector for the Nineteenth Ward in 1895. These photos, taken in the early 1900s, demonstrate that Addams and her political allies did not win the struggle for sanitary streets overnight.

Jane Addams Memorial Collection, Special Collections, The University Library, The University of Illinois at Chicago.

Chicago Historical Society, Negative no. CRC-143-D; Charles R. Clark, photographer.

Some such vague hope was in our minds when we started the Hull-House Coöperative Coal Association, which led a vigorous life for three years, and developed a large membership under the skillful advice of its one paid officer, an English workingman who had had experience in coöperative societies at "'ome." Some of the meetings of the association, in which people met to consider together their basic dependence upon fire and warmth, had a curious challenge of life about them. Because the coöperators knew what it meant to bring forth children in the midst of privation and to see the tiny creatures struggle for life, their recitals cut a cross section, as it were, in that world-old effort — the "dying to live" which so inevitably triumphs over poverty and suffering. And yet their very familiarity with hardship may have been responsible for that sentiment which traditionally ruins business, for a vote of the coöperators that the basket buyers be given one basket free out of every six, that the presentation of five purchase tickets should entitle the holders to a profit in coal instead of stock "because it would be a shame to keep them waiting for the dividend," was always pointed to by the conservative quarter-of-a-ton buyers as the beginning of the end. At any rate, at the close of the third winter, although the association occupied an imposing coal yard on the southeast corner of the Hull-House block and its gross receipts were between three and four hundred dollars a day, it became evident that the concern could not remain solvent if it continued its philanthropic policy, and the experiment was terminated by the coöperators taking up their stock in the remaining coal.

Our next coöperative experiment was much more successful, perhaps because it was much more spontaneous.

At a meeting of working girls held at Hull-House during a strike in a large shoe factory, the discussions made it clear that the strikers who had been most easily frightened, and therefore first to capitulate, were naturally those girls who were paying board and were afraid of being put out if they fell too far behind. After a recital of a case of peculiar hardship one of them exclaimed: "Wouldn't it be fine if we had a boarding club of our own, and then we could stand by each other in a time like this?" After that events moved quickly. We read aloud together Beatrice Potter's little book on "Coöperation," and discussed all the difficulties and fascinations of such an undertaking, and on the first of May, 1891, two comfortable apartments near Hull-House were rented and furnished. The Settlement was responsible for the furniture and paid the first month's rent, but beyond that the members managed the club themselves. The undertaking "marched," as the French say, from the very first, and always on its own feet. Although there were difficulties, none of them proved insurmountable, which was a matter for great satisfaction in the face of a statement made by the head of the United States Department of Labor, who, on a visit to the club when it was but two years old, said that his department had investigated many coöperative undertakings, and that none founded and managed by women had ever succeeded. At the end of the third year the club occupied all of the six apartments which the original building contained, and numbered fifty members.

It was in connection with our efforts to secure a building for the Jane Club that we first found ourselves in the dilemma between the needs of our neighbors and the kind-hearted response upon which we had already come to rely for their relief. The adapted apartments in which the Jane Club was housed were inevitably more or less uncomfortable, and we felt that the success of the club justified the erection of a building for its sole use.

Up to that time, our history had been as the minor peace of the early Church. We had had the most generous interpretation of our efforts. Of course, many people were indifferent to the idea of the Settlement; others looked on with tolerant and sometimes cynical amusement. . . .

The situation changed markedly after the Pullman strike,[36] and our efforts to secure factory legislation later brought upon us a certain amount of distrust and suspicion; until then we had been considered merely a kindly philanthropic undertaking whose new form gave us a certain idealistic glamour. But sterner tests were coming and one of the first was in connection with the new building for the Jane Club. A trustee of Hull-House came to see us one day with the good news that a friend of his was ready to give twenty thousand dollars with which to build the desired new clubhouse. When, however, he divulged the name of his generous friend, it proved to be that of a man who was notorious for underpaying the girls in his establishment and concerning whom there were even darker stories. It seemed clearly impossible to erect a

---

[36] The Pullman strike began in Chicago in May, 1894, as a local strike against the company George Pullman had created to design and build "Pullman cars" for passenger trains. The Pullman workers' situation was complicated by the fact that Mr. Pullman had built what he regarded as a "model industrial town" just south of Chicago, where the majority of workers lived. A key grievance in the initial strike was that Pullman refused to lower his rents even though the depression of 1893–94 drastically reduced Pullman workers' wages. Jane Addams, as a member of the Civic Federation, tried to mediate the strike but was rebuffed by Pullman.

The Pullman strike became a national strike in June, 1894, when the American Railway Union, led by Eugene V. Debs, called for a boycott of all trains carrying Pullman cars. In retaliation for the nationwide railway stoppage, President Grover Cleveland called federal troops to Chicago in early July. This ignited violence in the city and around the country, Debs was arrested and jailed for violating the first antistrike injunction in U.S. history, and the strike collapsed.

Jane Addams's indictment of George Pullman's conduct in the strike, "A Modern Lear," could not find a publisher until 1912, when it appeared in *Survey* magazine.

clubhouse for working girls with such money and we at once said that we must decline the offer. The trustee of Hull-House was put in the most embarrassing situation; he had, of course, induced the man to give the money, and had had no thought but that it would be eagerly received; he would now be obliged to return with the astonishing, not to say insulting, news that the money was considered unfit.

In the long discussion which followed, it gradually became clear to all of us that such a refusal could be valuable only as it might reveal to the man himself and to others, public opinion in regard to certain methods of money-making, but that from the very nature of the case our refusal of this money could not be made public because a representative of Hull-House had asked for it. However, the basic fact remained that we could not accept the money, and of this the trustee himself was fully convinced. This incident occurred during a period of much discussion concerning "tainted money," and is perhaps typical of the difficulty of dealing with it. It is impossible to know how far we may blame the individual for doing that which all of his competitors and his associates consider legitimate; at the same time, social changes can only be inaugurated by those who feel the unrighteousness of contemporary conditions, and the expression of their scruples may be the one opportunity for pushing forward moral tests into that dubious area wherein wealth is accumulated. . . .

There was room for discouragement in the many unsuccessful experiments in coöperation which were carried on in Chicago during the early nineties; a carpenter shop on Van Buren Street near Halsted, a labor exchange started by the unemployed, not so paradoxical an arrangement as it seems, and a very ambitious plan for a country colony which was finally carried out at Ruskin, Tennessee. In spite of failures, coöperative schemes went on, some of the same men appearing in one after another with irrepressible optimism. I remember during a coöperative congress, which met at Hull-House in the World's Fair summer that Mr. Henry D. Lloyd,[37] who collected records of coöperative experiments with the enthusiasm with which other men collect coins or pictures, put before the congress some of the remarkable successes in Ireland and north England, which he later embodied in his book on "Copartnership." One of the old-time coöperators denounced the modern method as "too much like cut-throat business" and declared himself in favor of "principles which may have failed over and over again, but are nevertheless

---

[37] Lloyd (1847–1903) was a muckraking journalist and radical social reformer in Chicago best known for his exposé on the Standard Oil Company, *Wealth against Commonwealth,* published in 1894 (New York: Harper & Brothers).

as sound as the law of gravitation." Mr. Lloyd and I agreed that the fiery old man presented as fine a spectacle of devotion to a lost cause as either of us had ever seen, although we both possessed memories well stored with such romantic attachments.

And yet this dream that men shall cease to waste strength in competition and shall come to pool their powers of production, is coming to pass all over the face of the earth. . . .

I have seldom been more infected by enthusiasm than I once was in Dulwich at a meeting of English coöperators where I was fairly overwhelmed by the fervor underlying the businesslike proceedings of the congress, and certainly when I served as a juror in the Paris Exposition of 1900, nothing in the entire display in the department of social economy was so imposing as the building housing the exhibit, which had been erected by coöperative trades-unions without the assistance of a single contractor.

And so one's faith is kept alive as one occasionally meets a realized ideal of better human relations. At least traces of successful coöperation are found even in individualistic America. . . .

Many experiments in those early years, although vivid, seemed to contain no illumination; nevertheless they doubtless permanently affected our judgments concerning what is called crime and vice. . . .

I recall our perplexity over the first girls who had "gone astray," — the poor, little, forlorn objects, fifteen and sixteen years old, with their moral natures apparently untouched and unawakened; one of them whom the police had found in a professional house and asked us to shelter for a few days until she could be used as a witness, was clutching a battered doll which she had kept with her during her six months of an "evil life." Two of these prematurely aged children came to us one day directly from the maternity ward of the Cook County Hospital, each with a baby in her arms, asking for protection, because they did not want to go home for fear of "being licked." . . .

But discouraging as these and other similar efforts often were, nevertheless the difficulties were infinitely less in those days when we dealt with "fallen girls" than in the years following when the "white slave traffic" became gradually established and when agonized parents, as well as the victims themselves, were totally unable to account for the situation. In the light of recent disclosures, it seems as if we were unaccountably dull not to have seen what was happening, especially to the Jewish girls among whom "the home trade of the white slave traffic" was first carried on and who were thus made to break through countless generations of chastity. We early encountered the difficulties of that old problem of restoring the woman, or even the child, into the society she has once outraged. I well remember our perplexity when we attempted to help two girls straight from a Virginia tobacco factory, who had been decoyed into a disreputable house when innocently seeking a lodging on the late evening of their arrival. Although they had been rescued promptly, the stigma remained, and we found it impossible to permit them to join any of the social clubs connected with Hull-House, not so much because there was danger of contamination, as because the parents of the club members would have resented their presence most hotly. One of our trustees succeeded in persuading a repentant girl, fourteen years old, whom we tried to give a fresh start in another part of the city, to attend a Sunday school class of a large Chicago church. The trustee hoped that the contact with nice girls, as well as the moral training, would help the poor child on her hard road. But unfortunately tales of her shortcomings reached the superintendent who felt obliged, in order to protect the other girls, to forbid her the school. She came back to tell us about it, defiant as well as discouraged, and had it not been for the experience with our own clubs, we could easily have joined her indignation over a church which "acted as if its Sunday school was a show window for candy kids."

In spite of poignant experiences or, perhaps, because of them, the memory of the first years at Hull-House is more or less blurred with fatigue, for we could of course become accustomed only gradually to the unending activity and to the confusion of a house constantly filling and refilling with groups of people. The little children who came to the kindergarten in the morning were followed by the afternoon clubs of older children, and those in turn made way for the educational and social organizations of adults, occupying every room in the house every evening. All one's habits of living had to be readjusted, and any student's tendency to sit with a book by the fire was of necessity definitely abandoned.

To thus renounce "the luxury of personal preference" was, however, a mere trifle compared to our perplexity over the problems of an industrial neighborhood situated in an unorganized city. Life pressed hard in many directions and yet it has always seemed to me rather interesting that when we were so distressed over its stern aspects and so impressed with the lack of municipal regulations, the first building erected for Hull-House should have been designed for an art gallery, for although it contained a reading-room on the first floor and a studio above, the largest space on the second floor was carefully designed and lighted for art exhibits, which had to do only with the cultivation of that which appealed to the powers of enjoyment as over against a wage-earning capacity. It was also significant that a Chicago business man, fond of pictures himself, responded to this first appeal of the new and certainly puzzling undertaking called a Settlement. . . .

These first buildings were very precious to us and it afforded us the greatest pride and pleasure as one building after another was added to the Hull-House group. They clothed in brick and mortar and made visible to the world that which we were trying to do; they stated to Chicago that education and recreation ought to be extended to the immigrants. The boys came in great numbers to our provisional gymnasium fitted up in a former saloon, and it seemed to us quite as natural that a Chicago man, fond of athletics, should erect a building for them, as that the boys should clamor for more room.

I do not wish to give a false impression, for we were often bitterly pressed for money and worried by the prospect of unpaid bills, and we gave up one golden scheme after another because we could not afford it; we cooked the meals and kept the books and washed the windows without a thought of hardship if we thereby saved money for the consummation of some ardently desired undertaking.

But in spite of our financial stringency, I always believed that money would be given when we had once clearly reduced the Settlement idea to the actual deed. This chapter, therefore, would be incomplete if it did not record a certain theory of nonresistance or rather universal good will which I had worked out in connection with the Settlement idea and which was later so often and so rudely disturbed. At that time I had come to believe that if the activities of Hull-House were ever misunderstood, it would be either because there was not time to fully explain or because our motives had become mixed, for I was convinced that disinterested action was like truth or beauty in its lucidity and power of appeal.

But more gratifying than any understanding or response from without could possibly be, was the consciousness that a growing group of residents was gathering at Hull-House, held together in that soundest of all social bonds, the companionship of mutual interests. These residents came primarily because they were genuinely interested in the social situation and believed that the Settlement was valuable as a method of approach to it. A house in which the men residents lived was opened across the street, and at the end of the first five years the Hull-House residential force numbered fifteen, a majority of whom still remain identified with the Settlement.

Even in those early years we caught glimpses of the fact that certain social sentiments, which are "the difficult and cumulating product of human growth" and which like all higher aims live only by communion and fellowship, are cultivated most easily in the fostering soil of a community life. . . .

In those early years at Hull-House we were, however, in no danger of losing ourselves in mazes of speculation or mysticism, and there was shrewd penetration in a compliment I received from one of our Scotch neighbors. He came down Polk Street as I was standing near the foundation of our new gymnasium, and in response to his friendly remark that "Hull-House was spreading out," I replied that "Perhaps we were spreading out too fast." "Oh, no," he rejoined, "you can afford to spread out wide, you are so well planted in the mud," giving the compliment, however, a practical turn, as he glanced at the deep mire on the then unpaved street. . . .

At the end of five years the residents of Hull-House published some first found facts and our reflections thereon in a book called "Hull-House Maps and Papers."[38] The maps were taken from information collected by one of the residents for the United States Bureau of Labor in the investigation into "the slums of great cities" and the papers treated of various neighborhood matters with candor and genuine concern if not with skill. The first edition became exhausted in two years, and apparently the Boston publisher did not consider the book worthy of a second.

CHAPTER 8
PROBLEMS OF POVERTY

That neglected and forlorn old age is daily brought to the attention of a Settlement which undertakes to bear its share of the neighborhood burden imposed by poverty, was pathetically clear to us during our first months of residence at Hull-House. One day a boy of ten led a tottering old lady into the House, saying that she had slept for six weeks in their kitchen on a bed made up next to the stove; that she had come when her son died, although none of them had ever seen her before; but because her son had "once worked in the same shop with Pa she thought of him when she had nowhere to go." The little fellow concluded by saying that our house was so much bigger than theirs that he thought we would have more room for beds. The old woman herself said absolutely nothing, but looking on with that gripping fear of the poorhouse in her eyes, she was a living embodiment of that dread which is so heart-breaking

---

[38] *Hull-House Maps and Papers* (Boston: Thomas Y. Crowell, 1895) was a collective effort by the settlement's residents. The book's ten chapters, including one by Addams on "The Settlement as a Factor in the Labor Movement," were described as "a presentation of nationalities and wages in a congested district of Chicago."

that the occupants of the County Infirmary themselves seem scarcely less wretched than those who are making their last stand against it.

This look was almost more than I could bear, for only a few days before some frightened women had bidden me come quickly to the house of an old German woman, whom two men from the county agent's office were attempting to remove to the County Infirmary. The poor old creature had thrown herself bodily upon a small and battered chest of drawers and clung there, clutching it so firmly that it would have been impossible to remove her without also taking the piece of furniture. She did not weep nor moan nor indeed make any human sound, but between her broken gasps for breath she squealed shrilly like a frightened animal caught in a trap. The little group of women and children gathered at her door stood aghast at this realization of the black dread which always clouds the lives of the very poor when work is slack, but which constantly grows more imminent and threatening as old age approaches. The neighborhood women and I hastened to make all sorts of promises as to the support of the old woman and the county officials, only too glad to be rid of their unhappy duty, left her to our ministrations. This dread of the poorhouse, the result of centuries of deterrent Poor Law [39] administration, seemed to me not without some justification one summer when I found myself perpetually distressed by the unnecessary idleness and forlornness of the old women in the Cook County Infirmary, many of whom I had known in the years when activity was still a necessity, and when they yet felt bustlingly important. To take away from an old woman whose life has been spent in household cares all the foolish little belongings to which her affections cling and to which her very fingers have become accustomed, is to take away her last incentive to activity, almost to life itself. To give an old woman only a chair and a bed, to leave her no cupboard in which her treasures may be stowed, not only that she may take them out when she desires occupation, but that her mind may dwell upon them in moments of revery, is to reduce living almost beyond the limit of human endurance.

The poor creature who clung so desperately to her chest of drawers was really clinging to the last remnant of normal living — a symbol of all she was asked to renounce. . . .

Even death itself sometimes fails to bring the dignity and serenity which one would fain associate with old age. I recall the dying hour of one old Scotchwoman whose long struggle to "keep respectable" had so embittered her, that her last words were gibes and taunts for those who were trying to minister to her. "So you came in yourself this morning, did

---

[39] The British Poor Law required that the destitute move into the local poorhouse.

you? You only sent things yesterday. I guess you knew when the doctor was coming. Don't try to warm my feet with anything but that old jacket that I've got there; it belonged to my boy who was drowned at sea nigh thirty years ago, but it's warmer yet with human feelings than any of your damned charity hot-water bottles." Suddenly the harsh gasping voice was stilled in death and I awaited the doctor's coming shaken and horrified.

The lack of municipal regulation was, in the early days of Hull-House, paralleled by the inadequacy of the charitable efforts of the city and an unfounded optimism that there was no real poverty among us. Twenty years ago there was no Charity Organization Society in Chicago and the Visiting Nurse Association had not yet begun its beneficent work, while the relief societies, although conscientiously administered, were inadequate in extent and antiquated in method. . . .

This lack of organization among the charitable forces of the city was painfully revealed in that terrible winter after the World's Fair, when the general financial depression throughout the country was much intensified in Chicago by the numbers of unemployed stranded at the close of the exposition. When the first cold weather came the police stations and the very corridors of the City Hall were crowded by men who could afford no other lodging. They made huge demonstrations on the lake front, reminding one of the London gatherings in Trafalgar Square.

It was the winter in which Mr. Stead[40] wrote his indictment of Chicago. . . .

Before he published "If Christ Came to Chicago" he made his attempt to rally the diverse moral forces of the city in a huge mass meeting, which resulted in a temporary organization, later developing into the Civic Federation.[41] I was a member of the committee of five appointed to carry out the suggestions made in this remarkable meeting, and our first concern was to appoint a committee to deal with the unemployed. But when has a committee ever dealt satisfactorily with the unemployed? Relief stations were opened in various parts of the city, temporary lodging houses were established, Hull-House undertaking to lodge the homeless women who could be received nowhere else, employment stations

---

[40]William Stead (1849–1912), a British journalist and social reformer, traveled to the United States in 1893 to see the World's Columbian Exposition in Chicago. His brief involvement with reform activism in the city led to publication of *If Christ Came to Chicago* (Chicago: Laird & Lee Publishers, 1894) wherein he attacked the city's industrial elites and praised reformers like Addams.

[41]The Civic Federation brought together civic-minded business leaders, labor unionists, and reformers to mediate labor disputes, investigate urban social conditions, and attack political corruption.

were opened giving sewing to the women, and street sweeping for the men was organized. It was in connection with the latter that the perplexing question of the danger of permanently lowering wages at such a crisis, in the praiseworthy effort to bring speedy relief, was brought home to me. I insisted that it was better to have the men work half a day for seventy-five cents than a whole day for a dollar, better that they should earn three dollars in two days than in three days. I resigned from the street cleaning committee in despair of making the rest of the committee understand that, as our real object was not street cleaning but the help of the unemployed, we must treat the situation in such wise that the men would not be worse off when they returned to their normal occupations. The discussion opened up situations new to me and carried me far afield in perhaps the most serious economic reading I have ever done.

A beginning also was then made toward a Bureau of Organized Charities, the main office being put in charge of a young man recently come from Boston, who lived at Hull-House. But to employ scientific methods for the first time at such a moment involved difficulties, and the most painful episode of the winter for me came from an attempt on my part to conform to carefully received instructions. A shipping clerk whom I had known for a long time had lost his place, as so many people had that year, and came to the relief station established at Hull-House four or five times to secure help for his family. I told him one day of the opportunity to work on the drainage canal and intimated that if any employment were obtainable, he ought to exhaust that possibility before asking for help. The man replied that he had always worked indoors and that he could not endure outside work in winter. I am grateful to remember that I was too uncertain to be severe, although I held to my instructions. He did not come again for relief, but worked for two days digging on the canal, where he contracted pneumonia and died a week later. I have never lost trace of the two little children he left behind him, although I cannot see them without a bitter consciousness that it was at their expense I learned that life cannot be administered by definite rules and regulations; that wisdom to deal with a man's difficulties comes only through some knowledge of his life and habits as a whole; and that to treat an isolated episode is almost sure to invite blundering.

It was also during this winter that I became permanently impressed with the kindness of the poor to each other; the woman who lives upstairs will willingly share her breakfast with the family below because she knows they "are hard up"; the man who boarded with them last winter will give a month's rent because he knows the father of the family is out of work; the baker across the street, who is fast being pushed to the wall by his downtown competitors, will send across three loaves of stale bread because he has seen the children looking longingly into his window and suspects they are hungry. There are also the families who, during times of business depression, are obliged to seek help from the county or some benevolent society, but who are themselves most anxious not to be confounded with the pauper class, with whom indeed they do not in the least belong. Charles Booth,[42] in his brilliant chapter on the unemployed, expressed regret that the problems of the working class are so often confounded with the problems of the inefficient and the idle, that although working people live in the same street with those in need of charity, to thus confound two problems is to render the solution of both impossible.

I remember one family in which the father had been out of work for this same winter, most of the furniture had been pawned, and as the worn-out shoes could not be replaced the children could not go to school. The mother was ill and barely able to come for the supplies and medicines. Two years later she invited me to supper one Sunday evening in the little home which had been completely restored, and she gave as a reason for the invitation that she couldn't bear to have me remember them as they had been during that one winter, which she insisted had been unique in her twelve years of married life. She said that it was as if she had met me, not as I am ordinarily, but as I should appear misshapen with rheumatism or with a face distorted by neuralgic pain; that it was not fair to judge poor people that way. She perhaps unconsciously illustrated the difference between the relief-station relation to the poor and the Settlement relation to its neighbors, the latter wishing to know them through all the varying conditions of life, to stand by when they are in distress, but by no means to drop intercourse with them when normal prosperity has returned, enabling the relation to become more social and free from economic disturbance. . . .

We early found ourselves spending many hours in efforts to secure support for deserted women, insurance for bewildered widows, damages for injured operators, furniture from the clutches of the installment store. The Settlement is valuable as an information and interpretation bureau. It constantly acts between the various institutions of the city and the people for whose benefit these institutions were erected. The hospitals, the county agencies, and state asylums are often but vague rumors

---

[42] A British social investigator (1840–1916) whose seventeen-volume work, *Life and Labour of the People of London* (London: Macmillan & Company, 1889–1903) pioneered new methods in the study of the poor and new theories on the causes of poverty.

to the people who need them most. Another function of the Settlement to its neighborhood resembles that of the big brother whose mere presence on the playground protects the little one from bullies.

We early learned to know the children of hard driven mothers who went out to work all day, sometimes leaving the little things in the casual care of a neighbor, but often locking them into their tenement rooms. The first three crippled children we encountered in the neighborhood had all been injured while their mothers were at work: one had fallen out of a third-story window, another had been burned, and the third had a curved spine due to the fact that for three years he had been tied all day long to the leg of the kitchen table, only released at noon by his older brother who hastily ran in from a neighboring factory to share his lunch with him. When the hot weather came the restless children could not brook the confinement of the stuffy rooms, and, as it was not considered safe to leave the doors open because of sneak thieves, many of the children were locked out. During our first summer an increasing number of these poor little mites would wander into the cool hallway of Hull-House. We kept them there and fed them at noon, in return for which we were sometimes offered a hot penny which had been held in a tight little fist "ever since mother left this morning, to buy something to eat with." Out of kindergarten hours our little guests noisily enjoyed the hospitality of our bedrooms under the so-called care of any resident who volunteered to keep an eye on them, but later they were moved into a neighboring apartment under more systematic supervision.

Hull-House was thus committed to a day nursery which we sustained for sixteen years first in a little cottage on a side street and then in a building designed for its use called the Children's House. It is now carried on by the United Charities of Chicago in a finely equipped building on our block, where the immigrant mothers are cared for as well as the children, and where they are taught the things which will make life in America more possible. Our early day nursery brought us into natural relations with the poorest women of the neighborhood, many of whom were bearing the burden of dissolute and incompetent husbands in addition to the support of their children. Some of them presented an impressive manifestation of that miracle of affection which outlives abuse, neglect, and crime,— the affection which cannot be plucked from the heart where it has lived, although it may serve only to torture and torment. "Has your husband come back?" you inquire of Mrs. S., whom you have known for eight years as an overworked woman bringing her three delicate children every morning to the nursery; she is bent under the double burden of earning the money which supports them and giving them the tender care which alone keeps them alive. The oldest two children have at last gone to work, and Mrs. S. has allowed herself the luxury of staying at home two days a week. And now the worthless husband is back again — the "gentlemanly gambler" type who, through all vicissitudes, manages to present a white shirtfront and a gold watch to the world, but who is dissolute, idle, and extravagant. You dread to think how much his presence will increase the drain upon the family exchequer, and you know that he stayed away until he was certain that the children were old enough to earn money for his luxuries. Mrs. S. does not pretend to take his return lightly, but she replies in all seriousness and simplicity, "You know my feeling for him has never changed. You may think me foolish, but I was always proud of his good looks and educated appearance. I was lonely and homesick during those eight years when the children were little and needed so much doctoring, but I could never bring myself to feel hard toward him, and I used to pray the good Lord to keep him from harm and bring him back to us; so, of course, I'm thankful now." She passes on with a dignity which gives one a new sense of the security of affection.

I recall a similar case of a woman who had supported her three children for five years, during which time her dissolute husband constantly demanded money for drink and kept her perpetually worried and intimidated. One Saturday, before the "blessed Easter," he came back from a long debauch, ragged and filthy, but in a state of lachrymose repentance. The poor wife received him as a returned prodigal, believed that his remorse would prove lasting, and felt sure that if she and the children went to church with him on Easter Sunday and he could be induced to take the pledge before the priest, all their troubles would be ended. After hours of vigorous effort and the expenditure of all her savings, he finally sat on the front doorstep the morning of Easter Sunday, bathed, shaved, and arrayed in a fine new suit of clothes. She left him sitting there in the reluctant spring sunshine while she finished washing and dressing the children. When she finally opened the front door with the three shining children that they might all set forth together, the returned prodigal had disappeared, and was not seen again until midnight, when he came back in a glorious state of intoxication from the proceeds of his pawned clothes and clad once more in the dingiest attire. She took him in without comment, only to begin again the wretched cycle. There were of course instances of the criminal husband as well as of the merely vicious. I recall one woman who, during seven years, never missed a visiting day at the penitentiary when she might see her husband, and whose little children in the nursery proudly reported the messages from father with no notion that he was in disgrace, so absolutely did they reflect the gallant spirit of their mother.

While one was filled with admiration for these heroic women, something was also to be said for some of the husbands, for the sorry men who, for one reason or another, had failed in the struggle of life. Sometimes this failure was purely economic and the men were competent to give the children, whom they were not able to support, the care and guidance and even education which were of the highest value. Only a few months ago I met upon the street one of the early nursery mothers who for five years had been living in another part of the city, and in response to my query as to the welfare of her five children, she bitterly replied, "All of them except Mary have been arrested at one time or another, thank you." In reply to my remark that I thought her husband had always had such admirable control over them, she burst out, "That has been the whole trouble. I got tired taking care of him and didn't believe that his laziness was all due to his health, as he said, so I left him and said that I would support the children, but not him. From that minute the trouble with the four boys began. I never knew what they were doing, and after every sort of a scrape I finally put Jack and the twins into institutions where I pay for them. Joe has gone to work at last, but with a disgraceful record behind him. I tell you I ain't so sure that because a woman can make big money that she can be both father and mother to her children."

As I walked on, I could but wonder in which particular we are most stupid,— to judge a man's worth so solely by his wage-earning capacity that a good wife feels justified in leaving him, or in holding fast to that wretched delusion that a woman can both support and nurture her children. . . .

With all the efforts made by modern society to nurture and educate the young, how stupid it is to permit the mothers of young children to spend themselves in the coarser work of the world! It is curiously inconsistent that with the emphasis which this generation has placed upon the mother and upon the prolongation of infancy, we constantly allow the waste of this most precious material. I cannot recall without indignation a recent experience. I was detained late one evening in an office building by a prolonged committee meeting of the Board of Education. As I came out at eleven o'clock, I met in the corridor of the fourteenth floor a woman whom I knew, on her knees scrubbing the marble tiling. As she straightened up to greet me, she seemed so wet from her feet up to her chin, that I hastily inquired the cause. Her reply was that she left home at five o'clock every night and had no opportunity for six hours to nurse her baby. Her mother's milk mingled with the very water with which she scrubbed the floors until she should return at midnight, heated and exhausted, to feed her screaming child with what remained within her breasts.

These are only a few of the problems connected with the lives of the poorest people with whom the residents in a Settlement are constantly brought in contact.

CHAPTER 9
A DECADE OF ECONOMIC DISCUSSION

The Hull-House residents were often bewildered by the desire for constant discussion which characterized Chicago twenty years ago, for although the residents in the early Settlements were in many cases young persons, who had sought relief from the consciousness of social maladjustment in the "anodyne of work" afforded by philanthropic and civic activities, their former experiences had not thrown them into company with radicals. The decade between 1890 and 1900 was, in Chicago, a period of propaganda as over against constructive social effort; the moment for marching and carrying banners, for stating general principles and making a demonstration, rather than the time for uncovering the situation and for providing the legal measures and the civic organization through which new social hopes might make themselves felt.

When Hull-House was established in 1889, the events of the Haymarket riot[43] were already two years old, but during that time Chicago had apparently gone through the first period of repressive measures, and in the winter of 1889–1890, by the advice and with the active participation of its leading citizens, the city had reached the conclusion that the only cure for the acts of anarchy was free speech and an open discussion of the ills of which the opponents of government complained. Great open meetings were held every Sunday evening in the recital hall of the then new auditorium, presided over by such representative citizens as Lyman Gage,[44] and every possible shade of opinion was freely expressed. A man who spoke constantly at these meetings used to be pointed out to the vis-

[43] The events surrounding a peaceful rally on May 4, 1886, in favor of the eight-hour day at which a dynamite bomb exploded, killing seven policemen and injuring sixty others. When eight Chicago anarchist leaders were arrested without evidence, and four were hanged, the incident came to symbolize police and media persecution of anarchists and foreigners to discredit labor activism.

[44] Gage (1836–1927) was a prominent banker in Chicago who advocated dialogue and mediation between labor and capital and was the first president of the Chicago Civic Federation. As a Republican, he served as secretary of the treasury under President William McKinley.

iting stranger as one who had been involved with the group of convicted anarchists, and who doubtless would have been arrested and tried, but for the accident of his having been in Milwaukee when the explosion occurred. One cannot imagine such meetings being held in Chicago today, nor that such a man should be encouraged to raise his voice in a public assemblage presided over by a leading banker. It is hard to tell just what change has come over our philosophy or over the minds of those citizens who were then convinced that if these conferences had been established earlier, the Haymarket riot and all its sensational results might have been avoided.

At any rate, there seemed a further need for smaller clubs, where men who differed widely in their social theories might meet for discussion, where representatives of the various economic schools might modify each other, and at least learn tolerance and the futility of endeavoring to convince all the world of the truth of one position. Fanaticism is engendered only when men, finding no contradiction to their theories, at last believe that the very universe lends itself as an exemplification of one point of view. "The Working People's Social Science Club" was organized at Hull-House in the spring of 1890 by an English workingman, and for seven years it held a weekly meeting. At eight o'clock every Wednesday night the secretary called to order from forty to one hundred people; a chairman for the evening was elected, a speaker was introduced who was allowed to talk until nine o'clock; his subject was then thrown open to discussion and a lively debate ensued until ten o'clock, at which hour the meeting was declared adjourned. The enthusiasm of this club seldom lagged. Its zest for discussion was unceasing, and any attempt to turn it into a study or reading club always met with the strong disapprobation of the members.

In these weekly discussions in the Hull-House drawing-room everything was thrown back upon general principles and all discussion save that which "went to the root of things," was impatiently discarded as an unworthy, halfway measure. I recall one evening in this club when an exasperated member had thrown out the statement that "Mr. B. believes that socialism will cure the toothache." Mr. B. promptly rose to his feet and said that it certainly would, that when every child's teeth were systematically cared for from the beginning, toothache would disappear from the face of the earth, belonging, as it did, to the extinct competitive order, as the black plague had disappeared from the earth with the ill-regulated feudal régime of the Middle Ages. "But," he added, "why do we spend time discussing trifles like the toothache when great social changes are to be considered which will of themselves reform these minor ills?" Even the man who had been humorous, fell into the solemn tone of the gathering. It was, perhaps, here that the socialist surpassed every one else in the fervor of economic discussion. He was usually a German or a Russian with a turn for logical presentation, who saw in the concentration of capital and the growth of monopolies an inevitable transition to the socialistic state. He pointed out that the concentration of capital in fewer hands but increased the mass of those whose interests were opposed to a maintenance of its power, and vastly simplified its final absorption by the community; that monopoly "when it is finished doth bring forth socialism." Opposite to him, springing up in every discussion was the individualist, or, as the socialist called him, the anarchist, who insisted that we shall never secure just human relations until we have equality of opportunity; that the sole function of the state is to maintain the freedom of each, guarded by the like freedom of all, in order that each man may be able to work out the problems of his own existence. . . .

It was doubtless owing largely to this club that Hull-House contracted its early reputation for radicalism. Visitors refused to distinguish between the sentiments expressed by its members in the heat of discussion and the opinions held by the residents themselves. At that moment in Chicago the radical of every shade of opinion was vigorous and dogmatic; of the sort that could not resign himself to the slow march of human improvement; of the type who knew exactly "in what part of the world Utopia standeth."

During this decade Chicago seemed divided into two classes; those who held that "business is business" and who were therefore annoyed at the very notion of social control,[45] and the radicals, who claimed that nothing could be done to really moralize the industrial situation until society should be reorganized.

A Settlement is above all a place for enthusiasms, a spot to which those who have a passion for the equalization of human joys and opportunities are early attracted. It is this type of mind which is in itself so often obnoxious to the man of conquering business faculty, to whom the practical world of affairs seems so supremely rational that he would never vote to change the type of it even if he could. The man of social enthusiasm is to him an annoyance and an affront. He does not like to hear him talk and considers him *per se* "unsafe." Such a business man would

---

[45] In contrast to modern usage, where *social control* often means moralistic regulation of the people, progressive reformers like Addams used the term to refer to legal regulation of business practices.

admit, as an abstract proposition, that society is susceptible of modification and would even agree that all human institutions imply progressive development, but at the same time he deeply distrusts those who seek to reform existing conditions. There is a certain common-sense foundation for this distrust, for too often the reformer is the rebel who defies things as they are because of the restraints which they impose upon his individual desires rather than because of the general defects of the system. When such a rebel poses for a reformer, his shortcomings are heralded to the world, and his downfall is cherished as an awful warning to those who refuse to worship "the god of things as they are." . . .

In the discussion of these themes, Hull-House was of course quite as much under the suspicion of one side as the other. I remember one night when I addressed a club of secularists, which met at the corner of South Halsted and Madison Streets, a rough looking man called out: "You are all right now, but, mark my words, when you are subsidized by the millionaires, you will be afraid to talk like this." The defense of free speech was a sensitive point with me, and I quickly replied that while I did not intend to be subsidized by millionaires, neither did I propose to be bullied by workingmen, and that I should state my honest opinion without consulting either of them. To my surprise, the audience of radicals broke into applause, and the discussion turned upon the need of resisting tyranny wherever found, if democratic institutions were to endure. This desire to bear independent witness to social righteousness often resulted in a sense of compromise difficult to endure, and at many times it seemed to me that we were destined to alienate everybody. I should have been most grateful at that time to accept the tenets of socialism, and I conscientiously made my effort, both by reading and by many discussions with the comrades. I found that I could easily give an affirmative answer to the heated question, "Don't you see that just as the hand mill created a society with a feudal lord, so the steam mill creates a society with an industrial capitalist?" But it was a little harder to give an affirmative reply to the proposition that the social relation thus established proceeds to create principles, ideas, and categories as merely historical and transitory products.

Of course I use the term "socialism" technically and do not wish to confuse it with the growing sensitiveness which recognizes that no personal comfort nor individual development can compensate a man for the misery of his neighbors, nor with the increasing conviction that social arrangements can be transformed through man's conscious and deliberate effort. Such a definition would not have been accepted for a moment by the Russians, who then dominated the Socialist Party[46] in Chicago and among whom a crude interpretation of the class conflict was the test of the faith.

During those first years on Halsted Street nothing was more painfully clear than the fact that pliable human nature is relentlessly pressed upon by its physical environment. I saw nowhere a more devoted effort to understand and relieve that heavy pressure than the socialists were making, and I should have been glad to have had the comradeship of that gallant company had they not firmly insisted that fellowship depends upon identity of creed. They repudiated similarity of aim and social sympathy as tests which were much too loose and wavering as they did that vague socialism which for thousands has come to be a philosophy or rather religion embodying the hope of the world and the protection of all who suffer.

I also longed for the comfort of a definite social creed, which should afford at one and the same time an explanation of the social chaos and the logical steps towards its better ordering. I came to have an exaggerated sense of responsibility for the poverty in the midst of which I was living and which the socialists constantly forced me to defend. My plight was not unlike that which might have resulted in my old days of skepticism regarding foreordination, had I then been compelled to defend the confusion arising from the clashing of free wills as an alternative to an acceptance of the doctrine. Another difficulty in the way of accepting this economic determinism, so baldly dependent upon the theory of class consciousness, constantly arose when I lectured in country towns and there had opportunities to read human documents of prosperous people as well as those of my neighbors who were crowded into the city. The former were stoutly unconscious of any classes in America, and the class consciousness of the immigrants was fast being broken into by the necessity for making new and unprecedented connections in the industrial life all about them.

In the meantime, although many men of many minds met constantly at our conferences, it was amazing to find the incorrigible good nature which prevailed. Radicals are accustomed to hot discussion and sharp differences of opinion and take it all in the day's work. I recall that the secretary of the Hull-House Social Science Club at the anniversary of the seventh year of its existence read a report in which he stated that, so far

---

[46]Refers here to the Socialist Labor Party, the more doctrinaire predecessor to Eugene V. Debs's Socialist Party, which was not founded until 1901. Addams would also find Debs's organization too ideologically rigid for her tastes.

as he could remember, but twice during that time had a speaker lost his temper, and in each case it had been a college professor who "wasn't accustomed to being talked back to."

He also added that but once had all the club members united in applauding the same speaker; only Samuel Jones,[47] who afterwards became "the golden rule" mayor of Toledo, had been able to overcome all their dogmatic differences, when he had set forth a plan of endowing a group of workingmen with a factory plant and a working capital for experimentation in hours and wages, quite as groups of scholars are endowed for research.

Chicago continued to devote much time to economic discussion and remained in a state of youthful glamour throughout the nineties. . . .

Trades-unionists, unless they were also socialists, were not prominent in those economic discussions, although they were steadily making an effort to bring order into the unnecessary industrial confusion. They belonged to the second of the two classes into which Mill[48] divides all those who are dissatisfied with human life as it is, and whose feelings are wholly identified with its radical amendment. He states that the thoughts of one class are in the region of ultimate aims, of "the highest ideals of human life," while the thoughts of the other are in the region of the "immediately useful, and practically attainable."

The meetings of our Social Science Club were carried on by men of the former class, many of them with a strong religious bias who constantly challenged the Church to assuage the human spirit thus torn and bruised "in the tumult of a time disconsolate." These men were so serious in their demand for religious fellowship, and several young clergymen were so ready to respond to the appeal, that various meetings were arranged at Hull-House, in which a group of people met together to consider the social question, not in a spirit of discussion, but in prayer and meditation. These clergymen were making heroic efforts to induce their churches to formally consider the labor situation, and during the years which have elapsed since then, many denominations of the Christian Church have organized labor committees; but at that time there was nothing of the sort beyond the society in the established Church of England "to consider the conditions of labor."

---

[47] Samuel "Golden Rule" Jones (1846–1904), a Welsh immigrant and self-made millionaire in the Ohio oil business, carried out a series of pro-labor, even anticapitalist, reforms as the activist mayor of Toledo, Ohio, between 1897 and 1907.

[48] John Stuart Mill (1806–73) was an English philosopher and political economist whose work reflected the tension between Utilitarian belief in the greatest good to the greatest number and the Liberal devotion to individual rights.

During that decade even the most devoted of that pioneer church society failed to formulate the fervid desire for juster social conditions into anything more convincing than a literary statement, and the Christian Socialists, at least when the American branch held its annual meeting at Hull-House, afforded but a striking portrayal of that "between-age mood" in which so many of our religious contemporaries are forced to live. . . .

On the other hand the workingmen who continue to demand help from the Church thereby acknowledge their kinship, as does the son who continues to ask bread from the father who gives him a stone. I recall an incident connected with a prolonged strike in Chicago on the part of the typographical unions for an eight-hour day. The strike had been conducted in a most orderly manner and the union men, convinced of the justice of their cause, had felt aggrieved because one of the religious publishing houses in Chicago had constantly opposed them. Some of the younger clergymen of the denominations who were friendly to the strikers' cause came to a luncheon at Hull-House, where the situation was discussed by the representatives of all sides. The clergymen, becoming much interested in the idealism with which an officer of the State Federation of Labor presented the cause, drew from him the story of his search for fraternal relation: he said that at fourteen years of age he had joined a church, hoping to find it there; he had later become a member of many fraternal organizations and mutual benefit societies, and, although much impressed by their rituals, he was disappointed in the actual fraternity. He had finally found, so it seemed to him, in the cause of organized labor, what these other organizations had failed to give him,—an opportunity for sacrificial effort.

Chicago thus took a decade to discuss the problems inherent in the present industrial organization and to consider what might be done, not so much against deliberate aggression as against brutal confusion and neglect; quite as the youth of promise passes through a mist of rose-colored hope before he settles in the land of achievement where he becomes all too dull and literal minded. And yet as I hastily review the decade in Chicago which followed this one given over to discussion, the actual attainment of these early hopes, so far as they have been realized at all, seems to have come from men of affairs rather than from those given to speculation. Was the whole decade of discussion an illustration of that striking fact which has been likened to the changing of swords in Hamlet; that the abstract minds at length yield to the inevitable or at least grow less ardent in their propaganda, while the concrete minds, dealing constantly with daily affairs, in the end demonstrate the reality of abstract notions? . . .

I am inclined to think that perhaps all this general discussion was inevitable in connection with the early Settlements, as they in turn were the inevitable result of theories of social reform, which in their full enthusiasm reached America by way of England, only in the last decade of the century. There must have been tough fiber somewhere; for, although the residents of Hull-House were often baffled by the radicalism within the Social Science Club and harassed by the criticism from outside, we still continued to believe that such discussion should be carried on, for if the Settlement seeks its expression through social activity, it must learn the difference between mere social unrest and spiritual impulse.

The group of Hull-House residents, which by the end of the decade comprised twenty-five, differed widely in social beliefs, from the girl direct from the country who looked upon all social unrest as mere anarchy, to the resident who had become a socialist when a student in Zurich, and who had long before translated from the German Engel's "Conditions of the Working Class in England," although at this time she had been read out of the Socialist Party because the Russian and German Impossibilists suspected her fluent English, as she always lightly explained.[49] Although thus diversified in social beliefs, the residents became solidly united through our mutual experience in an industrial quarter, and we became not only convinced of the need for social control and protective legislation but also of the value of this preliminary argument.

This decade of discussion between 1890 and 1900 already seems remote from the spirit of Chicago of to-day. So far as I have been able to reproduce this earlier period, it must reflect the essential provisionality of

---

[49] Florence Kelley (1859–1932) was a key influence in Jane Addams's political maturation. Kelley was the daughter of Philadelphia's legendary pro-labor congressman, William "Pig Iron" Kelley and the niece of Sarah Pugh, a well-known Philadelphia abolitionist. An 1882 graduate of Cornell University whose senior thesis on child labor was published, Kelley did advanced work at the University of Zurich where she became a socialist and worked with Friedrich Engels on the English translation of *The Condition of the Working Class in England* (New York: John W. Lovell, 1887). She left her abusive husband, Dr. Lazare Wischnewetzky, and arrived at Hull-House in the winter of 1891 with three small children in tow. Kelley was based at Hull-House until 1899, earning a law degree at Northwestern University Law School in 1894 and devoting her energies to factory labor legislation, child labor laws, and compulsory education laws. In 1899, she and the children moved to Henry Street Settlement in New York and Kelley became the general secretary of the National Consumers' League. She and Addams maintained a close personal and professional relationship throughout their lives.

everything; "the perpetual moving on to something future which shall supersede the present," that paramount impression of life itself, which affords us at one and the same time, ground for despair and for endless and varied anticipation.

CHAPTER 10
PIONEER LABOR LEGISLATION IN ILLINOIS

Our very first Christmas at Hull House, when we as yet knew nothing of child labor, a number of little girls refused the candy which was offered them as part of the Christmas good cheer, saying simply that they "worked in a candy factory and could not bear the sight of it." We discovered that for six weeks they had worked from seven in the morning until nine at night, and they were exhausted as well as satiated. The sharp consciousness of stern economic conditions was thus thrust upon us in the midst of the season of good will.

During the same winter three boys from a Hull-House club were injured at one machine in a neighboring factory for lack of a guard which would have cost but a few dollars. When the injury of one of these boys resulted in his death, we felt quite sure that the owners of the factory would share our horror and remorse, and that they would do everything possible to prevent the recurrence of such a tragedy. To our surprise they did nothing whatever, and I made my first acquaintance then with those pathetic documents signed by the parents of working children, that they will make no claim for damages resulting from "carelessness."

The visits we made in the neighborhood constantly discovered women sewing upon sweatshop work, and often they were assisted by incredibly small children. I remember a little girl of four who pulled out basting threads hour after hour, sitting on a stool at the feet of her Bohemian mother, a little bunch of human misery. But even for that there was no legal redress, for the only Child Labor Law in Illinois, with any provision for enforcement, had been secured by the coal miners' unions, and was confined to children employed in mines.

We learned to know many families in which the working children contributed to the support of their parents, not only because they spoke English better than the older immigrants and were willing to take lower wages, but because their parents gradually found it easy to live upon their earnings. A south Italian peasant who has picked olives and packed oranges from his toddling babyhood, cannot see at once the difference between the outdoor healthy work which he has performed in the varying seasons, and the long hours of monotonous factory life which his child encounters when he goes to work in Chicago. An Italian father came to us in great grief over the death of his eldest child, a little girl of twelve, who had brought the largest wages into the family fund. In the midst of his genuine sorrow he said: "She was the oldest kid I had. Now I shall have to go back to work again until the next one is able to take care of me." The man was only thirty-three and had hoped to retire from work at least during the winters. No foreman cared to have him in a factory, untrained and unintelligent as he was. It was much easier for his bright, English-speaking little girl to get a chance to paste labels on a box than for him to secure an opportunity to carry pig iron. The effect on the child was what no one concerned thought about, in the abnormal effort she made thus prematurely to bear the weight of life. Another little girl of thirteen, a Russian Jewish child employed in a laundry at a heavy task beyond her strength, committed suicide, because she had borrowed three dollars from a companion which she could not repay unless she confided the story to her parents and gave up an entire week's wages — but what could the family live upon that week in case she did! Her child mind, of course, had no sense of proportion, and carbolic acid appeared inevitable.

While we found many pathetic cases of child labor and hard-driven victims of the sweating system who could not possibly earn enough in the short busy season to support themselves during the rest of the year, it became evident that we must add carefully collected information to our general impression of neighborhood conditions if we would make it of any genuine value.

There was at that time no statistical information on Chicago industrial conditions, and Mrs. Florence Kelley, an early resident of Hull-House, suggested to the Illinois State Bureau of Labor that they investigate the sweating system in Chicago with its attendant child labor. The head of the bureau adopted this suggestion and engaged Mrs. Kelley to make the investigation. When the report was presented to the Illinois Legislature, a special committee was appointed to look into the Chicago conditions. I well recall that on the Sunday the members of this commission came to dine at Hull-House, our hopes ran high, and we believed that at last some of the worst ills under which our neighbors were suffering would be brought to an end.

As a result of its investigations, this committee recommended to the Legislature the provisions which afterwards became those of the first Factory Law of Illinois, regulating the sanitary conditions of the sweatshop and fixing fourteen as the age at which a child might be employed.

Before the passage of the law could be secured, it was necessary to appeal to all elements of the community, and a little group of us addressed the open meetings of trades-unions and of benefit societies, church organizations, and social clubs literally every evening for three months. Of course the most energetic help as well as intelligent understanding came from the trades-unions. The central labor body of Chicago, then called the Trades and Labor Assembly, had previously appointed a committee of investigation to inquire into the sweating system. This committee consisted of five delegates from the unions and five outside their membership. Two of the latter were residents of Hull-House, and continued with the unions in their well-conducted campaign until the passage of Illinois's first factory legislation was secured, a statute which has gradually been built upon by many public-spirited citizens until Illinois stands well among the states, at least in the matter of protecting her children. The Hull-House residents that winter had their first experience in lobbying. I remember that I very much disliked the word and still more the prospect of the lobbying itself, and we insisted that well-known Chicago women should accompany this first little group of Settlement folk who with trades-unionists moved upon the state capitol in behalf of factory legislation. The national or, to use its formal name, the General Federation of Women's Clubs had been organized in Chicago only the year before this legislation was secured. The federation was then timid in regard to all legislation because it was anxious not to frighten its new membership, although its second president, Mrs. Henrotin,[50] was most untiring in her efforts to secure this law.

It was, perhaps, a premature effort, though certainly founded upon a genuine need, to urge that a clause limiting the hours of all women working in factories or workshops to eight a day, or forty-eight a week, should be inserted in the first factory legislation of the state. Although we had lived at Hull-House but three years when we urged this legislation, we had known a large number of young girls who were constantly exhausted by night work; for whatever may be said in defense of night work for men, few women are able to endure it. A man who works by night sleeps regularly by day, but a woman finds it impossible to put aside the household duties which crowd upon her, and a conscientious

---

[50]Ellen Martin Henrotin (1847–1922) was a leader of the Chicago Woman's Club, the national General Federation of Women's Clubs, and the National Women's Trade Union League. Her wealthy background and marriage to the president of the Chicago Stock Exchange did not prevent her involvement with labor issues and working conditions or her close association with the reformers at Hull-House.

girl finds it hard to sleep with her mother washing and scrubbing within a few feet of her bed. One of the most painful impressions of those first years is that of pale, listless girls, who worked regularly in a factory of the vicinity which was then running full night time. These girls also encountered a special danger in the early morning hours as they returned from work, debilitated and exhausted, and only too easily convinced that a drink and a little dancing at the end of the balls in the saloon dance halls, was what they needed to brace them. One of the girls whom we then knew, whose name, Chloe, seemed to fit her delicate charm, craving a drink to dispel her lassitude before her tired feet should take the long walk home, had thus been decoyed into a saloon, where the soft drink was followed by an alcoholic one containing "knockout drops," and she awoke in a disreputable rooming house — too frightened and disgraced to return to her mother.

Thus confronted by that old conundrum of the interdependence of matter and spirit, the conviction was forced upon us that long and exhausting hours of work are almost sure to be followed by lurid and exciting pleasures; that the power to overcome temptation reaches its limit almost automatically with that of physical resistance. The eight-hour clause in this first Factory Law met with much less opposition in the Legislature than was anticipated, and was enforced for a year before it was pronounced unconstitutional by the Supreme Court of Illinois. During the halcyon months when it was a law, a large and enthusiastic Eight-Hour Club of working women met at Hull-House, to read the literature on the subject and in every way to prepare themselves to make public sentiment in favor of the measure which meant so much to them. The adverse decision in the test case, the progress of which they had most intelligently followed, was a matter of great disappointment. The entire experience left on my mind a distrust of all legislation which was not preceded by full discussion and understanding. A premature measure may be carried through a Legislature by perfectly legitimate means and still fail to possess vitality and a sense of maturity. . . .

Founded upon some such compunction, the sense that the passage of the Child Labor Law would in many cases work hardship, was never absent from my mind during the earliest years of its operation. I addressed as many mothers' meetings and clubs among working women as I could, in order to make clear the object of the law and the ultimate benefit to themselves as well as to their children. I am happy to remember that I never met with lack of understanding among the hard-working widows, in whose behalf many prosperous people were so eloquent. These widowed mothers would say, "Why, of course, that is what I am working for,— to give the children a chance. I want them to have more education than I had"; or another, "That is why we came to America, and I don't want to spoil his start, even although his father is dead"; or, "It's different in America. A boy gets left if he isn't educated." There was always a willingness, even among the poorest women, to keep on with the hard night scrubbing or the long days of washing for the children's sake.

The bitterest opposition to the law came from the large glass companies who were so accustomed to use the labor of children, that they were convinced the manufacturing of glass could not be carried on without it.

Fifteen years ago the state of Illinois, as well as Chicago, exhibited many characteristics of the pioneer country in which untrammeled energy and an "early start" were still the most highly prized generators of success. Although this first labor legislation was but bringing Illinois into line with the nations in the modern industrial world, which "have long been obliged for their own sakes to come to the aid of the workers by which they live,— that the child, the young person, and the woman may be protected from their own weakness and necessity," nevertheless from the first it ran counter to the instinct and tradition, almost to the very religion of the manufacturers of the state, who were for the most part self-made men.

This first attempt in Illinois for adequate factory legislation also was associated in the minds of business men with radicalism, because the law was secured during the term of Governor Altgeld and was first enforced during his administration. While nothing in its genesis or spirit could be further from "anarchy" than factory legislation, and while the first law in Illinois was still far behind Massachusetts and New York, the fact that Governor Altgeld pardoned from the state's prison the anarchists who had been sentenced there after the Haymarket riot, gave the opponents of this most reasonable legislation a quickly utilized opportunity to couple it with that detested word; the state document which accompanied Governor Altgeld's pardon gave these ungenerous critics a further opportunity, because a magnanimous action was marred by personal rancor, betraying for the moment the infirmity of a noble mind. For all of these reasons this first modification of the undisturbed control of the aggressive captains of industry, could not be enforced without resistance marked by dramatic episodes and revolts. The inception of the law had already become associated with Hull-House, and when its ministration was also centered there, we inevitably received all the odium which these first efforts entailed. Mrs. Kelley was appointed the first factory inspector with a deputy and a force of twelve inspectors to enforce the law.

Both Mrs. Kelley and her assistant, Mrs. Stevens,[51] lived at Hull-House; the office was on Polk Street directly opposite, and one of the most vigorous deputies was the president of the Jane Club. In addition, one of the early men residents, since dean of a state law school, acted as prosecutor in the cases brought against the violators of the law.

Chicago had for years been notoriously lax in the administration of law, and the enforcement of an unpopular measure was resented equally by the president of a large manufacturing concern and by the former victim of a sweatshop who had started a place of his own. Whatever the sentiments towards the new law on the part of the employers, there was no doubt of its enthusiastic reception by the trades-unions, as the securing of the law had already come from them, and through the years which have elapsed since, the experience of the Hull-House residents would coincide with that of an English statesman who said that "a common rule for the standard of life and the condition of labor may be secured by legislation, but it must be maintained by trades-unionism." . . .

In the first years of Hull-House we came across no trades-unions among the women workers, and I think, perhaps, that only one union, composed solely of women, was to be found in Chicago then,— that of the bookbinders. I easily recall the evening when the president of this pioneer organization accepted an invitation to take dinner at Hull-House.[52] She came in rather a recalcitrant mood, expecting to be patronized and so suspicious of our motives, that it was only after she had been persuaded to become a guest of the house for several weeks in order to find out about us for herself, that she was convinced of our sincerity and of the ability of "outsiders" to be of any service to working women. She afterward became closely identified with Hull-House, and her hearty coöperation was assured until she moved to Boston and became a general organizer for the American Federation of Labor.

The women shirt makers and the women cloak makers were both organized at Hull-House as was also the Dorcas Federal Labor Union,

---

[51] Alzina Stevens (1849–1900), a former factory worker and organizer for the Knights of Labor, became a resident of Hull-House in the early 1890s. In addition to working with Florence Kelley on passage and implementation of Illinois' short-lived Factory Inspection Act, Stevens worked on establishment of a Juvenile Court in Chicago and was its first probation officer.

[52] Mary Kenney (O'Sullivan) (1864–1943), the daughter of Irish immigrants, led the Chicago effort to organize female bookbinders. Kenney was initially suspicious of Jane Addams's overtures to her, but once she became convinced that Addams genuinely intended to aid the women workers she moved into Hull-House and based her organizing efforts there. Later, Kenney married and moved to Boston, serving as the first female organizer for the American Federation of Labor and then founding the National Women's Trade Union League. She appointed Jane Addams to the League's first Executive Council.

which had been founded through the efforts of a working woman, then one of the residents. The latter union met once a month in our drawing-room. It was composed of representatives from all the unions in the city which included women in their membership and also received other women in sympathy with unionism. It was accorded representation in the central labor body of the city, and later it joined its efforts with those of others to found the Woman's Union Label League. In what we considered a praiseworthy effort to unite it with other organizations, the president of a leading Women's Club applied for membership.[53] We were so sure of her election that she stood just outside of the drawing-room door, or, in trades-union language, "the wicket gate," while her name was voted upon. To our chagrin she did not receive enough votes to secure her admission, not because the working girls, as they were careful to state, did not admire her, but because she "seemed to belong to the other side." Fortunately, the big-minded woman so thoroughly understood the vote and her interest in working women was so genuine, that it was less than a decade afterward when she was elected to the presidency of the National Woman's Trades Union League. The incident and the sequel registers, perhaps, the change in Chicago towards the labor movement, the recognition of the fact that it is a general social movement concerning all members of society and not merely a class struggle.

Some such public estimate of the labor movement was brought home to Chicago during several conspicuous strikes; at least labor legislation has twice been inaugurated because its need was thus made clear. After the Pullman strike[54] various elements in the community were unexpectedly brought together that they might soberly consider and rectify the weaknesses in the legal structure which the strike had revealed. These citizens arranged for a large and representative convention to be held in Chicago on Industrial Conciliation and Arbitration. I served as secretary of the committee from the new Civic Federation having the matter in charge, and our hopes ran high when, as a result of the agitation, the Illinois Legislature passed a law creating a State Board of Conciliation and Arbitration. But even a State Board cannot accomplish more than public

[53] Margaret Dreier Robins (1868–1945), an upper-middle-class social reformer from New York who moved to Chicago in 1904 when she married Raymond Robins, the head resident at Northwestern University Settlement. She served as president of the Chicago branch of the Women's Trade Union League from 1907 to 1913. The WTUL, founded by Mary Kenney, was the national organization that brought middle-class supporters into a sometimes uneasy alliance with working women. Robins served as national president of the WTUL from 1913 to 1928. She shared Addams's devotion to cross-class cooperation but did not always feel Addams sided sufficiently with labor.

[54] See note 36.

sentiment authorizes and sustains, and we might easily have been discouraged in those early days could we have foreseen some of the industrial disturbances which have since disgraced Chicago. This law embodied the best provisions of the then existing laws for the arbitration of industrial disputes. At the time the word "arbitration" was still a word to conjure with, and many Chicago citizens were convinced, not only of the danger and futility involved in the open warfare of opposing social forces, but further believed that the search for justice and righteousness in industrial relations was made infinitely more difficult thereby.

The Pullman strike afforded much illumination to many Chicago people. Before it, there had been nothing in my experience to reveal that distinct cleavage of society, which a general strike at least momentarily affords. Certainly, during all those dark days of the Pullman strike, the growth of class bitterness was most obvious. The fact that the Settlement maintained avenues of intercourse with both sides seemed to give it opportunity for nothing but a realization of the bitterness and division along class lines. I had known Mr. Pullman and had seen his genuine pride and pleasure in the model town he had built with so much care; and I had an opportunity to talk to many of the Pullman employees during the strike when I was sent from a so-called "Citizens' Arbitration Committee" to their first meetings held in a hall in the neighboring village of Kensington, and when I was invited to the modest supper tables laid in the model houses. The employees then expected a speedy settlement and no one doubted but that all the grievances connected with the "straw bosses" would be quickly remedied and that the benevolence which had built the model town would not fail them. They were sure that the "straw bosses" had misrepresented the state of affairs, for this very first awakening to class consciousness bore many traces of the servility on one side and the arrogance on the other which had so long prevailed in the model town. The entire strike demonstrated how often the outcome of far-reaching industrial disturbances is dependent upon the personal will of the employer or the temperament of a strike leader. Those familiar with strikes know only too well how much they are influenced by poignant domestic situations, by the troubled consciences of the minority directors, by the suffering women and children, by the keen excitement of the struggle, by the religious scruples sternly suppressed but occasionally asserting themselves, now on one side and now on the other, and by that undefined psychology of the crowd which we understand so little. All of these factors also influence the public and do much to determine popular sympathy and judgment. In the early days of the Pullman strike, as I was coming down in the elevator of the Auditorium

Hotel from one of the futile meetings of the arbitration committee, I met an acquaintance, who angrily said that "the strikers ought all to be shot." As I had heard nothing so bloodthirsty as this either from the most enraged capitalist or from the most desperate of the men, and was interested to find the cause of such a senseless outbreak, I finally discovered that the first ten thousand dollars which my acquaintance had ever saved, requiring, he said, years of effort from the time he was twelve years old until he was thirty, had been lost as the result of a strike; he clinched his argument that he knew what he was talking about, with the statement that "no one need expect him to have any sympathy with strikers or with their affairs."

A very intimate and personal experience revealed, at least to myself, my constant dread of the spreading ill will. At the height of the sympathetic strike my oldest sister[55] who was convalescing from a long illness in a hospital near Chicago, became suddenly very much worse. While I was able to reach her at once, every possible obstacle of a delayed and blocked transportation system interrupted the journey of her husband and children who were hurrying to her bedside from a distant state. As the end drew nearer and I was obliged to reply to my sister's constant inquiries that her family had not yet come, I was filled with a profound apprehension lest her last hours should be touched with resentment towards those responsible for the delay; lest her unutterable longing should at the very end be tinged with bitterness. She must have divined what was in my mind, for at last she said each time after the repetition of my sad news, "I don't blame any one, I am not judging them." My heart was comforted and heavy at the same time; but how many more such moments of sorrow and death were being made difficult and lonely throughout the land, and how much would these experiences add to the lasting bitterness, that touch of self-righteousness which makes the spirit of forgiveness well-nigh impossible.

When I returned to Chicago from the quiet country I saw the federal troops encamped about the post office; almost every one on Halsted Street wearing a white ribbon, the emblem of the strikers' side; the res-

---

[55] Mary Addams Linn (1845–94), Jane Addams's eldest sister, was eighteen years old and Jane Addams two when their mother died. For the next six years, Mary functioned as Jane's surrogate mother until their father remarried and Mary herself married the Reverend John Linn, a Presbyterian minister whose career necessitated frequent moves in and around northern Illinois. Upon her death in 1894, Mary left four children ranging in age from 14 to 9. Jane Addams was actively involved in the children's lives and became the legal guardian of the youngest, Stanley.

idents at Hull-House divided in opinion as to the righteousness of this or that measure; and no one able to secure any real information as to which side was burning the cars. After the Pullman strike I made an attempt to analyze in a paper which I called "The Modern King Lear," the inevitable revolt of human nature against the plans Mr. Pullman had made for his employees, the miscarriage of which appeared to him such black ingratitude. It seemed to me unendurable not to make some effort to gather together the social implications of the failure of this benevolent employer and its relation to the demand for a more democratic administration of industry. Doubtless the paper represented a certain "excess of participation," to use a gentle phrase of Charles Lamb's in preference to a more emphatic one used by Mr. Pullman himself. The last picture of the Pullman strike which I distinctly recall was three years later when one of the strike leaders came to see me. Although out of work for most of the time since the strike, he had been undisturbed for six months in the repair shops of a street car company, under an assumed name, but he had at that moment been discovered and dismissed. He was a superior type of English workingman, but as he stood there, broken and discouraged, believing himself so black-listed that his skill could never be used again, filled with sorrow over the loss of his wife who had recently died after an illness with distressing mental symptoms, realizing keenly the lack of the respectable way of living he had always until now been able to maintain, he seemed to me an epitome of the wretched human waste such a strike implies. I fervently hoped that the new Arbitration Law would prohibit in Chicago forever more such brutal and ineffective methods of settling industrial disputes. And yet even as early as 1896, we found the greatest difficulty in applying the Arbitration Law to the garment workers' strike, although it was finally accomplished after various mass meetings had urged it. The cruelty and waste of the strike as an implement for securing the most reasonable demands, came to me at another time, during the long strike of the clothing cutters. They had protested, not only against various wrongs of their own, but against the fact that the tailors employed by the custom merchants were obliged to furnish their own workshops and thus bore a burden of rent which belonged to the employer. One of the leaders in this strike, whom I had known for several years as a sober, industrious, and unusually intelligent man, I saw gradually break down during the many trying weeks and at last suffer a complete moral collapse. . . .

But of all the aspects of social misery nothing is so heart-breaking as unemployment, and it was inevitable that we should see much of it in a neighborhood where low rents attracted the poorly paid worker and many newly arrived immigrants who were first employed in gangs upon railroad extensions and similar undertakings. The sturdy peasants eager for work were either the victims of the padrone who fleeced them unmercifully, both in securing a place to work and then in supplying them with food, or they became the mere sport of unscrupulous employment agencies. Hull-House made an investigation both of the padrone and of the agencies in our immediate vicinity, and the outcome confirming what we already suspected, we eagerly threw ourselves into a movement to procure free employment bureaus under state control until a law authorizing such bureaus and giving the officials intrusted with their management power to regulate private employment agencies, passed the Illinois Legislature in 1899. The history of these bureaus demonstrates the tendency we all have to consider a legal enactment in itself an achievement and to grow careless in regard to its administration and actual results; for an investigation into the situation ten years later discovered that immigrants were still shamefully imposed upon. A group of Bulgarians were found who had been sent to work in Arkansas where their services were not needed; they walked back to Chicago only to secure their next job in Oklahoma and to pay another railroad fare as well as another commission to the agency. Not only was there no method by which the men not needed in Arkansas could know that there was work in Oklahoma unless they came back to Chicago to find it out, but there was no certainty that they might not be obliged to walk back from Oklahoma because the Chicago agency had already sent out too many men.

This investigation of the employment bureau resources of Chicago was undertaken by the League for the Protection of Immigrants, with whom it is possible for Hull-House to coöperate whenever an investigation of the immigrant colonies in our immediate neighborhood seems necessary, as was recently done in regard to the Greek colonies of Chicago. The superintendent of this league, Miss Grace Abbott,[56] is a resident of Hull-House and all of our later attempts to secure justice and opportunity for immigrants are much more effective through the league, and when we speak before a Congressional Committee in Washington

---

[56] Abbott (1878–1939) was an educated, middle-class social reformer from Nebraska who, as a resident of Hull-House, served as head of the Immigrants' Protective League and lobbied for immigrants' rights. After World War I, she served as director of the Illinois State Immigrants' Commission and succeeded Julia Lathrop at the U.S. Children's Bureau, serving as director of that agency from 1921 to 1934 and lobbying for child labor laws and maternal and infant health programs. Her older sister, Edith, was also an associate of Jane Addams at Hull-House and was a founder of the University of Chicago's School of Social Work.

concerning the needs of Chicago immigrants, we represent the league as well as our own neighbors.

It is in connection with the first factory employment of newly arrived immigrants and the innumerable difficulties attached to their first adjustment, that some of the most profound industrial disturbances in Chicago have come about. Under any attempt at classification these strikes belong more to the general social movement than to the industrial conflict, for the strike is an implement used most rashly by unorganized labor who, after they are in difficulties, call upon the trades-unions for organization and direction. They are similar to those strikes which are inaugurated by the unions on behalf of unskilled labor. In neither case do the hastily organized unions usually hold after the excitement of the moment has subsided, and the most valuable result of such strikes is the expanding consciousness of the solidarity of the workers. . . .

Certainly the industrial conflict when epitomized in a strike, centers public attention on conditions as nothing else can do. A strike is one of the most exciting episodes in modern life and as it assumes the characteristics of a game, the entire population of a city becomes divided into two cheering sides. In such moments the fair-minded public, who ought to be depended upon as a referee, practically disappears. Any one who tries to keep the attitude of nonpartisanship, which is perhaps an impossible one, is quickly under suspicion by both sides. At least that was the fate of a group of citizens appointed by the mayor of Chicago to arbitrate during the stormy teamsters' strike which occurred in 1905. We sat through a long Sunday afternoon in the mayor's office in the City Hall, talking first with the labor men and then with the group of capitalists. The undertaking was the more futile in that we were all practically the dupes of a new type of "industrial conspiracy" successfully inaugurated in Chicago by a close compact between the coal teamsters' union and the coal team owners' association who had formed a kind of monopoly hitherto new to a monopoly-ridden public.

The stormy teamsters' strike, ostensibly undertaken in defense of the garment workers, but really arising from causes so obscure and dishonorable that they have never yet been made public, was the culmination of a type of trades-unions which had developed in Chicago during the preceding decade in which corruption had flourished almost as openly as it had previously done in the City Hall. . . .

At various times during these years the better types of trades-unionists had made a firm stand against this corruption and a determined effort to eradicate it from the labor movement, not unlike the general reform effort of many American cities against political corruption. This reform movement in the Chicago Federation of Labor had its martyrs, and more than one man nearly lost his life through the "slugging" methods employed by the powerful corruptionists. And yet even in the midst of these things were found touching examples of fidelity to the earlier principles of brotherhood totally untouched by the corruption. At one time the scrub women in the downtown office buildings had a union of their own affiliated with the elevator men and the janitors. Although the union was used merely as a weapon in the fight of the coal teamsters against the use of natural gas in downtown buildings, it did not prevent the women from getting their first glimpse into the fellowship and the sense of protection which is the great gift of trades-unionism to the unskilled, unbefriended worker. I remember in a meeting held at Hull-House one Sunday afternoon, that the president of a "local" of scrub women stood up to relate her experience. She told first of the long years in which the fear of losing her job and the fluctuating pay were harder to bear than the hard work itself, when she had regarded all the other women who scrubbed in the same building merely as rivals and was most afraid of the most miserable, because they offered to work for less and less as they were pressed harder and harder by debt. Then she told of the change that had come when the elevator men and even the lordly janitors had talked to her about an organization and had said that they must all stand together. She told how gradually she came to feel sure of her job and of her regular pay, and she was even starting to buy a house now that she could "calculate" how much she "could have for sure." Neither she nor any of the other members knew that the same combination which had organized the scrub women into a union later destroyed it during a strike inaugurated for their own purposes.

That a Settlement is drawn into the labor issues of its city can seem remote to its purpose only to those who fail to realize that so far as the present industrial system thwarts our ethical demands, not only for social righteousness but for social order, a Settlement is committed to an effort to understand and, as far as possible, to alleviate it. That in this effort it should be drawn into fellowship with the local efforts of trades-unions is most obvious. This identity of aim apparently commits the Settlement in the public mind to all the faiths and works of actual trades-unions. Fellowship has so long implied similarity of creed that the fact that the Settlement often differs widely from the policy pursued by trades-unionists and clearly expresses that difference, does not in the least change public opinion in regard to its identification. This is especially true in periods of industrial disturbance, although it is exactly at such moments that the trades-unionists themselves are suspicious of all but their "own kind." It is during the much longer periods between strikes that the Settlement's fellowship with trades-unions is most satisfactory in the agitation for labor legislation and similar undertakings. . . .

Nevertheless the reaction of strikes upon Chicago Settlements affords an interesting study in social psychology. For whether Hull-House is in any wise identified with the strike or not, makes no difference. When "Labor" is in disgrace we are always regarded as belonging to it and share the opprobrium. In the public excitement following the Pullman strike Hull-House lost many friends; later the teamsters' strike caused another such defection, although my office in both cases had been solely that of a duly appointed arbitrator. . . .

There has gradually developed between the various Settlements of Chicago a warm fellowship founded upon a like-mindedness resulting from similar experiences, quite as identity of interest and endeavor develop an enduring relation between the residents of the same Settlement. This sense of comradeship is never stronger than during the hardships and perplexities of a strike of unskilled workers revolting against the conditions which drag them even below the level of their European life. At such times the residents in various Settlements are driven to a standard of life argument running somewhat in this wise,— that as the very existence of the state depends upon the character of its citizens, therefore if certain industrial conditions are forcing the workers below the standard of decency, it becomes possible to deduce the right of state regulation. Even as late as the stockyard strike this line of argument was denounced as "socialism" although it has since been confirmed as wise statesmanship by a decision of the Supreme Court of the United States which was apparently secured through the masterly argument of the Brandeis brief[57] in the Oregon ten-hour case.

In such wise the residents of an industrial neighborhood gradually comprehend the close connection of their own difficulties with national and even international movements. The residents in the Chicago Settlements became pioneer members in the American branch of the International League for Labor Legislation, because their neighborhood experiences had made them only too conscious of the dire need for

---

[57] Written by Louis D. Brandeis (1856–1941), American lawyer and social reformer, whose innovative use of economic, historical, and sociological data in *Muller v. Oregon* (1908) transformed the nature of legal briefs and overturned legal precedent by upholding the state's right to establish maximum working hours for women. He was aided in this effort by Josephine Goldmark, his sister-in-law, and an aid to Florence Kelley at the National Consumers' League. Brandeis was appointed to the Supreme Court by President Woodrow Wilson; he was the first Jewish American to sit on the Supreme Court bench.

protective legislation. In such a league, with its ardent members in every industrial nation of Europe, with its encouraging reports of the abolition of all night work for women in six European nations, with its careful observations on the results of employer's liability legislation and protection of machinery, one becomes identified with a movement of world-wide significance and manifold manifestation.

CHAPTER 11
IMMIGRANTS AND THEIR CHILDREN

From our very first months at Hull-House we found it much easier to deal with the first generation of crowded city life than with the second or third, because it is more natural and cast in a simpler mold. The Italian and Bohemian peasants who live in Chicago, still put on their bright holiday clothes on a Sunday and go to visit their cousins. They tramp along with at least a suggestion of having once walked over plowed fields and breathed country air. The second generation of city poor too often have no holiday clothes and consider their relations a "bad lot." I have heard a drunken man in a maudlin stage, babble of his good country mother and imagine he was driving the cows home, and I knew that his little son who laughed loud at him, would be drunk earlier in life and would have no such pastoral interlude to his ravings. Hospitality still survives among foreigners, although it is buried under false pride among the poorest Americans. One thing seemed clear in regard to entertaining immigrants; to preserve and keep whatever of value their past life contained and to bring them in contact with a better type of Americans. For several years, every Saturday evening the entire families of our Italian neighbors were our guests. These evenings were very popular during our first winters at Hull-House. Many educated Italians helped us, and the house became known as a place where Italians were welcome and where national holidays were observed. They come to us with their petty lawsuits, sad relics of the *vendetta,* with their incorrigible boys, with their hospital cases, with their aspirations for American clothes, and with their needs for an interpreter. . . .

An evening similar in purpose to the one devoted to the Italians was organized for the Germans, in our first year. Owing to the superior education of our Teutonic guests and the clever leading of a cultivated German woman, these evenings reflected something of that cozy social intercourse which is found in its perfection in the fatherland. Our guests sang a great deal in the tender minor of the German folk song or in the rousing spirit of the Rhine, and they slowly but persistently pursued a course in German history and literature, recovering something of that poetry and romance which they had long since resigned with other good things. We found strong family affection between them and their English-speaking children, but their pleasures were not in common, and they seldom went out together. Perhaps the greatest value of the Settlement to them was in placing large and pleasant rooms with musical facilities at their disposal, and in reviving their almost forgotten enthusiasms. I have seen sons and daughters stand in complete surprise as their mother's knitting needles softly beat time to the song she was singing, or her worn face turned rosy under the hand-clapping as she made an old-fashioned courtsey at the end of a German poem. It was easy to fancy a growing touch of respect in her children's manner to her, and a rising enthusiasm for German literature and reminiscence on the part of all the family, an effort to bring together the old life and the new, a respect for the older cultivation, and not quite so much assurance that the new was the best. . . .

An overmastering desire to reveal the humbler immigrant parents to their own children lay at the base of what has come to be called the Hull-House Labor Museum. This was first suggested to my mind one early spring day when I saw an old Italian woman, her distaff against her homesick face, patiently spinning a thread by the simple stick spindle so reminiscent of all southern Europe. I was walking down Polk Street, perturbed in spirit, because it seemed so difficult to come into genuine relations with the Italian women and because they themselves so often lost their hold upon their Americanized children. It seemed to me that Hull-House ought to be able to devise some educational enterprise, which should build a bridge between European and American experiences in such wise as to give them both more meaning and a sense of relation. I meditated that perhaps the power to see life as a whole, is more needed in the immigrant quarter of a large city than anywhere else, and that the lack of this power is the most fruitful source of misunderstanding between European immigrants and their children, as it is between them and their American neighbors; and why should that chasm between fathers and sons, yawning at the feet of each generation, be made so unnecessarily cruel and impassable to these bewildered immigrants? Suddenly I looked up and saw the old woman with her distaff, sitting in the sun on the steps of a tenement house. She might have served as a model for one of Michael Angelo's [sic] Fates, but her face brightened as I passed and, holding up her spindle for me to see, she called out that when she had spun a little more yarn, she would knit a pair of stockings for her goddaughter. The occupation of the old woman gave me the clew that was needed. Could we not interest the young people working in the neighboring factories, in these older forms of industry, so that, through their own parents and grandparents, they would find a dramatic representation of the inherited resources of their daily occupation? If these young people could actually see that the complicated machinery of the factory had been evolved from simple tools, they might at least make a beginning towards that education which Dr. Dewey[58] defines as "a continuing reconstruction of experience." They might also lay a foundation for reverence of the past which Goethe declares to be the basis of all sound progress.

My exciting walk on Polk Street was followed by many talks with Dr. Dewey and with one of the teachers in his school who was a resident at Hull-House. Within a month a room was fitted up to which we might invite those of our neighbors who were possessed of old crafts and who were eager to use them.

We found in the immediate neighborhood, at least four varieties of these most primitive methods of spinning and three distinct variations of the same spindle in connection with wheels. It was possible to put these seven into historic sequence and order and to connect the whole with the present method of factory spinning. The same thing was done for weaving, and on every Saturday evening a little exhibit was made of these various forms of labor in the textile industry. Within one room a Syrian woman, a Greek, an Italian, a Russian, and an Irishwoman enabled even the most casual observer to see that there is no break in orderly evolution if we look at history from the industrial standpoint; that industry develops similarly and peacefully year by year among the workers of each nation, heedless of differences in language, religion, and political experiences. . . . Human progress is slow and perhaps never more cruel than in the advance of industry, but is not the worker comforted by knowing that other historical periods have existed similar to the one in which he finds himself, and that the readjustment may be shortened and alleviated by judicious action; and is he not entitled to the solace which an artistic portrayal of the situation might give him?

The textile museum is connected directly with the basket weaving, sewing, millinery, embroidery, and dressmaking constantly being

[58] John Dewey (1859–1952) was an American philosopher whose position as professor of philosophy, psychology, and pedagogy at the University of Chicago from 1894 to 1904 put him in close contact with Jane Addams and Hull-House. Dewey appealed to Addams because he argued that democratic practices and respect for experiential learning should shape all pedagogy.

When Jane Addams first established the Hull-House Labor Museum in 1900, the neighborhood's Italian and Greek immigrants made the most use of the museum's pottery, textile, basketry, and metalwork equipment. This 1920s photo of the members of the Mexican Men's Club engaged in ceramics serves as a visual reminder that though the immigrant population around the settlement was in constant flux, the interest in the offerings at Hull-House persisted.

Jane Addams Memorial Collection, Special Collections, The University Library, The University of Illinois at Chicago.

taught at Hull-House, and so far as possible with the other educational departments; we have also been able to make a collection of products, of early implements, and of photographs which are full of suggestion. Yet far beyond its direct educational value, we prize it because it so often puts the immigrants into the position of teachers, and we imagine that it affords them a pleasant change from the tutelage in which all Americans, including their own children, are so apt to hold them. I recall a number of Russian women working in a sewing-room near Hull-House, who heard one Christmas week that the House was going to give a party to which they might come. They arrived one afternoon when, unfortunately, there was no party on hand and, although the residents did their best to entertain them with impromptu music and refreshments, it was quite evident that they were greatly disappointed. Finally it was suggested that they be shown the Labor Museum — where gradually the thirty sodden, tired women were transformed. They knew how to use the spindles and were delighted to find the Russian spinning frame. Many of them had never seen the spinning wheel, which has not penetrated to certain parts of Russia, and they regarded it as a new and wonderful invention. They turned up their dresses to show their homespun petticoats; they tried the looms; they explained the difficulty of the old patterns; in short, from having been stupidly entertained, they themselves did the entertaining. Because of a direct appeal to former experiences, the immigrant visitors were able for the moment to instruct their American hostesses in an old and honored craft, as was indeed becoming to their age and experience.

In some such ways as these have the Labor Museum and the shops pointed out the possibilities which Hull-House has scarcely begun to develop, of demonstrating that culture is an understanding of the long-established occupations and thoughts of men, of the arts with which they have solaced their toil. A yearning to recover for the household arts something of their early sanctity and meaning, arose strongly within me one evening when I was attending a Passover Feast to which I had been invited by a Jewish family in the neighborhood, where the traditional and religious significance of woman's daily activity was still retained. The kosher food the Jewish mother spread before her family had been prepared according to traditional knowledge and with constant care in the use of utensils; upon her had fallen the responsibility to make all ready according to Mosaic instructions that the great crisis in a religious history might be fittingly set forth by her husband and son. Aside from the grave religious significance in the ceremony, my mind was filled with shifting pictures of woman's labor with which travel makes one familiar; the Indian women grinding grain outside of their huts as they sing praises to the sun and rain; a file of white-clad Moorish women whom I had once seen waiting their turn at a well in Tangiers; south Italian women kneeling in a row along the stream and beating their wet clothes against the smooth white stones; the milking, the gardening, the marketing in thousands of hamlets, which are such direct expressions of the solicitude and affection at the basis of all family life.

There has been some testimony that the Labor Museum has revealed the charm of woman's primitive activities. I recall a certain Italian girl who came every Saturday evening to a cooking class in the same building in which her mother spun in the Labor Museum exhibit; and yet Angelina always left her mother at the front door while she herself went around to a side door because she did not wish to be too closely identified in the eyes of the rest of the cooking class with an Italian woman who wore a kerchief over her head, uncouth boots, and short petticoats.

One evening, however, Angelina saw her mother surrounded by a group of visitors from the School of Education, who much admired the spinning, and she concluded from their conversation that her mother was "the best stick-spindle spinner in America." When she inquired from me as to the truth of this deduction, I took occasion to describe the Italian village in which her mother had lived, something of her free life, and how, because of the opportunity she and the other women of the village had to drop their spindles over the edge of a precipice, they had developed a skill in spinning beyond that of the neighboring towns. I dilated somewhat on the freedom and beauty of that life — how hard it must be to exchange it all for a two-room tenement, and to give up a beautiful homespun kerchief for an ugly department store hat. I intimated it was most unfair to judge her by these things alone, and that while she must depend on her daughter to learn the new ways, she also had a right to expect her daughter to know something of the old ways.

That which I could not convey to the child but upon which my own mind persistently dwelt, was that her mother's whole life had been spent in a secluded spot under the rule of traditional and narrowly localized observances, until her very religion clung to local sanctities, — to the shrine before which she had always prayed, to the pavement and walls of the low vaulted church, — and then suddenly she was torn from it all and literally put out to sea, straight away from the solid habits of her religious and domestic life, and she now walked timidly but with poignant sensibility upon a new and strange shore.

It was easy to see that the thought of her mother with any other background than that of the tenement was new to Angelina and at least two things resulted; she allowed her mother to pull out of the big box under the bed the beautiful homespun garments which had been previously hidden away as uncouth; and she openly came into the Labor Museum by the same door as did her mother, proud at least of the mastery of the craft which had been so much admired. . . .

The Labor Museum continually demanded more space as it was enriched by a fine textile exhibit lent by the Field Museum, and later by carefully selected specimens of basketry from the Philippines. The shops have finally included a group of three or four women, Irish, Italian, Danish, who have become a permanent working force in the textile department which has developed into a self-supporting industry through the sale of its homespun products.

These women and a few men, who come to the museum to utilize their European skill in pottery, metal, and wood, demonstrate that immigrant colonies might yield to our American life something very valuable, if their resources were intelligently studied and developed. I recall an Italian, who had decorated the doorposts of his tenement with a beautiful pattern he had previously used in carving the reredos of a Neapolitan church, who was "fired" by his landlord on the ground of destroying property. His feelings were hurt, not so much that he had been put out of his house, as that his work had been so disregarded; and he said that when people traveled in Italy they liked to look at wood carvings but that in America "they only made money out of you."

Sometimes the suppression of the instinct of workmanship is followed by more disastrous results. A Bohemian whose little girl attended classes at Hull-House, in one of his periodic drunken spells had literally almost choked her to death, and later had committed suicide when in delirium tremens. His poor wife, who stayed a week at Hull-House after the disaster until a new tenement could be arranged for her, one day showed me a gold ring which her husband had made for their betrothal. It exhibited the most exquisite workmanship, and she said that although in the old country he had been a goldsmith, in America he had for twenty years shoveled coal in a furnace room of a large manufacturing plant; that whenever she saw one of his "restless fits," which preceded his drunken periods, "coming on," if she could provide him with a bit of metal and persuade him to stay at home and work at it, he was all right and the time passed without disaster, but that "nothing else would do it." This story threw a flood of light upon the dead man's struggle and on the stupid maladjustment which had broken him down. Why had we never been told? Why had our interest in the remarkable musical ability of his child, blinded us to the hidden artistic ability of the father? We had forgotten that a long-established occupation may form the very foundations of the moral life, that the art with which a man has solaced his toil may be the salvation of his uncertain temperament.

There are many examples of touching fidelity to immigrant parents on the part of their grown children; a young man, who day after day, attends ceremonies which no longer express his religious convictions and who makes his vain effort to interest his Russian Jewish father in social problems; a daughter who might earn much more money as a stenographer could she work from Monday morning till Saturday night, but who quietly and docilely makes neckties for low wages because she can thus abstain from work Saturdays to please her father; these young people ... have reached the conclusion that pity, memory, and faithfulness are natural ties with paramount claims.

This faithfulness, however, is sometimes ruthlessly imposed upon by immigrant parents who, eager for money and accustomed to the patriarchal authority of peasant households, hold their children in a stern bondage which requires a surrender of all their wages and concedes no time or money for pleasures.

There are many convincing illustrations that this parental harshness often results in juvenile delinquency. A Polish boy of seventeen came to Hull-House one day to ask a contribution of fifty cents "towards a flower piece for the funeral of an old Hull-House club boy." A few questions made it clear that the object was fictitious, whereupon the boy broke down and half defiantly stated that he wanted to buy two twenty-five cent tickets, one for his girl and one for himself, to a dance of the Benevolent Social Twos; that he hadn't a penny of his own although he had worked in a brass foundry for three years and had been advanced twice, because he always had to give his pay envelope unopened to his father; "just look at the clothes he buys me" was his concluding remark.

Perhaps the girls are held even more rigidly. In a recent investigation of two hundred working girls it was found that only five per cent had the use of their own money and that sixty-two per cent turned in all they earned, literally every penny, to their mothers. It was through this little investigation that we first knew Marcella, a pretty young German girl who helped her widowed mother year after year to care for a large family of younger children. She was content for the most part although her mother's old-country notions of dress gave her but an infinitesimal amount of her own wages to spend on her clothes, and she was quite sophisticated as to proper dressing because she sold silk in a neighborhood department store. Her mother approved of the young man who was showing her various attentions and agreed that Marcella should accept his invitation to a ball, but would allow her not a penny towards a new gown to replace one impossibly plain and shabby. Marcella spent a sleepless night and wept bitterly, although she well knew that the doctor's bill for the children's scarlet fever was not yet paid. The next day as she was cutting off three yards of shining pink silk, the thought came to her that it would make her a fine new waist to wear to the ball. She wistfully saw it wrapped in paper and carelessly stuffed into the muff of the purchaser, when suddenly the parcel fell upon the floor. No one was looking and quick as a flash the girl picked it up and pushed it into her blouse. The theft was discovered by the relentless department store detective who, for "the sake of the example," insisted upon taking the case into court. The poor mother wept bitter tears over the downfall of her "frommes Mädchen" and no one had the heart to tell her of her own blindness.

I know a Polish boy whose earnings were all given to his father who gruffly refused all requests for pocket money. One Christmas his little sisters, having been told by their mother that they were too poor to have any Christmas presents, appealed to the big brother as to one who was earning money of his own. Flattered by the implication, but at the same time quite impecunious, the night before Christmas he nonchalantly walked through a neighboring department store and stole a manicure set for one little sister and a string of beads for the other. He was caught at the door by the house detective as one of those children whom each local department store arrests in the weeks before Christmas at the daily rate of eight to twenty. The youngest of these offenders are seldom taken into court but are either sent home with a warning or turned over to the officers of the Juvenile Protective Association. Most of these premature law breakers are in search of Americanized clothing and others are only looking for playthings. They are all distracted by the profusion and variety of the display, and their moral sense is confused by the general air of open-handedness.

These disastrous efforts are not unlike those of many younger children who are constantly arrested for petty thieving because they are too eager to take home food or fuel which will relieve the distress and need they so constantly hear discussed. The coal on the wagons, the vegetables displayed in front of the grocery shops, the very wooden blocks in the loosened street paving are a challenge to their powers to help out at home. A Bohemian boy who was out on parole from the old detention home of the Juvenile Court itself, brought back five stolen chickens to the matron for Sunday dinner, saying that he knew the committee were "having a hard time to fill up so many kids and perhaps these fowl would help out." The honest immigrant parents, totally ignorant of American laws and municipal regulations, often send a child to pick up coal on the railroad tracks or to stand at three o'clock in the morning before the side door of a restaurant which gives away broken food, or to collect grain for the chickens at the base of elevators and standing cars. The latter custom accounts for the large number of boys arrested for breaking the seals on grain freight cars. It is easy for a child thus trained to accept the proposition of a junk dealer to bring him bars of iron stored in freight yards. Four boys quite recently had thus carried away and sold to one man, two tons of iron.

Four fifths of the children brought into the Juvenile Court in Chicago are the children of foreigners. The Germans are the greatest offenders, Polish next. Do their children suffer from the excess of virtue in those parents so eager to own a house and lot? One often sees a grasping parent in the court, utterly broken down when the Americanized youth who has been brought to grief clings as piteously to his peasant father as if he were still a frightened little boy in the steerage.

Many of these children have come to grief through their premature fling into city life, having thrown off parental control as they have impatiently discarded foreign ways. Boys of ten and twelve will refuse to sleep at home, preferring the freedom of an old brewery vault or an empty warehouse to the obedience required by their parents, and for days these boys will live on the milk and bread which they steal from the back porches after the early morning delivery. Such children complain that there is "no fun" at home. One little chap who was given a vacant lot to cultivate by the City Garden Association, insisted upon raising only popcorn and tried to present the entire crop to Hull-House "to be used for the parties," with the stipulation that he would have "to be invited every single time." Then there are little groups of dissipated young men who pride themselves upon their ability to live without working, and who despise all the honest and sober ways of their immigrant parents. They are at once a menace and a center of demoralization. Certainly the bewildered parents, unable to speak English and ignorant of the city, whose children have disappeared for days or weeks, have often come to Hull-House, evincing that agony which fairly separates the marrow from the bone, as if they had discovered a new type of suffering, devoid of the healing in familiar sorrows. It is as if they did not know how to search for the children without the assistance of the children themselves. Perhaps the most pathetic aspect of such cases is their revelation of the premature dependence of the older and wiser upon the young and foolish, which is in itself often responsible for the situation because it has given the children an undue sense of their own importance and a false security that they can take care of themselves.

On the other hand, an Italian girl who has had lessons in cooking at the public school, will help her mother to connect the entire family with American food and household habits. That the mother has never baked bread in Italy — only mixed it in her own house and then taken it out to the village oven — makes all the more valuable her daughter's understanding of the complicated cooking stove. The same thing is true of the girl who learns to sew in the public school, and more than anything else, perhaps, of the girl who receives the first simple instruction in the care of little children, — that skillful care which every tenement-house baby requires if he is to be pulled through his second summer. As a result of this teaching I recall a young girl who carefully explained to her Italian mother that the reason the babies in Italy were so healthy and the babies in Chicago were so sickly, was not, as her mother had firmly insisted, because her babies in Italy had goat's milk and her babies in America had cow's milk, but because the milk in Italy was clean and the milk in Chicago was dirty. She said that when you milked your own goat before the door, you knew that the milk was clean, but when you bought milk from the grocery store after it had been carried for many miles in the country, you couldn't tell whether or not it was fit for the baby to drink until the men from the City Hall who had watched it all the way, said that it was all right.

Thus through civic instruction in the public schools, the Italian woman slowly became urbanized in the sense in which the word was used by her own Latin ancestors, and thus the habits of her entire family were modified. The public schools in the immigrant colonies deserve all the praise as Americanizing agencies which can be bestowed upon them, and there is little doubt that the fast-changing curriculum in the direction of the vacation-school experiments, will react still more directly upon such households.

It is difficult to write of the relation of the older and most foreign-looking immigrants to the children of other people, — the Italians whose fruit-carts are upset simply because they are "dagoes," or the Russian peddlers who are stoned and sometimes badly injured because it has become a code of honor in a gang of boys to thus express their derision. The members of a Protective Association of Jewish Peddlers organized at Hull-House, related daily experiences in which old age had been treated with such irreverence, cherished dignity with such disrespect. . . .

Doubtless these difficulties would be much minimized in America, if we faced our own race problem with courage and intelligence, and these very Mediterranean immigrants might give us valuable help. Certainly they are less conscious than the Anglo-Saxon of color distinctions, perhaps because of their traditional familiarity with Carthage and Egypt. They listened with respect and enthusiasm to a scholarly address delivered by Professor Du Bois[59] at Hull-House on a Lincoln's Birthday, with apparently no consciousness of that race difference which color seems to accentuate so absurdly, and upon my return from various conferences held in the interest of "the advancement of colored people," I have had many illuminating conversations with my cosmopolitan neighbors.

The celebration of national events has always been a source of new understanding and companionship with the members of the contiguous foreign colonies not only between them and their American neighbors but between them and their own children. One of our earliest Italian

---

[59] W. E. B. Du Bois (1868–1963) was a Harvard-trained African American sociologist, political theorist, historian, editor, and social activist. He was a founder of the NAACP in 1909, and editor of its journal, *The Crisis,* from 1910 to 1934, and worked with Addams in that organization. She spoke at his all-black home institution, Atlanta University, just as he spoke at Hull-House.

events was a rousing commemoration of Garibaldi's Birthday, and his imposing bust presented to Hull-House that evening, was long the chief ornament of our front hall. It called forth great enthusiasm from the *connazionali* whom Ruskin calls, not the "common people" of Italy, but the "companion people" because of their power for swift sympathy. . . .

To me personally the celebration of the hundredth anniversary of Mazzini's birth was a matter of great interest. Throughout the world that day Italians who believed in a United Italy came together. They recalled the hopes of this man who, with all his devotion to his country, was still more devoted to humanity and who dedicated to the workingmen of Italy, an appeal so philosophical, so filled with a yearning for righteousness, that it transcended all national boundaries and became a bugle call for "The Duties of Man." A copy of this document was given to every school child in the public schools of Italy on this one hundredth anniversary, and as the Chicago branch of the Society of Young Italy marched into our largest hall and presented to Hull-House an heroic bust of Mazzini, I found myself devoutly hoping that the Italian youth, who have committed their future to America, might indeed become "the Apostles of the fraternity of nations" and that our American citizenship might be built without disturbing these foundations which were laid of old time.

CHAPTER 12
TOLSTOYISM

The administration of charity in Chicago during the winter following the World's Fair had been of necessity most difficult for, although large sums had been given to the temporary relief organization which endeavored to care for the thousands of destitute strangers stranded in the city, we all worked under a sense of desperate need and a paralyzing consciousness that our best efforts were most inadequate to the situation.

During the many relief visits I paid that winter in tenement houses and miserable lodgings, I was constantly shadowed by a certain sense of shame that I should be comfortable in the midst of such distress. This resulted at times in a curious reaction against all the educational and philanthropic activities in which I had been engaged. In the face of the desperate hunger and need, these could not but seem futile and superficial. . . .

The dealing directly with the simplest human wants may have been responsible for an impression which I carried about with me almost constantly for a period of two years and which culminated finally in a visit to Tolstoy,— that the Settlement, or Hull-House at least, was a mere pretense and travesty of the simple impulse "to live with the poor," so long as the residents did not share the common lot of hard labor and scant fare.

Actual experience had left me in much the same state of mind I had been in after reading Tolstoy's "What to Do," which is a description of his futile efforts to relieve the unspeakable distress and want in the Moscow winter of 1881, and his inevitable conviction that only he who literally shares his own shelter and food with the needy, can claim to have served them.

Doubtless it is much easier to see "what to do" in rural Russia, where all the conditions tend to make the contrast as broad as possible between peasant labor and noble idleness, than it is to see "what to do" in the interdependencies of the modern industrial city. But for that very reason perhaps, Tolstoy's clear statement is valuable for that type of conscientious person in every land who finds it hard, not only to walk in the path of righteousness, but to discover where the path lies.

I had read the books of Tolstoy steadily all the years since "My Religion" had come into my hands immediately after I left college. The reading of that book had made clear that men's poor little efforts to do right are put forth for the most part in the chill of self-distrust; I became convinced that if the new social order ever came, it would come by gathering to itself all the pathetic human endeavor which had indicated the forward direction. But I was most eager to know whether Tolstoy's undertaking to do his daily share of the physical labor of the world, that labor which is "so disproportionate to the unnourished strength" of those by whom it is ordinarily performed, had brought him peace!

I had time to review carefully many things in my mind during the long days of convalescence following an illness of typhoid fever which I suffered in the autumn of 1895. The illness was so prolonged that my health was most unsatisfactory during the following winter, and the next May I went abroad with my friend Miss Smith, to effect if possible a more complete recovery.

The prospect of seeing Tolstoy filled me with the hope of finding a clew to the tangled affairs of city poverty. I was but one of thousands of our contemporaries who were turning towards this Russian, not as to a seer — his message is much too confused and contradictory for that — but as to a man who has had the ability to lift his life to the level of his conscience, to translate his theories into action.

We had letters of introduction to Mr. and Mrs. Aylmer Maude of Moscow, since well known as the translators of "Resurrection" and other of Tolstoy's later works, who at that moment were on the eve of leaving Russia in order to form an agricultural colony in south England where they might support themselves by the labor of their hands. We gladly accepted Mr. Maude's offer to take us to Yasnaya Polyana and to introduce us to Count Tolstoy, and never did a disciple journey towards his master with more enthusiasm than did our guide. When, however, Mr. Maude actually presented Miss Smith and myself to Count Tolstoy, knowing well his master's attitude toward philanthropy, he endeavored to make Hull-House appear much more noble and unique than I should have ventured to do.

Tolstoy standing by clad in his peasant garb, listened gravely but, glancing distrustfully at the sleeves of my traveling gown which unfortunately at that season were monstrous in size, he took hold of an edge and pulling out one sleeve to an interminable breadth, said quite simply that "there was enough stuff on one arm to make a frock for a little girl," and asked me directly if I did not find "such a dress" a "barrier to the people." I was too disconcerted to make a very clear explanation, although I tried to say that monstrous as my sleeves were they did not compare in size with those of the working girls in Chicago and that nothing would more effectively separate me from "the people" than a cotton blouse following the simple lines of the human form; even if I had wished to imitate him and "dress as a peasant," it would have been hard to choose which peasant among the thirty-six nationalities we had recently counted in our ward. Fortunately the countess came to my rescue with a recital of her former attempts to clothe hypothetical little girls in yards of material cut from a train and other superfluous parts of her best gown until she had been driven to a firm stand which she advised me to take at once. But neither Countess Tolstoy nor any other friend was on hand to help me out of my predicament later, when I was asked who "fed" me, and how did I obtain "shelter"? Upon my reply that a farm a hundred miles from Chicago supplied me with the necessities of life, I fairly anticipated the next scathing question: "So you are an absentee landlord? Do you think you will help the people more by adding yourself to the crowded city than you would by tilling your own soil?" This new sense of discomfort over a failure to till my own soil was increased when Tolstoy's second daughter appeared at the five-o'clock tea table set under the trees, coming straight from the harvest field where she had been working with a group of peasants since five o'clock in the morning, not pretending to work but really taking the place of a peasant woman who had hurt her foot. She was plainly much exhausted but neither expected nor received sympathy from the members of a family who were quite accustomed to see each other carry out their convictions in spite of discomfort and fatigue. The martyrdom of discomfort, however, was obviously much easier to bear than that to which, even to the eyes of the casual visitor, Count Tolstoy daily subjected himself, for his study in the basement of the conventional dwelling, with its short shelf of battered books and its scythe and spade leaning against the wall, had many times lent itself to that ridicule which is the most difficult form of martyrdom.

That summer evening as we sat in the garden with a group of visitors from Germany, from England, and America, who had traveled to the remote Russian village that they might learn of this man, one could not forbear the constant inquiry to one's self, as to why he was so regarded as sage and saint that this party of people should be repeated each day of the year. It seemed to me then that we were all attracted by this sermon of the deed, because Tolstoy had made the one supreme personal effort, one might almost say the one frantic personal effort, to put himself into right relations with the humblest people, with the men who tilled his soil, blacked his boots, and cleaned his stables. Doubtless the heaviest burden of our contemporaries is a consciousness of a divergence between our democratic theory on the one hand, that working people have a right to the intellectual resources of society, and the actual fact on the other hand, that thousands of them are so overburdened with toil that there is no leisure nor energy left for the cultivation of the mind. We constantly suffer from the strain and indecision of believing this theory and acting as if we did not believe it, and this man who years before had tried "to get off the backs of the peasants," who had at least simplified his life and worked with his hands, had come to be a prototype to many of his generation.

Doubtless all of the visitors sitting in the Tolstoy garden that evening had excused themselves from laboring with their hands upon the theory that they were doing something more valuable for society in other ways. No one among our contemporaries has dissented from this point of view so violently as Tolstoy himself, and yet no man might so easily have excused himself from hard and rough work on the basis of his genius and of his intellectual contributions to the world. So far, however, from considering his time too valuable to be spent in labor in the field or in making shoes, our great host was too eager to know life to be willing to give up this companionship of mutual labor. . . .

At the long dinner table laid in the garden were the various traveling guests, the grown-up daughters, and the younger children with their governess. The countess presided over the usual European dinner served by men, but the count and the daughter who had worked all day in the fields, ate only porridge and black bread and drank only kvas, the fare of the hay-making peasants. Of course we are all accustomed to the fact that those who perform the heaviest labor, eat the coarsest and simplest fare at the end of the day, but it is not often that we sit at the same table with them while we ourselves eat the more elaborate food prepared by some one else's labor. Tolstoy ate his simple supper without remark or comment upon the food his family and guests preferred to eat, assuming that they, as well as he, had settled the matter with their own consciences. . . .

The conversation at dinner and afterwards, although conducted with animation and sincerity, for the moment stirred vague misgivings within me. Was Tolstoy more logical than life warrants? Could the wrongs of life be reduced to the terms of unrequited labor and all be made right if each person performed the amount necessary to satisfy his own wants? Was it not always easy to put up a strong case if one took the naturalistic view of life? But what about the historic view, the inevitable shadings and modifications which life itself brings to its own interpretation? Miss Smith and I took a night train back to Moscow in that tumult of feeling which is always produced by contact with a conscience making one more of those determined efforts to probe to the very foundations of the mysterious world in which we find ourselves. A horde of perplexing questions, concerning those problems of existence of which in happier moments we catch but fleeting glimpses and at which we even then stand aghast, pursued us relentlessly on the long journey through the great wheat plains of south Russia, through the crowded Ghetto of Warsaw, and finally into the smiling fields of Germany where the peasant men and women were harvesting the grain. . . .

There grew up in my mind a conviction that what I ought to do upon my return to Hull-House, was to spend at least two hours every morning in the little bakery which we had recently added to the equipment of our coffee-house. Two hours' work would be but a wretched compromise, but it was hard to see how I could take more time out of each day. I had been taught to bake bread in my childhood not only as a household accomplishment, but because my father, true to his miller's tradition, had insisted that each one of his daughters on her twelfth birthday must present him with a satisfactory wheat loaf of her own baking, and he was most exigent as to the quality of this test loaf. What could be more in keeping with my training and tradition than baking bread? I did not quite see how my activity would fit in with that of the German union baker who presided over the Hull-House bakery but all such matters were secondary and certainly could be arranged. . . .

I held fast to the belief that I should do this, through the entire journey homeward, on land and sea, until I actually arrived in Chicago when suddenly the whole scheme seemed to me as utterly preposterous as it doubtless was. The half dozen people invariably waiting to see me after breakfast, the piles of letters to be opened and answered, the demand of actual and pressing human wants,—were these all to be pushed aside and asked to wait while I saved my soul by two hours' work at baking bread?

CHAPTER 13
PUBLIC ACTIVITIES AND INVESTIGATIONS

One of the striking features of our neighborhood twenty years ago, and one to which we never became reconciled, was the presence of huge wooden garbage boxes fastened to the street pavement in which the undisturbed refuse accumulated day by day. The system of garbage collecting was inadequate throughout the city, but it became the greatest menace in a ward such as ours, where the normal amount of waste was much increased by the decayed fruit and vegetables discarded by the Italian and Greek fruit peddlers, and by the residuum left over from the piles of filthy rags which were fished out of the city dumps and brought to the homes of the rag pickers for further sorting and washing.

The children of our neighborhood twenty years ago played their games in and around these huge garbage boxes. They were the first objects that a toddling child learned to climb; their bulk afforded a barricade and their contents provided missiles in all the battles of the older boys; and finally they became the seats upon which absorbed lovers held enchanted converse. We are obliged to remember that all children eat everything which they find and that odors have a curious and intimate power of entwining themselves into our tenderest memories, before even the residents of Hull-House can understand their own early enthusiasm for the removal of these boxes and the establishment of a better system of refuse collection.

It is easy for even the most conscientious citizen of Chicago to forget the foul smells of the stockyards and the garbage dumps, when he is living so far from them that he is only occasionally made conscious of their existence but the residents of a Settlement are perforce constantly surrounded by them. During our first three years on Halsted Street, we had established a small incinerator at Hull-House and we had many times reported the untoward conditions of the ward to the City Hall. We had also arranged many talks for the immigrants, pointing out that although a woman may sweep her own doorway in her native village and allow the refuse to innocently decay in the open air and sunshine, in a crowded city quarter, if the garbage is not properly collected and destroyed, a tenement-house mother may see her children sicken and die, and that the immigrants must therefore, not only keep their own houses clean, but must also help the authorities to keep the city clean.

Possibly our efforts slightly modified the worst conditions but they still remained intolerable, and the fourth summer the situation became for me absolutely desperate when I realized in a moment of panic that my delicate little nephew[60] for whom I was guardian, could not be with me at Hull-House at all unless the sickening odors were reduced. I may well be ashamed that other delicate children who were torn from their families, not into boarding school but into eternity, had not long before driven me to effective action. Under the direction of the first man who came as a resident to Hull-House we began a systematic investigation of the city system of garbage collection, both as to its efficiency in other wards and its possible connection with the death rate in the various wards of the city.

The Hull-House Women's Club had been organized the year before by the resident kindergartner who had first inaugurated a mothers' meeting. The members came together, however, in quite a new way that summer when we discussed with them the high death rate so persistent in our ward. After several club meetings devoted to the subject, despite the fact that the death rate rose highest in the congested foreign colonies and not in the streets in which most of the Irish American club women lived, twelve of their number undertook in connection with the residents, to carefully investigate the condition of the alleys. During August and September the substantiated reports of violations of the law sent in from Hull-House to the health department were one thousand and thirty-seven. For the club woman who had finished a long day's work of washing or ironing followed by the cooking of a hot supper, it would have

---

[60] Stanley Linn, the youngest child of Mary Addams Linn, for whom Jane Addams was made legal guardian after Mary's death in 1894. Stanley did not live at Hull-House permanently but visited regularly over the years.

been much easier to sit on her doorstep during a summer evening than to go up and down ill-kept alleys and get into trouble with her neighbors over the condition of their garbage boxes. It required both civic enterprise and moral conviction to be willing to do this three evenings a week during the hottest and most uncomfortable months of the year. Nevertheless, a certain number of women persisted, as did the residents, and three city inspectors in succession were transferred from the ward because of unsatisfactory services. Still the death rate remained high and the condition seemed little improved throughout the next winter. In sheer desperation, the following spring when the city contracts were awarded for the removal of garbage, with the backing of two well-known business men, I put in a bid for the garbage removal of the nineteenth ward. My paper was thrown out on a technicality but the incident induced the mayor to appoint me the garbage inspector of the ward.

The salary was a thousand dollars a year, and the loss of that political "plum" made a great stir among the politicians. The position was no sinecure whether regarded from the point of view of getting up at six in the morning to see that the men were early at work; or of following the loaded wagons, uneasily dropping their contents at intervals, to their dreary destination at the dump; or of insisting that the contractor must increase the number of his wagons from nine to thirteen and from thirteen to seventeen, although he assured me that he lost money on every one and that the former inspector had let him off with seven; or of taking careless landlords into court because they would not provide the proper garbage receptacles; or of arresting the tenant who tried to make the garbage wagons carry away the contents of his stable.

With the two or three residents who nobly stood by, we set up six of those doleful incinerators which are supposed to burn garbage with the fuel collected in the alley itself. The one factory in town which could utilize old tin cans was a window weight factory, and we deluged that with ten times as many tin cans as it could use — much less would pay for. We made desperate attempts to have the dead animals removed by the contractor who was paid most liberally by the city for that purpose but who, we slowly discovered, always made the police ambulances do the work, delivering the carcasses upon freight cars for shipment to a soap factory in Indiana where they were sold for a good price although the contractor himself was the largest stockholder in the concern. . . .

Many of the foreign-born women of the ward were much shocked by this abrupt departure into the ways of men, and it took a great deal of explanation to convey the idea even remotely that if it were a womanly task to go about in tenement houses in order to nurse the sick, it might be quite as womanly to go through the same district in order to prevent the breeding of so-called "filth diseases." While some of the women enthusiastically approved the slowly changing conditions and saw that their housewifely duties logically extended to the adjacent alleys and streets, they yet were quite certain that "it was not a lady's job."

And yet the spectacle of eight hours' work for eight hours' pay, the even-handed justice to all citizens irrespective of "pull," the dividing of responsibility between landlord and tenant, and the readiness to enforce obedience to law from both, was, perhaps, one of the most valuable demonstrations which could have been made. Such daily living on the part of the office holder is of infinitely more value than many talks on civics for, after all, we credit most easily that which we see. The careful inspection combined with other causes, brought about a great improvement in the cleanliness and comfort of the neighborhood and one happy day, when the death rate of our ward was found to have dropped from third to seventh in the list of city wards and was so reported to our Women's Club, the applause which followed recorded the genuine sense of participation in the result, and a public spirit which had "made good." But the cleanliness of the ward was becoming much too popular to suit our all-powerful alderman [61] and, although we felt fatuously secure under the regime of civil service, he found a way to circumvent us by eliminating the position altogether. He introduced an ordinance into the City Council which combined the collection of refuse with the cleaning and repairing of the streets, the whole to be placed under a ward superintendent. The office of course was to be filled under civil service regulations but only men were eligible to the examination. Although this latter regulation was afterwards modified in favor of one woman, it was retained long enough to put the nineteenth ward inspector out of office.

Of course our experience in inspecting only made us more conscious of the wretched housing conditions over which we had been distressed from the first. It was during the World's Fair summer that one of the Hull-House residents in a public address upon housing reform used as an example of indifferent landlordism a large block in the neighborhood occupied by small tenements and stables unconnected with a street sewer, as was much similar property in the vicinity. In the lecture the resident spared neither a description of the property nor the name of the owner.

[61] Johnny Powers, known as "De Pow." Powers was an Irish ward boss and saloon owner who controlled the Hull-House neighborhood and chaired the Finance Committee of the Chicago City Council. His corrupt economic interests often conflicted with Addams's desire to get streets cleaned, schools built, and local service improvements from municipal transit authorities.

The young man who owned the property was justly indignant at this public method of attack and promptly came to investigate the condition of the property. Together we made a careful tour of the houses and stables and in the face of the conditions that we found there, I could not but agree with him that supplying south Italian peasants with sanitary appliances seemed a difficult undertaking. Nevertheless he was unwilling that the block should remain in its deplorable state, and he finally cut through the dilemma with the rash proposition that he would give a free lease of the entire tract to Hull-House, accompanying the offer, however, with the warning remark, that if we should choose to use the income from the rents in sanitary improvements we should be throwing our money away.

Even when we decided that the houses were so bad that we could not undertake the task of improving them, he was game and stuck to his proposition that we should have a free lease. We finally submitted a plan that the houses should be torn down and the entire tract turned into a playground, although cautious advisers intimated that it would be very inconsistent to ask for subscriptions for the support of Hull-House when we were known to have thrown away an income of two thousand dollars a year. We, however, felt that a spectacle of inconsistency was better than one of bad landlordism and so the worst of the houses were demolished, the best three were sold and moved across the street under careful provision that they might never be used for junkshops or saloons, and a public playground was finally established. Hull-House became responsible for its management for ten years, at the end of which time it was turned over to the City Playground Commission, although from the first the city detailed a policeman who was responsible for its general order and who became a valued adjunct of the House.

During fifteen years this public-spirited owner of the property paid all the taxes, and when the block was finally sold he made possible the playground equipment of a near-by school yard. On the other hand, the dispossessed tenants, a group of whom had to be evicted by legal process before their houses could be torn down, have never ceased to mourn their former estates. . . .

The mere consistent enforcement of existing laws and efforts for their advance often placed Hull-House, at least temporarily, into strained relations with its neighbors. I recall a continuous warfare against local landlords who would move wrecks of old houses as a nucleus for new ones in order to evade the provisions of the building code, and a certain Italian neighbor who was filled with bitterness because his new rear tenement was discovered to be illegal. It seemed impossible to make him understand that the health of the tenants was in any wise as important as his undisturbed rents.

Nevertheless many evils constantly arise in Chicago from congested housing which wiser cities forestall and prevent; the inevitable boarders crowded into a dark tenement already too small for the use of the immigrant family occupying it; the surprisingly large number of delinquent girls who have become criminally involved with their own fathers and uncles; the school children who cannot find a quiet spot in which to read or study and who perforce go into the streets each evening; the tuberculosis superinduced and fostered by the inadequate rooms and breathing spaces. One of the Hull-House residents, under the direction of a Chicago physician who stands high as an authority on tuberculosis and who devotes a large proportion of his time to our vicinity, made an investigation into housing conditions as related to tuberculosis with a result as startling as that of the "lung block" in New York.

It is these subtle evils of wretched and inadequate housing which are often most disastrous. In the summer of 1902 during an epidemic of typhoid fever in which our ward, although containing but one thirty-sixth of the population of the city, registered one sixth of the total number of deaths, two of the Hull-House residents made an investigation of the methods of plumbing in the houses adjacent to conspicuous groups of fever cases. They discovered among the people who had been exposed to the infection, a widow who had lived in the ward for a number of years, in a comfortable little house of her own. Although the Italian immigrants were closing in all round her, she was not willing to sell her property and to move away until she had finished the education of her children. In the meantime she held herself quite aloof from her Italian neighbors and could never be drawn into any of the public efforts to secure a better code of tenement-house sanitation. Her two daughters were sent to an eastern college. One June when one of them had graduated and the other still had two years before she took her degree, they came to the spotless little house and to their self-sacrificing mother for the summer holiday. They both fell ill with typhoid fever and one daughter died because the mother's utmost efforts could not keep the infection out of her own house. The entire disaster affords, perhaps, a fair illustration of the futility of the individual conscience which would isolate a family from the rest of the community and its interests.

The careful information collected concerning the juxtaposition of the typhoid cases to the various systems of plumbing and nonplumbing, was made the basis of a bacteriological study by another resident, Dr. Alice Hamilton.[62] . . .

It was discovered that the wretched sanitary appliances through which alone the infection could have become so widely spread, would not have been permitted to remain, unless the city inspector had either been criminally careless or open to the arguments of favored landlords. The agitation finally resulted in a long and stirring trial before the Civil Service Board of half of the employees in the Sanitary Bureau, with the final discharge of eleven out of the entire force of twenty-four. . . .

We were amazed at the commercial ramifications which graft in the City Hall involved and at the indignation which interference with it produced. Hull-House lost some large subscriptions as the result of this investigation, a loss which, if not easy to bear, was at least comprehensible. We also uncovered unexpected graft in connection with the plumbers' unions, and but for the fearless testimony of one of their members, could never have brought the trial to a successful issue.

Inevitable misunderstanding also developed in connection with the attempt on the part of Hull-House residents to prohibit the sale of cocaine to minors, which brought us into sharp conflict with many druggists. I recall an Italian druggist living on the edge of the neighborhood, who finally came with a committee of his fellow countrymen to see what Hull-House wanted of him, thoroughly convinced that no such effort could be disinterested. One dreary trial after another had been lost through the inadequacy of the existing legislation and after many attempts to secure better legal regulation of its sale, a new law with the coöperation of many agencies was finally secured in 1907. Through all this the Italian druggist, who had greatly profited by the sale of cocaine to boys, only felt outraged and abused. And yet the thought of this campaign brings before my mind with irresistible force, a young Italian boy who died,—a victim to the drug at the age of seventeen. He had been in our kindergarten as a handsome merry child, in our clubs as a vivacious boy, and then gradually there was an eclipse of all that was animated and joyous and promising, and when I at last saw him in his coffin, it was im-

---

[62]Alice Hamilton (1869–1970) became a resident at Hull-House in 1897 after graduating from medical school at the University of Michigan and accepting a position as professor of pathology at the Woman's Medical School of Northwestern University. She stayed at Hull-House for twenty-two years, becoming an expert in the epidemiology of "industrial diseases." Her book, *Exploring the Dangerous Trades: The Autobiography of Alice Hamilton, M.D.* (Boston: Little, Brown & Co., 1943), traced her career as an influential lobbyist for legal health standards in industry. In 1919, she became the first woman to join the faculty at Harvard University.

possible to connect that haggard shriveled body with what I had known before.

A midwife investigation, undertaken in connection with the Chicago Medical Society, while showing the great need of further state regulation in the interest of the most ignorant mothers and helpless children, brought us into conflict with one of the most venerable of all customs. Was all this a part of the unending struggle between the old and new, or were these oppositions so unexpected and so unlooked for merely a reminder of that old bit of wisdom that "there is no guarding against interpretations"? Perhaps more subtle still, they were due to that very superrefinement of disinterestedness which will not justify itself, that it may feel superior to public opinion. . . .

For many years we have administered a branch station of the federal post office at Hull-House, which we applied for in the first instance because our neighbors lost such a large percentage of the money they sent to Europe, through the commissions to middle men. The experience in the post office constantly gave us data for urging the establishment of postal savings as we saw one perplexed immigrant after another turning away in bewilderment when he was told that the United States post office did not receive savings.

We find increasingly, however, that the best results are to be obtained in investigations as in other undertakings, by combining our researches with those of other public bodies or with the state itself. When all the Chicago Settlements found themselves distressed over the condition of the newsboys who, because they are merchants and not employees, do not come under the provisions of the Illinois Child Labor Law, they united in the investigation of a thousand young newsboys, who were all interviewed on the streets during the same twenty-four hours. Their school and domestic status was easily determined later, for many of the boys lived in the immediate neighborhoods of the ten Settlements which had undertaken the investigation. The report embodying the results of the investigation recommended a city ordinance containing features from the Boston and Buffalo regulations, and although an ordinance was drawn up and a strenuous effort was made to bring it to the attention of the aldermen, none of them would introduce it into the City Council without newspaper backing. We were able to agitate for it again at the annual meeting of the National Child Labor Committee which was held in Chicago in 1908, and which was of course reported in papers throughout the entire country. This meeting also demonstrated that local measures can sometimes be urged most effectively when joined to the efforts of a national body. Undoubtedly the best discussions ever held upon the operation and status of the Illinois law, were those which took place then. The needs of the Illinois children were regarded in connection with the children of the nation and advanced health measures for Illinois were compared with those of other states. The investigations of Hull-House thus tend to be merged with those of larger organizations, from the investigation of the social value of saloons made for the Committee of Fifty in 1896, to the one on infant mortality in relation to nationality, made for the American Academy of Science in 1909. This is also true of Hull-House activities in regard to public movements, some of which are inaugurated by the residents of other Settlements, as the Chicago School of Civics and Philanthropy, founded by the splendid efforts of Dr. Graham Taylor, for many years head of the Chicago Commons.[63] All of our recent investigations into housing have been under the department of investigation of this school with which several of the Hull-House residents are identified, quite as our active measures to secure better housing conditions have been carried on with the City Homes Association and through the coöperation of one of our residents who several years ago was appointed a sanitary inspector on the city staff. . . .

Mr. Howells[64] has said that we are all so besotted with our novel reading that we have lost the power of seeing certain aspects of life with any sense of reality because we are continually looking for the possible romance. The description might apply to the earlier years of the American Settlement, but certainly the later years are filled with discoveries in actual life as romantic as they are unexpected. If I may illustrate one of these romantic discoveries from my own experience, I would cite the indications of an internationalism as sturdy and virile as it is unprecedented which I have seen in our cosmopolitan neighborhood: when a south Italian Catholic is forced by the very exigencies of the situation to make friends with an Austrian Jew representing another nationality and another religion, both of which cut into all his most cherished prejudices, he finds it harder to utilize them a second time and gradually loses them. He thus modifies his provincialism for if an old enemy working by

---

[63]Taylor (1851–1938) was founder and director of the Chicago Commons Settlement and the Chicago School of Civics and Philanthropy and one of Addams's closest colleagues in Chicago settlement work.

[64]William Dean Howells (1837–1920) was an American novelist and critic who championed literary realism and the Naturalistic school of fiction, which illuminated social problems.

his side has turned into a friend, almost anything may happen. When, therefore, I became identified with the peace movement both in its International and National Conventions, I hoped that this internationalism engendered in the immigrant quarters of American cities might be recognized as an effective instrument in the cause of peace. I first set it forth with some misgiving before the convention held in Boston in 1904 and it is always a pleasure to recall the hearty assent given to it by Professor William James.[65]

I have always objected to the phrase "sociological laboratory" applied to us, because Settlements should be something much more human and spontaneous than such a phrase connotes, and yet it is inevitable that the residents should know their own neighborhoods more thoroughly than any other, and that their experiences there should affect their convictions.

Years ago I was much entertained by a story told at the Chicago Women's Club by one of its ablest members in the discussion following a paper of mine on "The Outgrowths of Toynbee Hall." She said that when she was a little girl playing in her mother's garden, she one day discovered a small toad who seemed to her very forlorn and lonely, although as she did not in the least know how to comfort him, she reluctantly left him to his fate; later in the day, quite at the other end of the garden, she found a large toad, also apparently without family and friends. With a heart full of tender sympathy, she took a stick and by exercising infinite patience and some skill, she finally pushed the little toad through the entire length of the garden into the company of the big toad, when, to her inexpressible horror and surprise, the big toad opened his mouth and swallowed the little one. The moral of the tale was clear applied to people who lived "where they did not naturally belong," although I protested that was exactly what we wanted — to be swallowed and digested, to disappear into the bulk of the people.

Twenty years later I am willing to testify that something of the sort does take place after years of identification with an industrial community.

---

[65] Harvard-based philosopher (1842–1910) who developed his philosophy of Pragmatism from the same cultural and ideological tools Addams and John Dewey were using in Chicago. Like them, James assessed meaning and value from the consequences of an act or idea. The "assent" to which Addams refers here came in a letter from James in January of 1907. In response to Addams's book *Newer Ideals of Peace,* James wrote: "I do not know why you should always be right, but you always are. You inhabit reality."

CHAPTER 14
CIVIC COÖPERATION

One of the first lessons we learned at Hull-House was that private beneficence is totally inadequate to deal with the vast numbers of the city's disinherited. We also quickly came to realize that there are certain types of wretchedness from which every private philanthropy shrinks and which are cared for only in those wards of the County Hospital provided for the wrecks of vicious living or in the city's isolation hospital for smallpox patients.

I have heard a broken-hearted mother exclaim when her erring daughter came home at last too broken and diseased to be taken into the family she had disgraced, "There is no place for her but the top floor of the County Hospital; they will have to take her there," and this only after every possible expedient had been tried or suggested. This aspect of governmental responsibility was unforgettably borne in upon me during the smallpox epidemic following the World's Fair, when one of the residents, Mrs. Kelley, as state factory inspector was much concerned in discovering and destroying clothing which was being finished in houses containing unreported cases of smallpox. The deputy most successful in locating such cases lived at Hull-House during the epidemic because he did not wish to expose his own family. Another resident, Miss [Julia C.] Lathrop,[66] as a member of the State Board of Charities, went back and forth to the crowded pest house which had been hastily constructed on a stretch of prairie west of the city. As Hull-House was already so exposed, it seemed best for the special smallpox inspectors from the Board of Health to take their meals and change their clothing there before they went to their respective homes. All of these officials had accepted without question and as implicit in public office, the obligation to carry on the dangerous and difficult undertakings for which private philanthropy is unfitted, as if the commonalty of compassion represented by the state was more comprehending than that of any individual group.

It was as early as our second winter on Halsted Street that [Miss Lathrop] received an appointment from the Cook County agent as a county

---

[66]Julia Clifford Lathrop (1858–1932) was one of Addams's closest associates at Hull-House. As the daughter of a Republican party activist and one-time congressman from Rockford, Illinois, her background was similar to Addams's. Lathrop attended Rockford Female Seminary for one year before transferring to Vassar College where she earned her bachelor's degree in 1880. As a resident of Hull-House, she served on the Illinois Board of Charities, was active in the Immigrants' Protective League and Juvenile Court, and served as the first head of the United States Children's Bureau from 1912 to 1921. Jane Addams's last book, published soon after her death in 1935, was *My Friend, Julia Lathrop.*

visitor. She reported at the agency each morning, and all the cases within a radius of ten blocks from Hull-House were given to her for investigation. This gave her a legitimate opportunity for knowing the poorest people in the neighborhood and also for understanding the county method of outdoor relief. The commissioners were at first dubious of the value of such a visitor and predicted that a woman would be a perfect "coal chute" for giving away county supplies, but they gradually came to depend upon her suggestion and advice.

In 1893 . . . Miss Lathrop was appointed by the governor a member of the Illinois State Board of Charities. She served in this capacity for two consecutive terms and was later reappointed to a third term. Perhaps her most valuable contribution towards the enlargement and reorganization of the charitable institutions of the state came through her intimate knowledge of the beneficiaries, and her experience demonstrated that it is only through long residence among the poor that an official could have learned to view public institutions as she did, from the standpoint of the inmates rather than from that of the managers. Since that early day, residents of Hull-House have spent much time in working for the civil service methods of appointment for employees in the county and state institutions; for the establishment of state colonies for the care of epileptics; and for a dozen other enterprises which occupy that borderland between charitable effort and legislation. In this borderland we coöperate in many civic enterprises for I think we may claim that Hull-House has always held its activities lightly, ready to hand them over to whosoever would carry them on properly. . . .

In our first two summers we had maintained three baths in the basement of our own house for the use of the neighborhood and they afforded some experience and argument for the erection of the first public bathhouse in Chicago, which was built on a neighboring street and opened under the City Board of Health. The lot upon which it was erected belonged to a friend of Hull-House who offered it to the city without rent, and this enabled the city to erect the first public bath from the small appropriation of ten thousand dollars. Great fear was expressed by the public authorities that the baths would not be used and the old story of the bathtubs in model tenements which had been turned into coal bins was often quoted to us. We were supplied, however, with the incontrovertible argument that in our adjacent third square mile there were in 1892 but three bathtubs and that this fact was much complained of by many of the tenement-house dwellers. Our contention was justified by the immediate and overflowing use of the public baths, as we had before been sustained in the contention that an immigrant population would respond to opportunities for reading when the Public Library Board had established a branch reading room at Hull-House.

We also quickly discovered that nothing brought us so absolutely into comradeship with our neighbors as mutual and sustained effort such as the paving of a street, the closing of a gambling house, or the restoration of a veteran police sergeant.

Several of these earlier attempts at civic coöperation were undertaken in connection with the Hull-House Men's Club which had been organized in the spring of 1893, had been incorporated under a State Charter of its own, and had occupied a club room in the gymnasium building. This club obtained an early success in one of the political struggles in the ward and thus fastened upon itself a specious reputation for political power. It was at last so torn by the dissensions of two political factions which attempted to capture it that, although it is still an existing organization, it has never regained the prestige of its first five years. Its early political success came in a campaign Hull-House had instigated against a powerful alderman who has held office for more than twenty years in the nineteenth ward, and who, although notoriously corrupt, is still firmly intrenched among his constituents.[67]

Hull-House has had to do with three campaigns organized against him. In the first one he was apparently only amused at our "Sunday school" effort and did little to oppose the election to the aldermanic office of a member of the Hull-House Men's Club who thus became his colleague in the City Council. When Hull-House, however, made an effort in the following spring against the reëlection of the alderman himself, we encountered the most determined and skillful opposition. In these campaigns we doubtless depended too much upon the idealistic appeal for we did not yet comprehend the element of reality always brought into the political struggle in such a neighborhood where politics deal so directly with getting a job and carning a living.

We soon discovered that approximately one out of every five voters in the nineteenth ward at that time held a job dependent upon the good will of the alderman. There were no civil service rules to interfere and the unskilled voter swept the street and dug the sewer, as secure in his position as the more sophisticated voter who tended a bridge or occupied an office chair in the City Hall. The alderman was even more fortunate in finding places with the franchise-seeking corporations; it took us some time to understand why so large a proportion of our neighbors were

---

[67] Another reference to Alderman Johnny Powers, the ward boss who controlled the Hull-House neighborhood. (See note 61.)

street-car employees and why we had such a large club composed solely of telephone girls. Our powerful alderman had various methods of intrenching himself. Many people were indebted to him for his kindly services in the police station and the justice courts, for in those days Irish constituents easily broke the peace, and before the establishment of the Juvenile Court, boys were arrested for very trivial offenses; added to these were hundreds of constituents indebted to him for personal kindness from the peddler who received a free license, to the business man who had a railroad pass to New York. Our third campaign against him, when we succeeded in making a serious impression upon his majority, evoked from his henchmen the same sort of hostility which a striker so inevitably feels against the man who would take his job, even sharpened by the sense that the movement for reform came from an alien source.

Another result of the campaign was an expectation on the part of our new political friends that Hull-House would perform like offices for them, and there resulted endless confusion and misunderstanding because in many cases we could not even attempt to do what the alderman constantly did with a right good will. When he protected a law breaker from the legal consequences of his act, his kindness appeared, not only to himself but to all beholders, like the deed of a powerful and kindly statesman. When Hull-House on the other hand insisted that a law must be enforced, it could but appear like the persecution of the offender. We were certainly not anxious for consistency nor for individual achievement, but in a desire to foster a higher political morality and not to lower our standards, we constantly clashed with the existing political code. We also unwittingly stumbled upon a powerful combination of which our alderman was the political head, with its banking, its ecclesiastical, and its journalistic representatives, and as we followed up the clew and naïvely told all we discovered, we of course laid the foundations for opposition which has manifested itself in many forms; the most striking expression of it was an attack upon Hull-House lasting through weeks and months by a Chicago daily newspaper which has since ceased publication. . . .

These campaigns were not without their rewards; one of them was a quickened friendship both with the more substantial citizens in the ward and with a group of fine young voters whose devotion to Hull-House has never since failed; another was a sense of identification with public-spirited men throughout the city who contributed money and time to what they considered a gallant effort against political corruption. I remember a young professor from the University of Chicago who with his wife came to live at Hull-House, traveling the long distance every day throughout the autumn and winter that he might qualify as a nineteenth-ward voter in the spring campaign. He served as a watcher at the polls and it was but a poor reward for his devotion that he was literally set upon and beaten up, for in those good old days such things frequently occurred. Many another case of devotion to our standard so recklessly raised might be cited but perhaps more valuable than any of these was the sense of identification we obtained with the rest of Chicago.

So far as a Settlement can discern and bring to local consciousness neighborhood needs which are common needs, and can give vigorous help to the municipal measures through which such needs shall be met, it fulfills its most valuable function. To illustrate from our first effort to improve the street paving in the vicinity, we found that when we had secured the consent of the majority of the property owners on a given street for a new paving, the alderman checked the entire plan through his kindly service to one man who had appealed to him to keep the assessments down. The street long remained a shocking mass of wet, dilapidated cedar blocks, where children were sometimes mired as they floated a surviving block in the water which speedily filled the holes whence other blocks had been extracted for fuel. And yet when we were able to demonstrate that the street paving had thus been reduced into cedar pulp by the heavily loaded wagons of an adjacent factory, that the expense of its repaving should be borne from a general fund and not by the poor property owners, we found that we could all unite in advocating reform in the method of repaving assessments, and the alderman himself was obliged to come into such a popular movement. The Nineteenth Ward Improvement Association which met at Hull-House during two winters, was the first body of citizens able to make a real impression upon the local paving situation. They secured an expert to watch the paving as it went down to be sure that their half of the paving money was well expended. In the belief that property values would be thus enhanced, the common aim brought together the more prosperous people of the vicinity, somewhat as the Hull-House Coöperative Coal Association brought together the poorer ones. . . .

Certainly the need for civic coöperation was obvious in many directions, and in none more strikingly than in that organized effort which must be carried on unceasingly if young people are to be protected from the darker and coarser dangers of the city. The coöperation between Hull-House and the Juvenile Protective Association came about gradually, and it seems now almost inevitably. From our earliest days we saw many boys constantly arrested, and I had a number of most enlightening experiences in the police station with an Irish lad whose mother upon her deathbed had begged me "to look after him." We were distressed by the gangs of very little boys who would sally forth with an enterprising leader in search of old brass and iron, sometimes breaking into empty houses for the sake of the faucets or lead pipe which they would sell for a good price to a junk dealer. With the money thus obtained they would buy cigarettes and beer or even candy, which could be conspicuously consumed in the alleys where they might enjoy the excitement of being seen and suspected by the "coppers." From the third year of Hull-House, one of the residents held a semi-official position in the nearest police station, at least the sergeant agreed to give her provisional charge of every boy and girl under arrest for a trivial offense.

Mrs. Stevens [see note 51], who performed this work for several years, became the first probation officer of the Juvenile Court when it was established in Cook County in 1899. She was the sole probation officer at first, but at the time of her death, which occurred at Hull-House in 1900, she was the senior officer of a corps of six. Her entire experience had fitted her to deal wisely with wayward children. She had gone into a New England cotton mill at the age of thirteen, where she had promptly lost the index finger of her right hand through "carelessness," she was told, and no one then seemed to understand that freedom from care was the prerogative of childhood. Later she became a typesetter and was one of the first women in America to become a member of the typographical union, retaining her "card" through all the later years of editorial work. As the Juvenile Court developed, the committee of public-spirited citizens who first supplied only Mrs. Stevens's salary, later maintained a corps of twenty-two such officers; several of these were Hull-House residents who brought to the house for many years a sad little procession of children struggling against all sorts of handicaps. When legislation was secured which placed the probation officers upon the pay roll of the county, it was a challenge to the efficiency of the civil service method of appointment to obtain by examination, men and women fitted for this delicate human task. As one of five people asked by the Civil Service Commission to conduct this first examination for probation officers, I became convinced that we were but at the beginning of the nonpolitical method of selecting public servants, but even stiff and unbending as the examination may be, it is still our hope of political salvation.

In 1907 the Juvenile Court was housed in a model court building of its own, containing a detention home and equipped with a competent staff. The committee of citizens largely responsible for this result, thereupon turned their attention to the conditions which the records of the court indicated had led to the alarming amount of juvenile delinquency and crime. They organized the Juvenile Protective Association, whose twenty-two officers meet weekly at Hull-House with their executive committee to report what they have found and to discuss city conditions affecting the lives of children and young people.

The association discovers that there are certain temptations into which children so habitually fall that it is evident that the average child cannot withstand them. An overwhelming mass of data is accumulated showing the need of enforcing existing legislation and of securing new legislation, but it also indicates a hundred other directions in which the young people who so gayly walk our streets, often to their own destruction, need safeguarding and protection.

The effort of the association to treat the youth of the city with consideration and understanding, has rallied the most unexpected forces to its standard. Quite as the basic needs of life are supplied solely by those who make money out of the business, so the modern city has assumed that the craving for pleasure must be ministered to only by the sordid. This assumption, however, in a large measure broke down as soon as the Juvenile Protective Association courageously put it to the test. After persistent prosecutions, but also after many friendly interviews, the Druggists' Association itself prosecutes those of its members who sell indecent postal cards; the Saloon Keepers' Protective Association not only declines to protect members who sell liquor to minors, but now takes drastic action to prevent such sales; the Retail Grocers' Association forbids the selling of tobacco to minors; the Association of Department Store Managers not only increased the vigilance in their waiting rooms by supplying more matrons, but as a body they have become regular contributors to the association; the special watchmen in all the railroad yards agree not to arrest trespassing boys but to report them to the association; the firms manufacturing moving picture films not only submit their films to a volunteer inspection committee, but ask for suggestions in regard to new matter; and the five-cent theaters arrange for "stunts" which shall deal with the subject of public health and morals when the lecturers provided are entertaining as well as instructive. . . .

It was not without hope that I might be able to forward in the public school system the solution of some of these problems of delinquency so dependent upon truancy and ill-adapted education, that I became a member of the Chicago Board of Education in July, 1905. It is impossible to write of the situation as it became dramatized in half a dozen strong personalities, but the entire experience was so illuminating as to the difficulties and limitations of democratic government, that it would be unfair in a chapter on Civic Coöperation not to attempt an outline.

Even the briefest statement, however, necessitates a review of the preceding few years. For a decade the Chicago school teachers, or rather a majority of them who were organized into the Teachers' Federation, had been engaged in a conflict with the Board of Education both for more adequate salaries and for more self-direction in the conduct of the schools. In pursuance of the first object, they had attacked the tax dodger along the entire line of his defense, from the curbstone to the Supreme Court. They began with an intricate investigation which uncovered the fact that in 1899, two hundred thirty-five million dollars of value of public utility corporations paid nothing in taxes. The Teachers' Federation brought a suit which was prosecuted through the Supreme Court of Illinois and resulted in an order entered against the State Board of Equalization, demanding that it tax the corporations mentioned in the bill. In spite of the fact that the defendant companies sought federal aid and obtained an order which restrained the payment of a portion of the tax, each year since 1900, the Chicago Board of Education has benefited to the extent of more than a quarter of a million dollars. Although this result has been attained through the unaided efforts of the teachers, to their surprise and indignation their salaries were not increased. The Teachers' Federation, therefore, brought a suit against the Board of Education for the advance which had been promised them three years earlier but never paid. The decision of the lower court was in their favor but the Board of Education appealed the case, and this was the situation when the seven new members appointed by Mayor Dunne[68] in 1905 took their seats. The conservative public suspected that these new members were merely representatives of the Teachers' Federation. . . .

The new appointees to the School Board represented no concerted policy of any kind, but were for the most part adherents to the new education. The teachers, confident that their cause was identical with the principles advocated by such educators as Colonel Parker,[69] were therefore sure that the plans of the "new education" members would of necessity coincide with the plans of the Teachers' Federation. In one sense the situation was an epitome of Mayor Dunne's entire administration, which was founded upon the belief that if those citizens representing social ideals and reform principles were but appointed to office, public welfare must be established.

[68] Edward Dunne was a reform mayor in Chicago from 1905 to 1907. During his brief and relatively unsuccessful administration, he advocated municipal ownership of the city's transit system and an end to political corruption of the school system, transit system, and sanitation system.

[69] Colonel Parker (1837–1902) was a leader of the progressive education movement, which emphasized students' individuality, experiential learning, and parent–teacher cooperation. At the turn of the century, when Jane Addams and John Dewey were closely involved with the University of Chicago, Parker was the first director of the university's School of Education.

During my tenure of office I many times talked to the officers of the Teachers' Federation, but I was seldom able to follow their suggestions and, although I gladly coöperated in their plans for a better pension system and other matters, only once did I try to influence the policy of the federation. When the withheld salaries were finally paid to the representatives of the federation who had brought suit and were divided among the members who had suffered both financially and professionally during this long legal struggle, I was most anxious that the division should voluntarily be extended to all of the teachers who had experienced a loss of salary although they were not members of the federation. It seemed to me a striking opportunity to refute the charge that the federation was self-seeking and to put the whole long effort in the minds of the public, exactly where it belonged, as one of devoted public service. But it was doubtless much easier for me to urge this altruistic policy than it was for those who had borne the heat and burden of the day, to act upon it. . . .

The difficulties between the majority of the grade school teachers and the Chicago School Board . . . lay far back in the long effort of public school administration in America to free itself from the rule and exploitation of politics. In every city for many years the politician had secured positions for his friends as teachers and janitors; he had received a rake-off in the contract for every new building or coal supply or adoption of school-books. In the long struggle against this political corruption, the one remedy continually advocated was the transfer of authority in all educational matters from the board to the superintendent. The one cure for "pull" and corruption was the authority of the "expert." The rules and records of the Chicago Board of Education are full of relics of this long struggle honestly waged by honest men, who unfortunately became content with the ideals of an "efficient business administration." These business men established an able superintendent with a large salary, with his tenure of office secured by state law so that he would not be disturbed by the wrath of the balked politician. They instituted impersonal examinations for the teachers both as to entrance into the system and promotion, and they proceeded "to hold the superintendent responsible" for smooth-running schools. All this however dangerously approximated the commercialistic ideal of high salaries only for the management with the final test of a small expense account and a large output.

In this long struggle for a quarter of a century to free the public schools from political interference, in Chicago at least, the high wall of defense erected around the school system in order "to keep the rascals out," unfortunately so restricted the teachers inside the system that they had no space in which to move about freely and the more adventurous of them fairly panted for light and air. Any attempt to lower the wall for the sake of the teachers within, was regarded as giving an opportunity to the politicians without, and they were often openly accused, with a show of truth, of being in league with each other. Whenever the Dunne members of the board attempted to secure more liberty for the teachers, we were warned by tales of former difficulties with the politicians, and it seemed impossible that the struggle so long the focus of attention, should recede into the dullness of the achieved and allow the energy of the board to be free for new effort.

The whole situation between the superintendent supported by a majority of the board, and the Teachers' Federation had become an epitome of the struggle between efficiency and democracy; on one side a well-intentioned expression of the bureaucracy necessary in a large system but which under pressure had become unnecessarily self-assertive, and on the other side a fairly militant demand for self-government made in the name of freedom. Both sides inevitably exaggerated the difficulties of the situation and both felt that they were standing by important principles.

I certainly played a most inglorious part in this unnecessary conflict; I was chairman of the School Management Committee during one year when a majority of the members seemed to me exasperatingly conservative, and during another year when they were frustratingly radical, and I was of course highly unsatisfactory to both. . . .

Before my School Board experience, I thought that life had taught me at least one hard-earned lesson, that existing arrangements and the hoped for improvements must be mediated and reconciled to each other, that the new must be dovetailed into the old as it were, if it were to endure; but on the School Board I discerned that all such efforts were looked upon as compromising and unworthy, by both partisans. In the general disorder and public excitement resulting from the illegal dismissal of a majority of the "Dunne" board and their reinstatement by a court decision, I found myself belonging to neither party. During the months following the upheaval and the loss of my most vigorous colleagues, under the régime of men representing the leading Commercial Club of the city who honestly believed that they were rescuing the schools from a condition of chaos, I saw one beloved measure after another withdrawn. Although the new president scrupulously gave me the floor in the defense of each, it was impossible to consider them upon their merits in the lurid light which at the moment enveloped all the plans of the "uplifters." Thus the building of smaller schoolrooms, . . . the extension of the truant rooms so successfully inaugurated, the multiplication of school playgrounds, and many another cherished plan was thrown out or at least indefinitely postponed. . . .

As I myself was treated with uniform courtesy by the leading papers, I may perhaps here record my discouragement over this complicated difficulty of open discussion, for democratic government is founded upon the assumption that differing policies shall be freely discussed and that each party shall have an opportunity for at least a partisan presentation of its contentions. This attitude of the newspapers was doubtless intensified because the Dunne School Board had instituted a lawsuit challenging the validity of the lease for the school ground occupied by a newspaper building. This suit has since been decided in favor of the newspaper, and it may be that in their resentment they felt justified in doing everything possible to minimize the prosecuting School Board. I am, however, inclined to think that the newspapers but reflected an opinion honestly held by many people, and that their constant and partisan presentation of this opinion clearly demonstrates one of the greatest difficulties of governmental administration in a city grown too large for verbal discussions of public affairs.

It is difficult to close this chapter without a reference to the efforts made in Chicago to secure the municipal franchise for women. During two long periods of agitation for a new City Charter, a representative body of women appealed to the public, to the Charter Convention, and to the Illinois Legislature for this very reasonable provision. During the campaign when I acted as chairman of the federation of a hundred women's organizations, nothing impressed me so forcibly as the fact that the response came from bodies of women representing the most varied traditions. We were joined by a church society of hundreds of Lutheran women, because Scandinavian women had exercised the municipal franchise since the seventeenth century and had found American cities strangely conservative; by organizations of working women who had keenly felt the need of the municipal franchise in order to secure for their workshops the most rudimentary sanitation and the consideration which the vote alone obtains for workingmen; by federations of mothers meetings, who were interested in clean milk and the extension of kindergartens; by property-owning women, who had been powerless to protest against unjust taxation; by organizations of professional women, of university students, and of collegiate alumnae; and by women's clubs interested in municipal reforms. There was a complete absence of the traditional women's rights clamor but much impressive testimony from busy and useful women that they had reached the place where they needed the franchise in order to carry on their own affairs. A striking witness as to the need of the ballot, even for the women who are restricted to the most primitive and traditional activities, occurred when some Russian women waited upon me to ask whether under the new charter, they could vote for covered markets and so get rid of the shocking Chicago grime upon all their food; and when some neighboring Italian women sent me word that they would certainly vote for public washhouses if they ever had the chance to vote at all. It was all so human, so spontaneous, and so direct that it really seemed as if the time must be ripe for political expression of that public concern on the part of women which has so long been forced to seek indirection. None of these busy women wished to take the place of men nor to influence them in the direction of men's affairs, but they did seek an opportunity to coöperate directly in civic life through the use of the ballot in regard to their own affairs.

A Municipal Museum which was established in the Chicago Public Library building several years ago, largely through the activity of a group of women who had served as jurors in the departments of social economy, of education, and of sanitation in the World's Fair at St. Louis, showed nothing more clearly than that it is impossible to divide any of these departments from the political life of the modern city which is constantly forced to enlarge the boundary of its activity.

CHAPTER 15
THE VALUE OF SOCIAL CLUBS

From the early days at Hull-House, social clubs composed of English-speaking American born young people grew apace. So eager were they for social life that no mistakes in management could drive them away. I remember one enthusiastic leader who read aloud to a club a translation of "Antigone," which she had selected because she believed that the great themes of the Greek poets were best suited to young people. She came into the club room one evening in time to hear the president call the restive members to order with the statement, "You might just as well keep quiet for she is bound to finish it, and the quicker she gets to reading, the longer time we'll have for dancing." And yet the same club leader had the pleasure of lending four copies of the drama to four of the members, and one young man almost literally committed the entire play to memory.

On the whole we were much impressed by the great desire for self-improvement, for study and debate, exhibited by many of the young men. This very tendency, in fact, brought one of the most promising of our earlier clubs to an untimely end. The young men in the club, twenty in number, had grown much irritated by the frivolity of the girls during their long debates, and had finally proposed that three of the most "frivolous" be expelled. Pending a final vote, the three culprits appealed to certain of their friends who were members of the Hull-House Men's Club, between whom and the debating young men the incident became the cause of a quarrel so bitter that at length it led to a shooting. Fortunately the shot missed fire, or it may have been true that it was "only intended for a scare," but at any rate, we were all thoroughly frightened by this manifestation of the hot blood which the defense of woman has so often evoked. After many efforts to bring about a reconciliation, the debating club of twenty young men and the seventeen young women, who either were or pretended to be sober minded, rented a hall a mile west of Hull-House severing their connection with us because their ambitious and right-minded efforts had been unappreciated, basing this on the ground that we had not urged the expulsion of the so-called "tough" members of the Men's Club, who had been involved in the difficulty. The seceding club invited me to the first meeting in their new quarters that I might present to them my version of the situation and set forth the incident from the standpoint of Hull-House. The discussion I had with the young people that evening has always remained with me as one of the moments of illumination which life in a Settlement so often affords. In response to my position that a desire to avoid all that was "tough" meant to walk only in the paths of smug self-seeking and personal improvement leading straight into the pit of self-righteousness and petty achievement and was exactly what the Settlement did not stand for, they contended with much justice that ambitious young people were obliged for their own reputation, if not for their own morals, to avoid all connection with that which bordered on the tough, and that it was quite another matter for the Hull-House residents who could afford a more generous judgment. It was in vain I urged that life teaches us nothing more inevitably than that right and wrong are most confusingly confounded; that the blackest wrong may be within our own motives, and that at the best, right will not dazzle us by its radiant shining, and can only be found by exerting patience and discrimination. They still maintained their wholesome bourgeois position, which I am now quite ready to admit was most reasonable. . . .

Having lived in a Settlement twenty years, I see scores of young people who have successfully established themselves in life, and in my travels in the city and outside, I am constantly cheered by greetings from the rising young lawyer, the scholarly rabbi, the successful teacher, the prosperous young matron buying clothes for her blooming children.

The Hull-House Boys' Club organized its own Boys' Band in 1907. The band quickly became one of the settlement's most popular activities. Addams happily raised funds for instruments and uniforms because the band diverted boys' interests away from militaristic games and toward artistic endeavor. This photo was taken in the 1920s, when the Hull-House Boys' Band counted among its members future stars of the "big band era" such as Paul Whiteman and Benny Goodman.

Jane Addams Memorial Collection, Special Collections, The University Library, The University of Illinois at Chicago.

"Don't you remember me? I used to belong to a Hull-House club." I once asked one of these young people, a man who held a good position on a Chicago daily, what special thing Hull-House had meant to him, and he promptly replied, "It was the first house I had ever been in where books and magazines just lay around as if there were plenty of them in the world. Don't you remember how much I used to read at that little round table at the back of the library? To have people regard reading as a reasonable occupation changed the whole aspect of life to me and I began to have confidence in what I could do." ...

In addition to these rising young people given to debate and dramatics, and to the members of the public school alumni associations which meet in our rooms, there are hundreds of others who for years have come to Hull-House frankly in search of that pleasure and recreation which all young things crave and which those who have spent long hours in a factory or shop demand as a right. . . .

The residents at Hull-House, in their efforts to provide opportunities for clean recreation, receive the most valued help from the experienced wisdom of the older women of the neighborhood. Bowen Hall is constantly used for dancing parties with soft drinks established in its foyer. The parties given by the Hull-House clubs are by invitation and the young people themselves carefully maintain their standard of entrance so that the most cautious mother may feel safe when her daughter goes to one of our parties. No club festivity is permitted without the presence of a director; no young man under the influence of liquor is allowed; certain types of dancing often innocently started are strictly prohibited; and above all, early closing is insisted upon. This standardizing of pleasure has always seemed an obligation to the residents of Hull-House, but we are, I hope, saved from that priggishness which young people so heartily resent, by the Mardi Gras dance and other festivities which the residents themselves arrange and successfully carry out.

In spite of our belief that the standards of a ball may be almost as valuable to those without as to those within, the residents are constantly concerned for those many young people in the neighborhood who are too hedonistic to submit to the discipline of a dancing class or even to the claim of a pleasure club, but who go about in freebooter fashion to find pleasure wherever it may be cheaply on sale.

Such young people, well meaning but impatient of control, become the easy victims of the worst type of public dance halls and of even darker places, whose purposes are hidden under music and dancing. We were thoroughly frightened when we learned that during the year which ended last December, more than twenty-five thousand young people under the age of twenty-five passed through the Juvenile and Municipal Courts of Chicago — approximately one out of every eighty of the entire population, or one out of every fifty-two of those under twenty-five years of age. One's heart aches for these young people caught by the outside glitter of city gayety, who make such a feverish attempt to snatch it for themselves. The young people in our clubs are comparatively safe, but many instances come to the knowledge of Hull-House residents which make us long for the time when the city, through more small parks, municipal gymnasiums, and schoolrooms open for recreation, can guard from disaster these young people who walk so carelessly on the edge of the pit. . . .

Then there is the ever recurring difficulty about dress; the insistence of the young to be gayly bedecked to the utter consternation of the hard-working parents who are paying for a house and lot. The Polish girl who stole five dollars from her employer's till with which to buy a white dress for a church picnic was turned away from home by her indignant father who replaced the money to save the family honor, but would harbor no "thief" in a household of growing children who, in spite of the sister's revolt, continued to be dressed in dark heavy clothes through all the hot summer. There are a multitude of working girls who for hours carry hair ribbons and jewelry in their pockets or stockings, for they can wear them only during the journey to and from work. Sometimes this desire to taste pleasure, to escape into a world of congenial companionship takes more elaborate forms and often ends disastrously. . . .

I was grimly reminded of that . . . when I heard the tale of this seventeen-year-old girl, who had worked steadily in the same factory for four years before she resolved "to see life." In order not to arouse her parents' suspicions, she borrowed thirty dollars from one of those loan sharks who require no security from a pretty girl, so that she might start from home every morning as if to go to work. For three weeks she spent the first part of each dearly bought day in a department store where she lunched and unfortunately made some dubious acquaintances; in the afternoon she established herself in a theater and sat contentedly hour after hour watching the endless vaudeville until the usual time for returning home. At the end of each week she gave her parents her usual wage, but when her thirty dollars was exhausted it seemed unendurable that she should return to the monotony of the factory. In the light of her newly acquired experience she had learned that possibility which the city ever holds open to the restless girl.

That more such girls do not come to grief is due to those mothers who understand the insatiable demand for a good time, and if all of the mothers did understand, those pathetic statistics which show that four fifths of all prostitutes are under twenty years of age would be marvelously changed. We are told that "the will to live" is aroused in each baby by his mother's irresistible desire to play with him, the physiological value of joy that a child is born, and that the high death rate in institutions is increased by "the discontented babies" whom no one persuades into living. Something of the same sort is necessary in that second birth at adolescence. The young people need affection and understanding each one for himself, if they are to be induced to live in an inheritance of decorum and safety and to understand the foundations upon which this orderly world rests. No one comprehends their needs so sympathetically as those mothers who iron the flimsy starched finery of their grown-up daughters late into the night, and who pay for a red velvet parlor set on the installment plan, although the younger children may sadly need new shoes. These mothers apparently understand the sharp demand for social pleasure and do their best to respond to it, although at the same time they constantly minister to all the physical needs of an exigent family of little children. . . .

We are slowly learning that social advance depends quite as much upon an increase in moral sensibility as it does upon a sense of duty, and of this one could cite many illustrations. I was at one time chairman of the Child Labor Committee in the General Federation of Women's Clubs, which sent out a schedule asking each club in the United States to report as nearly as possible all the working children under fourteen living in its vicinity. A Florida club filled out the schedule with an astonishing number of Cuban children who were at work in sugar mills, and the club members registered a complaint that our committee had sent the schedule too late, for if they had realized the conditions earlier, they might have presented a bill to the Legislature which had now adjourned. Of course the children had been working in the sugar mills for years, and had probably gone back and forth under the very eyes of the club women, but the women had never seen them, much less felt any obligation to protect them, until they joined a club, and the club joined a federation, and the federation appointed a Child Labor Committee who sent them a schedule. With their quickened perceptions they then saw the rescue of these familiar children in the light of a social obligation. Through some such experiences the members of the Hull-House Women's Club have obtained the power of seeing the concrete through the general and have entered into various undertakings. . . .

The leader of the Social Extension Committee has also been able, through her connection with the vacant lot garden movement in Chicago, to maintain a most flourishing "friendly club" largely composed of people who cultivate these garden plots. During the club evening at least, they regain something of the ease of the man who is being estimated by the bushels per acre of potatoes he has raised, and not by that flimsy city judgment so often based upon store clothes. Their jollity and enthusiasm are unbounded, expressing itself in clog dances and rousing old songs often in sharp contrast to the overworked, worn aspects of the members.

Of course there are surprising possibilities discovered through other clubs, in one of Greek women or in the *circolo Italiano,* for a social club often affords a sheltered space in which the gentler social usages may be exercised, as the more vigorous clubs afford a point of departure into larger social concerns. . . .

Thus the value of social clubs broadens out in one's mind to an instrument of companionship through which many may be led from a sense of isolation to one of civic responsibility, even as another type of club provides recreational facilities for those who have had only meaningless excitements, or, as a third type, opens new and interesting vistas of life to those who are ambitious.

The social clubs form a basis of acquaintanceship for many people living in other parts of the city. Through friendly relations with individuals, which is perhaps the sanest method of approach, they are thus brought into contact, many of them for the first time, with the industrial and social problems challenging the moral resources of our contemporary life. During our twenty years hundreds of these nonresidents have directed clubs and classes, and have increased the number of Chicago citizens who are conversant with adverse social conditions and conscious that only by the unceasing devotion of each, according to his strength, shall the compulsions and hardships, the stupidities and cruelties of life be overcome. The number of people thus informed is constantly increasing in all our American cities, and they may in time remove the reproach of social neglect and indifference which has so long rested upon the citizens of the new world. . . .

The entire social development of Hull-House is so unlike what I predicted twenty years ago, that I venture to quote from that ancient writing as an end to this chapter.[70]

> The social organism has broken down through large districts of our great cities. Many of the people living there are very poor, the majority of them without leisure or energy for anything but the gain of subsistence.
>
> They live for the moment side by side, many of them without knowledge of each other, without fellowship, without local tradition or public spirit, without social organization of any kind. Practically nothing is done to remedy this. The people who might do it, who have the social tact and training, the large houses, and the traditions and customs of hospitality, live in other parts of the city. The clubhouses, libraries, galleries, and semi-public conveniences for social life are also blocks away. We find workingmen organized into armies of producers because men of executive ability and business sagacity have found it

[70] Refers to Addams's 1893 essay, "The Subjective Necessity for Social Settlements."

to their interests thus to organize them. But these workingmen are not organized socially; although lodging in crowded tenement houses, they are living without a corresponding social contact. The chaos is as great as it would be were they working in huge factories without foreman or superintendent. Their ideas and resources are cramped, and the desire for higher social pleasure becomes extinct. They have no share in the traditions and social energy which make for progress. Too often their only place of meeting is a saloon, their only host a bartender; a local demagogue forms their public opinion. Men of ability and refinement, of social power and university cultivation, stay away from them. Personally, I believe the men who lose most are those who thus stay away. But the paradox is here: when cultivated people do stay away from a certain portion of the population, when all social advantages are persistently withheld, it may be for years, the result itself is pointed to as a reason and is used as an argument, for the continued withholding.

It is constantly said that because the masses have never had social advantages, they do not want them, that they are heavy and dull, and that it will take political or philanthropic machinery to change them. This divides a city into rich and poor; into the favored, who express their sense of the social obligation by gifts of money, and into the unfavored, who express it by clamoring for a "share"— both of them actuated by a vague sense of justice. This division of the city would be more justifiable, however, if the people who thus isolate themselves on certain streets and use their social ability for each other, gained enough thereby and added sufficient to the sum total of social progress to justify the withholding of the pleasures and results of that progress, from so many people who ought to have them. But they cannot accomplish this for the social spirit discharges itself in many forms, and no one form is adequate to its total expression.

CHAPTER 16
ARTS AT HULL-HOUSE

The first building erected for Hull-House contained an art gallery well lighted for day and evening use and our first exhibit of loaned pictures was opened in June, 1891. . . .

We took pride in the fact that our first exhibit contained some of the best pictures Chicago afforded, and we conscientiously insured them against fire and carefully guarded them by night and day.

We had five of these exhibits during two years, after the gallery was completed: two of oil paintings, one of old engravings and etchings, one of water colors, and one of pictures especially selected for use in the public schools. These exhibits were surprisingly well attended and thousands of votes were cast for the most popular pictures. Their value to the neighborhood of course had to be determined by each one of us according to the value he attached to beauty and the escape it offers from dreary reality into the realm of the imagination. Miss Starr always insisted that the arts should receive adequate recognition at Hull-House and urged that one must always remember "the hungry individual soul which without art will have passed unsolaced and unfed, followed by other souls who lack the impulse his should have given."

The exhibits afforded pathetic evidence that the older immigrants do not expect the solace of art in this country; an Italian expressed great surprise when he found that we, although Americans, still liked pictures, and said quite naïvely that he didn't know that Americans cared for anything but dollars — that looking at pictures was something people only did in Italy.

The extreme isolation of the Italian colony was demonstrated by the fact that he did not know that there was a public art gallery in the city nor any houses in which pictures were regarded as treasures.

A Greek was much surprised to see a photograph of the Acropolis at Hull-House because he had lived in Chicago for thirteen years and had never before met any Americans who knew about this foremost glory of the world. Before he left Greece he had imagined that Americans would be most eager to see pictures of Athens, and as he was a graduate of a school of technology, he had prepared a book of colored drawings and had made a collection of photographs which he was sure Americans would enjoy. But although from his fruit stand near one of the large railroad stations he had conversed with many Americans and had often tried to lead the conversation back to ancient Greece, no one had responded, and he had at last concluded that "the people of Chicago knew nothing of ancient times."

The loan exhibits were continued until the Chicago Art Institute was opened free to the public on Sunday afternoons and parties were arranged at Hull-House and conducted there by a guide. In time even these parties were discontinued as the galleries became better known in all parts of the city and the Art Institute management did much to make pictures popular.

From the first a studio was maintained at Hull-House which was developed through the changing years under the direction of Miss Benedict, one of the residents who is a member of the faculty in the Art Institute.[71] Buildings on the Hull-House quadrangle furnish studios for artists who find something of the same spirit in the contiguous Italian

---

[71] Enella Benedict was the head of the Hull-House art studio from 1892 until 1943.

colony that the French artist is traditionally supposed to discover in his beloved Latin Quarter. These artists uncover something of the picturesque in the foreign colonies, which they have reproduced in painting, etching, and lithography. They find their classes filled not only by young people possessing facility and sometimes talent, but also by older people to whom the studio affords the one opportunity of escape from dreariness; a widow with four children who supplemented a very inadequate income by teaching the piano, for six years never missed her weekly painting lesson because it was "her one pleasure"; another woman whose youth and strength had gone into the care of an invalid father, poured into her afternoon in the studio once a week, all of the longing for self-expression which she habitually suppressed.

Perhaps the most satisfactory results of the studio have been obtained through the classes of young men who are engaged in the commercial arts, and who are glad to have an opportunity to work out their own ideas. This is true of young engravers and lithographers; of the men who have to do with posters and illustrations in various ways. The little pile of stones and the lithographer's hand-press in a corner of the studio have been used in many an experiment, as has a set of beautiful type loaned to Hull-House by a bibliophile.

The work of the studio almost imperceptibly merged into the crafts and well within the first decade a shop was opened at Hull-House under the direction of several residents who were also members of the Chicago Arts and Crafts Society. This shop is not merely a school where people are taught and then sent forth to use their teaching in art according to their individual initiative and opportunity, but where those who have already been carefully trained, may express the best they can in wood or metal. The Settlement soon discovers how difficult it is to put a fringe of art on the end of a day spent in a factory. We constantly see young people doing overhurried work. Wrapping bars of soap in pieces of paper might at least give the pleasure of accuracy and repetition if it could be done at a normal pace, but when paid for by the piece, speed becomes the sole requirement and the last suggestion of human interest is taken away. In contrast to this the Hull-House shop affords many examples of the restorative power in the exercise of a genuine craft; a young Russian who, like too many of his countrymen, had made a desperate effort to fit himself for a learned profession, and who had almost finished his course in a night law school, used to watch constantly the work being done in the metal shop at Hull-House. One evening in a moment of sudden resolve, he took off his coat, sat down at one of the benches, and began to work, obviously as a very clever silversmith. He had long concealed his craft because he thought it would hurt his efforts as a lawyer and because he imagined an office more honorable and "more American" than a shop. As he worked on during his two leisure evenings each week, his entire bearing and conversation registered the relief of one who abandons the effort he is not fitted for and becomes a man on his own feet, expressing himself through a familiar and delicate technique. . . .

From the very first winter, concerts which are still continued were given every Sunday afternoon in the Hull-House drawing-room and later, as the audiences increased, in the larger halls. . . .

It was in connection with these first choruses that a public-spirited citizen of Chicago offered a prize for the best labor song, competition to be open to the entire country. The responses to the offer literally filled three large barrels and speaking at least for myself as one of the bewildered judges, we were more disheartened by their quality than even by their overwhelming bulk. Apparently the workers of America are not yet ready to sing, although I recall a creditable chorus trained at Hull-House for a large meeting in sympathy with the anthracite coal strike in which the swinging lines

> Who was it made the coal?
> Our God as well as theirs.

seemed to relieve the tension of the moment. Miss Eleanor Smith, the head of the Hull-House Music School, who had put the words to music, performed the same office for the "Sweatshop" of the Yiddish poet, the translation of which presents so graphically the bewilderment and tedium of the New York shop that it might be applied to almost any other machine industry as the first verse indicates:—

> The roaring of the wheels has filled my ears,
> The clashing and the clamor shut me in,
> Myself, my soul, in chaos disappears,
> I cannot think or feel amid the din.

It may be that this plaint explains the lack of labor songs in this period of industrial maladjustment when the worker is overmastered by his very tools. . . .

From the beginning we had classes in music, and the Hull-House Music School, which is housed in quarters of its own in our quieter court, was opened in 1893. The school is designed to give a thorough musical instruction to a limited number of children. From the first lessons they are taught to compose and to reduce to order the musical suggestions which may come to them, and in this wise the school has sometimes been able to recover the songs of the immigrants through their children. . . .

The recitals and concerts given by the school are attended by large and appreciative audiences. On the Sunday before Christmas the program of Christmas songs draws together people of the most diverging faiths. In the deep tones of the memorial organ erected at Hull-House, we realize that music is perhaps the most potent agent for making the universal appeal and inducing men to forget their differences.

Some of the pupils in the music school have developed during the years into trained musicians and are supporting themselves in their chosen profession. On the other hand, we constantly see the most promising musical ability extinguished when the young people enter industries which so sap their vitality that they cannot carry on serious study in the scanty hours outside of factory work. Many cases indisputably illustrate this: a Bohemian girl, who, in order to earn money for pressing family needs, first ruined her voice in a six months' constant vaudeville engagement, returned to her trade working overtime in a vain effort to continue the vaudeville income; another young girl whom Hull-House had sent to the high school so long as her parents consented, because we realized that a beautiful voice is often unavailable through lack of the informing mind, later extinguished her promise in a tobacco factory; . . .

Even that bitter experience did not prepare us for the sorrowful year when six promising pupils out of a class of fifteen, developed tuberculosis. It required but little penetration to see that during the eight years the class of fifteen school children had come together to the music school, they had approximately an even chance, but as soon as they reached the legal working age only a scanty moiety of those who became self-supporting could endure the strain of long hours and bad air. . . .

It has been pointed out many times that Art lives by devouring her own offspring and the world has come to justify even that sacrifice, but we are unfortified and unsolaced when we see the children of Art devoured, not by her, but by the uncouth stranger, Modern Industry, who, needlessly ruthless and brutal to her own children, is quickly fatal to the offspring of the gentler mother. And so schools in art for those who go to work at the age when more fortunate young people are still sheltered and educated, constantly epitomize one of the haunting problems of life; why do we permit the waste of this most precious human faculty, this consummate possession of civilization? When we fail to provide the vessel in which it may be treasured, it runs out upon the ground and is irretrievably lost.

The universal desire for the portrayal of life lying quite outside of personal experience evinces itself in many forms. One of the conspicuous features of our neighborhood, as of all industrial quarters, is the persistency with which the entire population attends the theater. The very first day I saw Halsted Street a long line of young men and boys stood outside the gallery entrance of the Bijou Theater, waiting for the Sunday matinée to begin at two o'clock, although it was only high noon. This waiting crowd might have been seen every Sunday afternoon during the twenty years which have elapsed since then. Our first Sunday evening in Hull-House, when a group of small boys sat on our piazza and told us "about things around here," their talk was all of the theater and of the astonishing things they had seen that afternoon.

But quite as it was difficult to discover the habits and purposes of this group of boys because they much preferred talking about the theater to contemplating their own lives, so it was all along the line; the young men told us their ambitions in the phrases of stage heroes, and the girls, so far as their romantic dreams could be shyly put into words, possessed no others but those soiled by long use in the melodrama. All of these young people looked upon an afternoon a week in the gallery of a Halsted Street theater as their one opportunity to see life. The sort of melodrama they see there has recently been described as "the Ten Commandments written in red fire." Certainly the villain always comes to a violent end, and the young and handsome hero is rewarded by marriage with a beautiful girl, usually the daughter of a millionaire, but after all that is not a portrayal of the morality of the Ten Commandments any more than of life itself.

Nevertheless the theater, such as it was, appeared to be the one agency which freed the boys and girls from that destructive isolation of those who drag themselves up to maturity by themselves, and it gave them a glimpse of that order and beauty into which even the poorest drama endeavors to restore the bewildering facts of life. . . .

In . . . illustration of an overmastering desire to see life as portrayed on the stage are two young girls whose sober parents did not approve of the theater and would allow no money for such foolish purposes. In sheer desperation the sisters evolved a plot that one of them would feign a toothache, and while she was having her tooth pulled by a neighboring dentist the other would steal the gold crowns from his table, and with the money thus procured they could attend the vaudeville theater every night on their way home from work. Apparently the pain and wrongdoing did not weigh for a moment against the anticipated pleasure. The plan was carried out to the point of selling the gold crowns to a pawn-broker when the disappointed girls were arrested.

All this effort to see the play took place in the years before the five-cent theaters had become a feature of every crowded city thoroughfare and before their popularity had induced the attendance of two and a quarter million people in the United States every twenty-four hours. The eagerness of the penniless children to get into these magic spaces is re-sponsible for an entire crop of petty crimes made more easy because two children are admitted for one nickel at the last performance when the hour is late and the theater nearly deserted. The Hull-House residents were aghast at the early popularity of these mimic shows, and in the days before the inspection of films and the present regulations for the five-cent theaters we established at Hull-House a moving picture show. Al-though its success justified its existence, it was so obviously but one in the midst of hundreds that it seemed much more advisable to turn our attention to the improvement of all of them or rather to assist as best we could, the successful efforts in this direction by the Juvenile Protective Association.

However, long before the five-cent theater was even heard of, we had accumulated much testimony as to the power of the drama, and we would have been dull indeed if we had not availed ourselves of the use of the play at Hull-House, not only as an agent of recreation and education, but as a vehicle of self-expression for the teeming young life all about us.

Long before the Hull-House theater was built we had many plays, first in the drawing-room and later in the gymnasium. The young people's clubs never tired of rehearsing and preparing for these dramatic occa-sions, and we also discovered that older people were almost equally ready and talented. We quickly learned that no celebration at Thanks-giving was so popular as a graphic portrayal on the stage of the Pilgrim Fathers, and we were often put to it to reduce to dramatic effects the great days of patriotism and religion. . . .

The immigrants in the neighborhood of Hull-House have utilized our little stage in an endeavor to reproduce the past of their own nations through those immortal dramas which have escaped from the restrain-ing bond of one country into the land of the universal.

A large colony of Greeks near Hull-House, who often feel that their history and classic background are completely ignored by Americans, and that they are easily confused with the more ignorant immigrants from other parts of southeastern Europe, welcome an occasion to pre-sent Greek plays in the ancient text. With expert help in the difficulties of staging and rehearsing a classic play, they reproduced the "Ajax" of Sophocles upon the Hull-House stage. It was a genuine triumph to the actors who felt that they were "showing forth the glory of Greece" to "ignorant Americans." The scholar who came with a copy of Sophocles in hand and followed the play with real enjoyment, did not in the least realize that the revelation of the love of Greek poets was mutual between the audience and the actors. The Greeks have quite recently assisted an enthusiast in producing "Electra," while the Lithuanians, the Poles, and other Russian subjects often use the Hull-House stage to present plays in their own tongue, which shall at one and the same time keep alive their sense of participation in the great Russian Revolution and relieve their feelings in regard to it. There is something still more appealing in the yearning efforts the immigrants sometimes make to formulate their situation in America. I recall a play written by an Italian playwright of our neighborhood, which depicted the insolent break between Americanized sons and old country parents, so touchingly that it moved to tears all the older Italians in the audience. Did the tears of each express relief in finding that others had had the same experience as himself, and did the knowledge free each one from a sense of isolation and an injured belief that his children were the worst of all?

This effort to understand life through its dramatic portrayal, to see one's own participation intelligibly set forth, becomes difficult when one enters the field of social development, but even here it is not impossible if a Settlement group is constantly searching for new material.

A labor story appearing in the *Atlantic Monthly* was kindly dramatized for us by the author who also superintended its presentation upon the Hull-House stage. The little drama presented the untutored effort of a trades-union man to secure for his side the beauty of self-sacrifice, the glamour of martyrdom, which so often seems to belong solely to the nonunion forces. The presentation of the play was attended by an audience of trades-unionists and employers and those other people who are supposed to make public opinion. Together they felt the moral beauty of the man's conclusion that "it's the side that suffers most that will win out in this war — the saints is the only ones that has got the world under their feet — we've got to do the way they done if the unions is to stand," so completely that it seemed quite natural that he should forfeit his life upon the truth of this statement. . . .

I have come to believe, however, that the stage may do more than teach, that much of our current moral instruction will not endure the test of being cast into a lifelike mold, and when presented in dramatic form will reveal itself as platitudinous and effete. That which may have sounded like righteous teaching when it was remote and wordy, will be challenged afresh when it is obliged to simulate life itself.

This function of the stage, as a reconstructing and reorganizing agent of accepted moral truths, came to me with overwhelming force as I listened to the Passion Play at Oberammergau one beautiful summer's day in 1900. The peasants who portrayed exactly the successive scenes of the wonderful Life, who used only the very words found in the accepted version of the Gospels, yet curiously modernized and reorientated the message. They made clear that the opposition to the young Teacher sprang from the merchants whose traffic in the temple He had disturbed and from the Pharisees who were dependent upon them for support. Their query was curiously familiar, as they demanded the antecedents of the Radical who dared to touch vested interests, who presumed to dictate the morality of trade, and who insulted the marts of honest merchants by calling them "a den of thieves." As the play developed, it became clear that this powerful opposition had friends in Church and State, that they controlled influences which ramified in all directions. They obviously believed in their statement of the case and their very wealth and position in the community gave their words such weight that finally all of their hearers were convinced that the young Agitator must be done away with in order that the highest interests of society might be conserved. These simple peasants made it clear that it was the money power which induced one of the Agitator's closest friends to betray Him, and the villain of the piece, Judas himself, was only a man who was so dazzled by money, so under the domination of all it represented, that he was perpetually blind to the spiritual vision unrolling before him. As I sat through the long summer day, seeing the shadows on the beautiful mountain back of the open stage shift from one side to the other and finally grow long and pointed in the soft evening light, my mind was filled with perplexing questions. Did the dramatization of the life of Jesus set forth its meaning more clearly and conclusively than talking and preaching could possibly do as a shadowy following of the command "to do the will"?

The peasant actors whom I had seen returning from mass that morning had prayed only to portray the life as He had lived it and, behold, out of their simplicity and piety arose this modern version which even Harnack was only then venturing to suggest to his advanced colleagues in Berlin. Yet the Oberammergau folk were very like thousands of immigrant men and women of Chicago, both in their experiences and in their familiarity with the hard facts of life, and throughout that day as my mind dwelt on my far-away neighbors, I was reproached with the sense of an ungarnered harvest.

Of course such a generally uplifted state comes only at rare moments, while the development of the little theater at Hull-House has not depended upon the moods of any one, but upon the genuine enthusiasm and sustained effort of a group of residents, several of them artists who have ungrudgingly given their time to it year after year. This group has long fostered junior dramatic associations, through which it seems possible to give a training in manners and morals more directly than through any other medium. . . .

This group of Hull-House artists have filled our little foyer with a series of charming playbills and by dint of painting their own scenery and making their own costumes have obtained beguiling results in stage setting. Sometimes all the artistic resources of the House unite in a Wagnerian combination; thus the text of the "Troll's Holiday" was written by one resident, set to music by another; sung by the music school, and placed upon the stage under the careful direction and training of the dramatic committee; and the little brown trolls could never have tumbled about so gracefully in their gleaming caves unless they had been taught in the gymnasium.

Some such synthesis takes place every year at the Hull-House annual exhibition, when an effort is made to bring together in a spirit of holiday the nine thousand people who come to the House every week during duller times. Curiously enough the central feature at the annual exhibition seems to be the brass band of the Boys' Club which apparently dominates the situation by sheer size and noise, but perhaps their fresh boyish enthusiasm expresses that which the older people take more soberly.

As the stage of our little theater had attempted to portray the heroes of many lands, so we planned one early spring seven years ago, to carry out a scheme of mural decoration upon the walls of the theater itself, which should portray those cosmopolitan heroes who have become great through identification with the common lot, in preference to the heroes of mere achievement. In addition to the group of artists living at Hull-House several others were in temporary residence, and they all threw themselves enthusiastically into the plan. The series began with Tolstoy plowing his field, which was painted by an artist of the Glasgow school, and the next was of the young Lincoln pushing his flatboat down the Mississippi River at the moment he received his first impression of the "great iniquity." This was done by a promising young artist of Chicago, and the wall spaces nearest to the two selected heroes were quickly filled with their immortal sayings.

A spirited discussion thereupon ensued in regard to the heroes for the two remaining large wall spaces, when to the surprise of all of us the group of twenty-five residents who had lived in unbroken harmony for more than ten years, suddenly broke up into cults and even camps of hero worship. . . .

When we were all fatigued and hopeless of compromise, we took refuge in a series of landscapes connected with our two heroes by a quotation from Wordsworth slightly distorted to meet our dire need, but still stating his impassioned belief in the efficacious spirit capable of companionship with man which resides in "particular spots." Certainly peace emanates from the particular folding of the hills in one of our treasured mural landscapes, yet occasionally when a guest with a bewildered air looks from one side of the theater to the other, we are forced to conclude that the connection is not convincing.

In spite of its stormy career this attempt at mural decoration connects itself quite naturally with the spirit of our earlier efforts to make Hull-House as beautiful as we could, which had in it a desire to embody in the outward aspect of the House something of the reminiscence and aspiration of the neighborhood life. . . .

Perhaps the early devotion of the Hull-House residents to the pre-Raphaelites recognized that they above all English-speaking poets and painters reveal "the sense of the expressiveness of outward things" which is at once the glory and the limitation of the arts.

CHAPTER 17
ECHOES OF THE RUSSIAN REVOLUTION

The residents of Hull-House have always seen many evidences of the Russian Revolution,[72] a forlorn family of little children whose parents have been massacred at Kishinev are received and supported by their relatives in our Chicago neighborhood; or a Russian woman, her face streaming with tears of indignation and pity, asks you to look at the scarred back of her sister, a young girl, who has escaped with her life

---

[72] Addams was referring to a two-year period of demonstrations, general strikes, and insurrections that were met with violent repression in czarist Russia. The groundwork for the 1917 Russian Revolution was laid in this tumultuous time.

from the whips of the Cossack soldiers; or a studious young woman suddenly disappears from the Hull-House classes because she has returned to Kiev to be near her brother while he is in prison, that she may earn money for the nourishing food which alone will keep him from contracting tuberculosis; or we attend a protest meeting against the newest outrages of the Russian government in which the speeches are interrupted by the groans of those whose sons have been sacrificed and by the hisses of others who cannot repress their indignation. At such moments an American is acutely conscious of our ignorance of this greatest tragedy of modern times, and at our indifference to the waste of perhaps the noblest human material among our contemporaries. Certain it is, as the distinguished Russian revolutionists have come to Chicago, they have impressed me, as no one else ever has done, as belonging to that noble company of martyrs who have ever and again poured forth blood that human progress might be advanced. Sometimes these men and women have addressed audiences gathered quite outside the Russian colony and have filled to overflowing Chicago's largest halls with American citizens deeply touched by this message of martyrdom. . . .

In this wonderful procession of revolutionists, Prince Kropotkin, or, as he prefers to be called, Peter Kropotkin,[73] was doubtless the most distinguished. When he came to America to lecture, he was heard throughout the country with great interest and respect; that he was a guest of Hull-House during his stay in Chicago attracted little attention at the time, but two years later, when the assassination of President McKinley occurred, the visit of this kindly scholar, who had always called himself an "anarchist" and had certainly written fiery tracts in his younger manhood, was made the basis of an attack upon Hull-House by a daily newspaper, which ignored the fact that while Prince Kropotkin had addressed the Chicago Arts and Crafts Society at Hull-House, . . . he had also spoken at the State Universities of Illinois and Wisconsin and before the leading literary and scientific societies of Chicago. These institutions and societies were not, therefore, called anarchistic. Hull-House had doubtless laid itself open to this attack through an incident connected with the imprisonment of the editor of an anarchistic paper,[74] who was arrested in Chicago immediately after the assassination of President

---

[73] A Russian prince (1842–1921) who renounced his aristocratic privilege and devoted himself to the cause of anarchist communism. Having escaped imprisonment in Russia for his views, he lived in exile until the Russian Revolution of 1917.

[74] Abraham Isaaks, the editor of *Free Society,* a journal of philosophical anarchy published in Chicago.

McKinley. In the excitement following the national calamity and the avowal by the assassin of the influence of the anarchistic lecture to which he had listened, arrests were made in Chicago of every one suspected of anarchy, in the belief that a widespread plot would be uncovered. The editor's house was searched for incriminating literature, his wife and daughter taken to a police station, and his son and himself, with several other suspected anarchists, were placed in the disused cells in the basement of the City Hall.

It is impossible to overstate the public excitement of the moment and the unfathomable sense of horror with which the community regarded an attack upon the chief executive of the nation, as a crime against government itself which compels an instinctive recoil from all law-abiding citizens. . . .

Both the hatred and the determination to punish reached the highest pitch in Chicago after the assassination of President McKinley, and the group of wretched men detained in the old-fashioned, scarcely habitable cells, had not the least idea of their ultimate fate. They were not allowed to see an attorney and were kept "in communicado" as their excited friends called it. I had seen the editor and his family only during Prince Kropotkin's stay at Hull-House, when they had come to visit him several times. The editor had impressed me as a quiet, scholarly man, challenging the social order by the philosophic touchstone of Bakunin[75] and of Herbert Spencer,[76] somewhat startled by the radicalism of his fiery young son and much comforted by the German domesticity of his wife and daughter. Perhaps it was but my hysterical symptom of the universal excitement, but it certainly seemed to me more than I could bear when a group of his individualistic friends, who had come to ask for help, said: "You see what becomes of your boasted law; the authorities won't even allow an attorney, nor will they accept bail for these men, against whom nothing can be proved, although the veriest criminals are not denied such a right." Challenged by an anarchist, one is always sensitive for the honor of legally constituted society, and I replied that of course the men could have an attorney, that the assassin himself would eventually be furnished with one, that the fact that a man was an anarchist had nothing to do with his rights before the law! I was met with the retort that

[75] Mikhail Aleksandrovich Bakunin (1814–76) was a Russian anarchist philosopher who clashed with Marx over questions of centralization, authority, and control.

[76] British philosopher (1820–1903) whose philosophy of "social Darwinism" argued that the rule of survival of the fittest ensured beneficial social evolution. Spencer espoused the primacy of individual interests over communal interests. In coupling Spencer with Bakunin, Addams is classifying Spencer's laissez-faire thinking as a type of anarchism.

that might do for a theory, but that the fact still remained that these men had been absolutely isolated, seeing no one but policemen, who constantly frightened them with tales of public clamor and threatened lynching.

This conversation took place on Saturday night and, as the final police authority rests in the mayor, with a friend who was equally disturbed over the situation, I repaired to his house on Sunday morning to appeal to him in the interest of a law and order that should not yield to panic. We contended that to the anarchist above all men it must be demonstrated that law is impartial and stands the test of every strain. The mayor heard us through with the ready sympathy of the successful politician. He insisted, however, that the men thus far had merely been properly protected against lynching, but that it might now be safe to allow them to see some one; he would not yet, however, take the responsibility of permitting an attorney, but if I myself chose to see them on the humanitarian errand of an assurance of fair play, he would write me a permit at once. I promptly fell into the trap, if trap it was, and within half an hour was in a corridor in the City Hall basement, talking to the distracted editor and surrounded by a cordon of police, who assured me that it was not safe to permit him out of his cell. The editor, who had grown thin and haggard under his suspense, asked immediately as to the whereabouts of his wife and daughter, concerning whom he had heard not a word since he had seen them arrested. Gradually he became composed as he learned, not that his testimony had been believed to the effect that he had never seen the assassin but once, and had then considered him a foolish half-witted creature, but that the most thoroughgoing "dragnet" investigations on the part of the united police of the country had failed to discover a plot and that the public was gradually becoming convinced that the dastardly act was that of a solitary man with no political or social affiliations.

The entire conversation was simple and did not seem to me unlike, in motive or character, interviews I had had with many another forlorn man who had fallen into prison. I had scarce returned to Hull-House, however, before it was filled with reporters, and I at once discovered that whether or not I had helped a brother out of a pit, I had fallen into a deep one myself. A period of sharp public opprobrium followed, traces of which, I suppose, will always remain. . . .

Although one or two ardent young people rushed into print to defend me from the charge of "abetting anarchy," it seemed to me at the time that mere words would not avail. I had felt that the protection of the law itself extended to the most unpopular citizen was the only reply to the anarchistic argument, to the effect that this moment of panic revealed the truth of their theory of government; . . .

At that moment I was firmly convinced that the public could only be convicted of the blindness of its course, when a body of people with a hundred-fold of the moral energy possessed by a Settlement group, should make clear that there is no method by which any community can be guarded against sporadic efforts on the part of half-crazed, discouraged men, save by a sense of mutual rights and securities which will include the veriest outcast.

It seemed to me then that in the millions of words uttered and written at that time, no one adequately urged that public-spirited citizens set themselves the task of patiently discovering how these sporadic acts of violence against government may be understood and averted. We do not know whether they occur among the discouraged and unassimilated immigrants who might be cared for in such a way as enormously to lessen the probability of these acts, or whether they are the result of anarchistic teaching. By hastily concluding that the latter is the sole explanation for them, we make no attempt to heal and cure the situation. Failure to make a proper diagnosis may mean treatment of a disease which does not exist, or it may furthermore mean that the dire malady from which the patient is suffering be permitted to develop unchecked. And yet as the details of the meager life of the President's assassin were disclosed, they were a challenge to the forces for social betterment in American cities. Was it not an indictment to all those whose business it is to interpret and solace the wretched, that a boy should have grown up in an American city so uncared for, so untouched by higher issues, his wounds of life so unhealed by religion that the first talk he ever heard dealing with life's wrongs, although anarchistic and violent, should yet appear to point a way of relief? . . .

The attempt a Settlement makes to interpret American institutions to those who are bewildered concerning them either because of their personal experiences, or because of preconceived theories, would seem to lie in the direct path of its public obligation, and yet it is apparently impossible for the overwrought community to distinguish between the excitement the Settlements are endeavoring to understand and to allay and the attitude of the Settlement itself. At times of public panic, fervid denunciation is held to be the duty of every good citizen, and if a Settlement is convinced that the incident should be used to vindicate the law and does not at the moment give its strength to denunciation, its attitude is at once taken to imply a championship of anarchy itself. The public mind at such a moment falls into the old medieval confusion — he who feeds or shelters a heretic is upon *prima facie* evidence a heretic himself — he who knows intimately people among whom anarchists arise, is therefore an anarchist. . . .

Whether or not Hull-House has accomplished anything by its method of meeting such a situation, or at least attempting to treat it in a way which will not destroy confidence in the American institutions so adored by refugees from foreign governmental oppression, it is of course impossible for me to say.

And yet it was in connection with an effort to pursue an intelligent policy in regard to a so-called "foreign anarchist" that Hull-House again became associated with that creed six years later. This again was an echo of the Russian Revolution, but in connection with one of its humblest representatives. A young Russian Jew named Averbuch appeared in the early morning at the house of the Chicago chief of police upon an obscure errand. It was a moment of panic everywhere in regard to anarchists because of a recent murder in Denver which had been charged to an Italian anarchist, and the chief of police, assuming that the dark young man standing in his hallway was an anarchist bent upon his assassination, hastily called for help. In a panic born of fear and self-defense, young Averbuch was shot to death. The members of the Russian Jewish colony on the West Side of Chicago were thrown into a state of intense excitement as soon as the nationality of the young man became known. They were filled with dark forebodings from a swift prescience of what it would mean to them were the odium of anarchy rightly or wrongly attached to one of their members. It seemed to the residents of Hull-House most important that every effort should be made to ascertain just what did happen, that every means of securing information should be exhausted before a final opinion should be formed, and this odium fastened upon a colony of law-abiding citizens. The police might be right or wrong in their assertion that the man was an anarchist. It was, to our minds, also most unfortunate that the Chicago police in the determination to uncover an anarchistic plot should have utilized the most drastic methods of search within the Russian Jewish colony composed of families only too familiar with the methods of the Russian police. Therefore, when the Chicago police ransacked all the printing offices they could locate in the colony, when they raided a restaurant which they regarded as suspicious because it had been supplying food at cost to the unemployed, when they searched through private houses for papers and photographs of revolutionaries, when they seized the library of the Edelstadt group and carried the books, including Shakespeare and Herbert Spencer, to the City Hall, when they arrested two friends of young

Averbuch and kept them in the police station forty-eight hours, when they mercilessly "sweated" the sister, Olga, that she might be startled into a confession — all these things so poignantly reminded them of Russian methods, that indignation fed both by old memory and bitter disappointment in America, swept over the entire colony. The older men asked whether constitutional rights gave no guarantee against such violent aggression of police power, and the hot-headed younger ones cried out at once that the only way to deal with the police was to defy them, which was true of police the world over. It was said many times that those who are without influence and protection in a strange country fare exactly as hard as do the poor in Europe; that all the talk of guaranteed protection through political institutions is nonsense.

Every Settlement has classes in citizenship in which the principles of American institutions are expounded and of these the community, as a whole, approves. But the Settlements know better than any one else that while these classes and lectures are useful, nothing can possibly give lessons in citizenship so effectively and make so clear the constitutional basis of a self-governing community as the current event itself. The treatment at a given moment of that foreign colony which feels itself outraged and misunderstood, either makes its constitutional rights clear to it, or forever confuses it on the subject.

The only method by which a reasonable and loyal conception of government may be substituted for the one formed upon Russian experiences, is that the actual experience of refugees with government in America shall gradually demonstrate what a very different thing government means here. Such an event as the Averbuch affair affords an unprecedented opportunity to make clear this difference and to demonstrate beyond the possibility of misunderstanding that the guarantee of constitutional rights implies that officialism shall be restrained and guarded at every point, that the official represents, not the will of a small administrative body, but the will of the entire people, and that methods therefore have been constituted by which official aggression may be restrained. The Averbuch incident gave an opportunity to demonstrate this to that very body of people who need it most; to those who have lived in Russia where autocratic officers represent autocratic power and where government is officialism. It seemed to the residents in the Settlements nearest the Russian Jewish colony that it was an obvious piece of public spirit to try out all the legal value involved, to insist that American institutions were stout enough not to break down in times of stress and public panic.

CHAPTER 18
SOCIALIZED EDUCATION

In a paper written years ago I deplored at some length the fact that educational matters are more democratic in their political than in their social aspect. . . .

In line with this declaration, Hull-House in the very beginning opened what we called College Extension classes with a faculty finally numbering thirty-five college men and women, many of whom held their pupils for consecutive years. As these classes antedated in Chicago the University Extension and Normal Extension classes and supplied a demand for stimulating instruction, the attendance strained to their utmost capacity the spacious rooms in the old house. The relation of students and faculty to each other and to the residents was that of guest and hostess and at the close of each term the residents gave a reception to students and faculty which was one of the chief social events of the season. Upon this comfortable social basis some very good work was done. . . .

Every Thursday evening during the first years, a public lecture came to be an expected event in the neighborhood, and Hull-House became one of the early University Extension Centers, first in connection with an independent society and later with the University of Chicago. One of the Hull-House trustees was so impressed with the value of this orderly and continuous presentation of economic subjects that he endowed three courses in a downtown center, in which the lectures were free to any one who chose to come. He was much pleased that these lectures were largely attended by workingmen who ordinarily prefer that an economic subject shall be presented by a partisan, and who are supremely indifferent to examinations and credits. They also dislike the balancing of pro and con which scholarly instruction implies, and prefer to be "inebriated on raw truth" rather than to sip a carefully prepared draught of knowledge.

Nevertheless Bowen Hall, which seats seven hundred and fifty people, is often none too large to hold the audiences of men who come to Hull-House every Sunday evening during the winter to attend the illustrated lectures provided by the faculty of the University of Chicago, and others who kindly give their services. . . .

In spite of the success of these Sunday evening courses, it has never been an easy undertaking to find acceptable lecturers. A course of lectures on astronomy illustrated by stereopticon slides will attract a large audience the first week, who hope to hear of the wonders of the heavens and the relation of our earth thereto, but instead are treated to spectrum analyses of star dust, or the latest theory concerning the Milky Way. The habit of research and the desire to say the latest word upon any subject often overcomes the sympathetic understanding of his audience which the lecturer might otherwise develop, and he insensibly drops into the dull terminology of the classroom. There are, of course, notable exceptions; we had twelve gloriously popular talks on organic evolution, but the lecturer was not yet a professor — merely a university instructor — and his mind was still eager over the marvel of it all. Fortunately there are an increasing number of lecturers whose matter is so real, so definite, and so valuable, that in an attempt to give it an exact equivalence in words, they utilize the most direct forms of expression.

It sometimes seems as if the men of substantial scholarship were content to leave to the charlatan the teaching of those things which deeply concern the welfare of mankind, and that the mass of men get their intellectual food from the outcasts of scholarship, who provide millions of books, pictures, and shows, not to instruct and guide, but for the sake of their own financial profit. A Settlement soon discovers that simple people are interested in large and vital subjects and the Hull-House residents themselves at one time, with only partial success, undertook to give a series of lectures on the history of the world, beginning with the nebular hypothesis and reaching Chicago itself in the twenty-fifth lecture! Absurd as the hasty review appears, there is no doubt that the beginner in knowledge is always eager for the general statement, as those wise old teachers of the people well knew, when they put the history of creation on the stage and the monks themselves became the actors. I recall that in planning my first European journey I had soberly hoped in two years to trace the entire pattern of human excellence as we passed from one country to another, in the shrines popular affection had consecrated to the saints, in the frequented statues erected to heroes, and in the "worn blasonry of funeral brasses," — an illustration that when we are young we all long for those mountain tops upon which we may soberly stand and dream of our own ephemeral and uncertain attempts at righteousness. . . .

The residents of Hull-House place increasing emphasis upon the great inspirations and solaces of literature and are unwilling that it should ever languish as a subject for class instruction or for reading parties. The Shakespeare Club has lived a continuous existence at Hull-House for sixteen years during which time its members have heard the leading interpreters of Shakespeare, both among scholars and players. I recall that one of its earliest members said that her mind was peopled with Shakespeare characters during her long hours of sewing in a shop, that she couldn't remember what she thought about before she joined the club, and concluded that she hadn't thought about anything at all. To feed the mind of the worker, to lift it above the monotony of his task, and to connect it with the larger world, outside of his immediate surroundings, has always been the object of art, perhaps never more nobly fulfilled than by the great English bard. Miss Starr has held classes in Dante and Browning for many years and the great lines are conned with never failing enthusiasm. I recall Miss Lathrop's Plato Club and an audience who listened to a series of lectures by Dr. John Dewey on "Social Psychology," as genuine intellectual groups consisting largely of people from the immediate neighborhood, who were willing to make "that effort from which we all shrink, the effort of thought." But while we prize these classes as we do the help we are able to give to the exceptional young man or woman who reaches the college and university and leaves the neighborhood of his childhood behind him, the residents of Hull-House feel increasingly that the educational efforts of a Settlement should not be directed primarily to reproduce the college type of culture, but to work out a method and an ideal adapted to the immediate situation. They feel that they should promote a culture which will not set its possessor aside in a class with others like himself, but which will, on the contrary, connect him with all sorts of people by his ability to understand them as well as by his power to supplement their present surroundings with the historic background. Among the hundreds of immigrants who have for years attended classes at Hull-House designed primarily to teach the English language, dozens of them have struggled to express in the newly acquired tongue some of those hopes and longings which had so much to do with their emigration. . . .

The teacher in a Settlement is constantly put upon his mettle to discover methods of instruction which shall make knowledge quickly available to his pupils, and I should like here to pay my tribute of admiration to the dean of our educational department, Miss Landsberg,[77] and to the many men and women who every winter come regularly to Hull-House, putting untiring energy into the endless task of teaching the newly arrived immigrant the first use of a language of which he has such desperate need. Even a meager knowledge of English may mean an opportunity to work in a factory *versus* nonemployment, or it may mean a

---

[77] Clara Landsberg (1873–1966) moved to Hull-House in 1899 after graduation from Bryn Mawr College. She was in charge of the settlement's adult education program until 1920 but also served as one of Addams's secretaries, keeping up with correspondence and various writing projects.

question of life or death when a sharp command must be understood in order to avoid the danger of a descending crane.

In response to a demand for an education which should be immediately available, classes have been established and grown apace in cooking, dressmaking, and millinery. A girl who attends them will often say that she "expects to marry a workingman next spring," and because she has worked in a factory so long she knows "little about a house." Sometimes classes are composed of young matrons of like factory experiences. I recall one of them whose husband had become so desperate after two years of her unskilled cooking that he had threatened to desert her and go where he could get "decent food," as she confided to me in a tearful interview, when she followed my advice to take the Hull-House courses in cooking, and at the end of six months reported a united and happy home.

Two distinct trends are found in response to these classes; the first is for domestic training, and the other is for trade teaching which shall enable the poor little milliner and dressmaker apprentices to shorten the two years of errand running which is supposed to teach them their trade.

The beginning of trade instruction has been already evolved in connection with the Hull-House Boys' Club. The ample Boys' Club building presented to Hull-House three years ago by one of our trustees has afforded well-equipped shops for work in wood, iron, and brass; for smithing in copper and tin; for commercial photography, for printing, for telegraphy, and electrical construction. These shops have been filled with boys who are eager for that which seems to give them a clew to the industrial life all about them. These classes meet twice a week and are taught by intelligent workingmen who apparently give the boys what they want better than do the strictly professional teachers. While these classes in no sense provide a trade training, they often enable a boy to discover his aptitude and help him in the selection of what he "wants to be" by reducing the trades to embryonic forms. . . .

It sometimes happens that boys are held in the Hull-House classes for weeks by their desire for the excitement of placing burglar alarms under the door mats. But to enable the possessor of even a little knowledge to thus play with it, is to decoy his feet at least through the first steps of the long, hard road of learning, although even in this, the teacher must proceed warily. A typical street boy who was utterly absorbed in a wood-carving class, abruptly left never to return when he was told to use some simple calculations in the laying out of the points. He evidently scented the approach of his old enemy, arithmetic, and fled the field. On the other hand, we have come across many cases in which boys have vainly tried to secure such opportunities for themselves. During the trial of a boy of ten recently arrested for truancy, it developed that he had spent many hours watching the electrical construction in a downtown building, and many others in the public library "reading about electricity." Another boy who was taken from school early, when his father lost both of his legs in a factory accident, tried in vain to find a place for himself "with machinery." He was declared too small for any such position, and for four years worked as an errand boy, during which time he steadily turned in his unopened pay envelope for the use of the household. At the end of the fourth year the boy disappeared, to the great distress of his invalid father and his poor mother whose day washings became the sole support of the family. He had beaten his way to Kansas City, hoping "they wouldn't be so particular there about a fellow's size." He came back at the end of six weeks because he felt sorry for his mother who, aroused at last to a realization of his unbending purpose, applied for help to the Juvenile Protective Association. They found a position for the boy in a machine shop and an opportunity for evening classes.

Out of the fifteen hundred members of the Hull-House Boys' Club, hundreds seem to respond only to the opportunities for recreation, and many of the older ones apparently care only for the bowling and the billiards. And yet tournaments and match games under supervision and regulated hours are a great advance over the sensual and exhausting pleasures to be found so easily outside the club. These organized sports readily connect themselves with the Hull-House gymnasium and with all those enthusiasms which are so mysteriously aroused by athletics.

Our gymnasium has been filled with large and enthusiastic classes for eighteen years in spite of the popularity of dancing and other possible substitutes, while the Saturday evening athletic contests have become a feature of the neighborhood. The Settlement strives for that type of gymnastics which is at least partly a matter of character, for that training which presupposes abstinence and the curbing of impulse, as well as for those athletic contests in which the mind of the contestant must be vigilant to keep the body closely to the rules of the game. . . .

When the men and boys from the Hull-House gymnasium bring back their cups and medals, one's mind is filled with something like foreboding in the reflection that too much success may lead the winners into that professionalism which is so associated with betting and so close to pugilism. Candor, however, compels me to state that a long acquaintance with the acrobatic folk who have to do with the circus, a large number of whom practice in our gymnasium every winter, has raised our estimate of that profession.

Young people who work long hours at sedentary occupations, factories and offices, need perhaps more than anything else the freedom and ease to be acquired from a symmetrical muscular development and are quick to respond to that fellowship which athletics apparently afford more easily than anything else. The Greek immigrants form large classes and are eager to reproduce the remnants of old methods of wrestling, and other bits of classic lore which they still possess, and when one of the Greeks won a medal in a wrestling match which represented the championship of the entire city, it was quite impossible that he should present it to the Hull-House trophy chest without a classic phrase which he recited most gravely and charmingly.

It was in connection with a large association of Greek lads that Hull-House finally lifted its long restriction against military drill. If athletic contests are the residuum of warfare first waged against the conqueror without and then against the tyrants within the State, the modern Greek youth is still in the first stage so far as his inherited attitude against the Turk is concerned. Each lad believes that at any moment he may be called home to fight this long time enemy of Greece. With such a genuine motive at hand, it seemed mere affectation to deny the use of our Boys' Club building and gymnasium for organized drill, although happily it forms but a small part of the activities of the Greek Educational Association.

Having thus confessed to military drill countenanced if not encouraged at Hull-House, it is perhaps only fair to relate an early experience of mine with the "Columbian Guards," an organization of the World's Fair summer. Although the Hull-House squad was organized as the others were with the motto of a clean city, it was very anxious for military drill. This request not only shocked my nonresistant principles, but seemed to afford an opportunity to find a substitute for the military tactics which were used in the boys' brigades everywhere, even in those connected with churches. As the cleaning of the filthy streets and alleys was the ostensible purpose of the Columbian Guards, I suggested to the boys that we work out a drill with sewer spades, which with their long narrow blades and shortened handles were not so unlike bayoneted guns in size, weight, and general appearance, but that much of the usual military drill could be readapted. While I myself was present at the gymnasium to explain that it was nobler to drill in imitation of removing disease-breeding filth than to drill in simulation of warfare; while I distractedly readapted tales of chivalry to this modern rescuing of the endangered and distressed, the new drill went forward in some sort of fashion, but so surely as I withdrew, the drillmaster would complain that our troops would first grow self-conscious, then demoralized, and finally flatly refuse to go on. Throughout the years since the failure of this quixotic experiment, I occasionally find one of these sewer spades in a Hull-House storeroom, too truncated to be used for its original purpose and too prosaic to serve the purpose for which it was bought. I can only look at it in the forlorn hope that it may foreshadow that piping time when the weapons of warfare shall be turned into the implements of civic salvation. . . .

Throughout the history of Hull-House many inquiries have been made concerning the religion of the residents, and the reply that they are as diversified in belief and in the ardor of the inner life as any like number of people in a college or similar group, apparently does not carry conviction. I recall that after a house for men residents had been opened on Polk Street and the residential force at Hull-House numbered twenty, we made an effort to come together on Sunday evenings in a household service, hoping thus to express our moral unity in spite of the fact that we represented many creeds. But although all of us reverently knelt when the High Church resident read the evening service and bowed our heads when the evangelical resident led in prayer after his chapter, and although we sat respectfully through the twilight when a resident read her favorite passages from Plato and another from Abt Vogler, we concluded at the end of the winter that this was not religious fellowship and that we did not care for another reading club. So it was reluctantly given up, and we found that it was quite as necessary to come together on the basis of the deed and our common aim inside the household as it was in the neighborhood itself. I once had a conversation on the subject with the warden of Oxford House, who kindly invited me to the evening service held for the residents in a little chapel on the top floor of the Settlement. All the residents were High Churchmen to whom the service was an important and reverent part of the day. Upon my reply to a query of the warden that the residents of Hull-House could not come together for religious worship because there were among us Jews, Roman Catholics, English Churchmen, Dissenters, and a few agnostics, and that we had found unsatisfactory the diluted form of worship which we could carry on together, he replied that it must be most difficult to work with a group so diversified, for he depended upon the evening service to clear away any difficulties which the day had involved and to bring the residents to a religious consciousness of their common aim. I replied that this diversity of creed was part of the situation in American Settlements, as it was our task to live in a neighborhood of many nationalities and faiths, and that it might be possible that among such diversified people it was

The Residents' Dining Hall was one of the first additions built on to Hull-House. Addams knew that the settlement's collective spirit needed to be encouraged by regular gatherings for meals and conversation. In this photo, taken around 1930, Addams is pictured on the right, at the head of the back table. Every evening she was in Chicago, she presided over dinner at Hull-House. Always seated among the residents were visitors from around the city, the U.S., and the world.

Jane Addams Memorial Collection, Special Collections, The University Library, The University of Illinois at Chicago.

better that the Settlement corps should also represent varying religious beliefs.

A wise man has told us that "men are once for all so made that they prefer a rational world to believe in and to live in," but that it is no easy matter to find a world rational as to its intellectual, aesthetic, moral, and practical aspects. Certainly it is no easy matter if the place selected is of the very sort where the four aspects are apparently furthest from perfection, but an undertaking resembling this is what the Settlement gradually becomes committed to, as its function is revealed through the reaction on its consciousness of its own experiences. Because of this fourfold undertaking, the Settlement has gathered into residence people of widely diversified tastes and interests and in Hull-House, at least, the group has been surprisingly permanent. The majority of the present corps of forty residents support themselves by their business and professional occupations in the city giving only their leisure time to Settlement undertakings. This in itself tends to continuity of residence and has certain advantages. Among the present staff of whom the larger number have been in residence for more than twelve years, there are the secretary of the City Club, two practicing physicians, several attorneys, newspaper men, business men, teachers, scientists, artists, musicians, lecturers in the School of Civics and Philanthropy, officers in the Juvenile Protective Association and in the League for the Protection of Immigrants, a visiting nurse, a sanitary inspector, and others.

We have also worked out during our years of residence a plan of living which may be called coöperative, for the families and individuals who rent the Hull-House apartments have the use of the central kitchen and dining room so far as they care for them; many of them work for hours every week in the studios and shops; the theater and drawing-rooms are available for such social organization as they care to form; the entire group of thirteen buildings is heated and lighted from a central plant. During the years, the common human experiences have gathered about the House; funeral services have been held there, marriages and christenings, and many memories hold us to each other as well as to our neighbors. Each resident, of course, carefully defrays his own expenses, and his relations to his fellow residents are not unlike those of a college professor to his colleagues. The depth and strength of his relation to the neighborhood must depend very largely upon himself and upon the genuine friendships he has been able to make. His relation to the city as a whole comes largely through his identification with those groups who are carrying forward the reforms which a Settlement neighborhood so sadly needs and with which residence has made him familiar.

Life in the Settlement discovers above all what has been called "the extraordinary pliability of human nature," and it seems impossible to set any bounds to the moral capabilities which might unfold under ideal civic and educational conditions. But in order to obtain these conditions, the Settlement recognizes the need of coöperation, both with the radical and the conservative, and from the very nature of the case the Settlement cannot limit its friends to any one political party or economic school.

The Settlement casts aside none of those things which cultivated men have come to consider reasonable and goodly, but it insists that those belong as well to that great body of people who, because of toilsome and underpaid labor, are unable to procure them for themselves. Added to this is a profound conviction that the common stock of intellectual enjoyment should not be difficult of access because of the economic position of him who would approach it, that those "best results of civilization" upon which depend the finer and freer aspects of living must be incorporated into our common life and have free mobility through all elements of society if we would have our democracy endure.

The educational activities of a Settlement, as well as its philanthropic, civic, and social undertakings, are but differing manifestations of the attempt to socialize democracy, as is the very existence of the Settlement itself.

PART THREE

Related Documents

1

Hull-House Weekly Program

March 1, 1892

*A Social Settlement
at 335 So. Halsted Street, Chicago*

Weekly Program of Lectures, Clubs, Classes, Etc.

The best way to imagine the breadth of programs and level of activity at Hull-House is to read through the settlement's weekly schedule. The schedule provided here is from 1892 — just three years after Jane Addams and Ellen Gates Starr opened Hull-House. Schedules from later years would run to several more pages. This document invites multiple interpretations. For example, what do you make of the fact that Jane Addams's name appears in only two places in the schedule — as the secretary of the "Working People's Social Science Club" and as the convenor of "The Pansy Club," one of the settlement's social clubs for school girls? And if her name is not on the weekly program, what other sources could you consult to find out what she did all day? Addams did not teach classes, but a visitor to Hull-House during this week in 1892 could have taken classes from a wide assortment of individuals. What significance do you place on the evidence here that Hull-House neighbors in March of 1892 could take classes from a University of Chicago professor (John Dewey), a divorced Socialist (Florence Kelley), a wealthy, volunteer socialite (Mary Wilmarth), a labor leader (Samuel Gompers), or a capitalist (George F. Stone)?

EVENINGS

Monday

Hull-House Social Club — Drawing Room — 8 to 10

This club has a membership of thirty girls, between the ages of sixteen and twenty, who have met every week for two years. The primary object of the club is profitable social intercourse. The first hour of each evening is devoted to reading and discussion; the second to amusement, in which they are joined by the members of the Debating Club. Dancing every fourth Monday. Miss McDowell is at present the leading honorary member.

Hull-House Debating Club — Art Exhibit Room, Butler Gallery — 8 to 10

This club has a membership of thirty young men, who have met weekly for a year. They devote the first hour of each evening to debates, largely upon topics of national and municipal interest; the second hour they join the Hull-House Social Club. This Club has its own officers, elected for a term of three months. Mr. Robert Hamill is the honorary member.

Men's Athletic Class — Gymnasium — 8 to 10

Mr. Frank Eikenkoeter, Director.

Drawing Class — Studio — 7:30 to 9:30

Mr. R. P. Lamont (B.S. University of Michigan).

Greek Art — Reception Room (College Extension)

Miss Ellen Gates Starr.

Arithmetic, Geometry — Dining Room — 7 to 8; 8 to 9 (College Extension)

Mr. A. M. Underwood (A.B. Williams College).

English Composition — Octagon — 8 to 9 (College Extension)

Miss Ada Woolfolk (B.S. Wellesley College).

Tuesday

Working People's Social Science Club — Drawing Room — 8 to 10

This club was organized at Hull-House in April, 1890, and has met weekly, except during the months of July and August, since that time. An address of forty-five minutes' length on some subject relating to economics, is followed by an hour of free discussion. The Club has only one permanent officer — the Secretary. The Chairman is elected for one evening only. Speakers are secured by the Executive Committee. The Club has collected a small library of books and pamphlets for circulation among its members.

SECRETARY: Jane Addams.

EXECUTIVE COMMITTEE: Alexander A. McCormick, T. W. Crowell, Jane Addams.

PROGRAM FOR TWELVE WEEKS.

Feb. 2	"Child Labor"	Mrs. Florence Kelley.
Feb. 9	"Our Jury System"	Mr. Sigmund Zeisler.
Feb. 16	"The Chicago Police"	Major R. R. McClaughry, Supt. of Police.
Feb. 23	"Labor Organizations"	Mr. Samuel Gompers Pres. American Federation of Labor.
Mar. 1	"Competition"	Col. Aldace F. Walker, Chairman Western Traffic Association.
Mar. 8	"Single Tax"	Mr. John Z. White.
Mar. 15	"Some Phases of Business Done on the Chicago Board of Trade"	Mr. George F. Stone, Sec'y Board of Trade.
Mar. 22	"Rules of the House"	Hon. George E. Adams, Pres. Union League Club.
Mar. 29	"The Cook County Courts"	Judge M. F. Tuley.
April 5	"What Can the Law Do for the Poor Man"	Mr. I. K. Boyesen.
April 12	"The Cook County House of Correction"	Mr. Mark Crawford, Supt. of Bridewell.
April 19	"The Municipal Control of Heat, Light, and Transportation"	Col. Augustus Jacobson.

The Young Citizens' Club — Gymnasium — 7:30 to 9:30

This Club has a membership limited to thirty. Its members are boys between fourteen and eighteen years of age. Most of them have belonged to the Club for two years. The first hour is given to gymnastics; the second to discussion of subjects supposed to be of interest to young citizens. This Club occasionally gives a "party" to its friends.

Mr. Frank Nichols and Mr. William Monroe are the "advisory committee" of the Young Citizens' Club.

Drawing — Studio, Butler Gallery — 7 to 9

Miss Belle Barnum.

Cooking Class — Diet Kitchen — 7 to 9

Miss Fanny Gary.

American History — Art Exhibit Room, Butler Gallery — 8 to 9 (College Extension)

Mr. Wm. H. Day (A.B. Amherst College).

Reading Party — Reception Room — 8 to 9 (Lowell: "Bigelow Papers")

Mr. Allen B. Pond (A.B. University of Michigan).

Cæsar — Octagon — 7 to 8 (College Extension)

Mr. Louis M. Greeley (A.B. Harvard College).

Latin Grammar — Dining Room — 7 to 8 (College Extension)

Mr. C. C. Arnold (A.B. Hamilton College).

Political Economy — Dining Room — 8 to 9 (College Extension)

Miss Alice M. Miller (A.B. Smith College).

Modern History — Upper Hall — 7:30 to 8:30 (College Extension)

Miss Mary Ware Howe (B.S. Wellesley College).

Wednesday

Drawing — Studio, Butler Gallery — 7:30 to 9 (College Extension)

Miss Alice D. Kellogg.

Classes in Singing — Drawing Room — 7 to 9 (College Extension)

Miss Eleanor Smith.

Needlework (German Method) — Art Exhibit Room, Butler Gallery — 7 to 9

Fraulein Amalie Hannig.

Reading Party, "Felix Holt"— Octagon — 7 to 8 (College Extension)
Miss Jane Addams (B.A. Rockford Seminary).

Hull-House Columbian Guards — Gymnasium — 7 to 8
Drillmaster, Mr. T. W. Allinson.
Civic Instructor, Mr. J. P. Cary.
The Columbian Guards is a company of twenty-five lads who are organized under the constitution issued by the Municipal Order Committee of the World's Fair Auxiliary. They are pledged to good citizenship and a clean city.

Mothers' Evening Club — Diet Kitchen — 7:30 to 9
This Club is composed of women who are occupied during the day. They have at present elected a course in cooking with Miss Nason as teacher. Other courses will follow.

Women's Gymnastic Classes — Gymnasium — 8 to 9 (For College Extension Students)
Miss Isabel Stone.
Pianist, Miss Sophie Ware.

Physiography — Reception Room — 8 to 9 (College Extension)
Mr. R. M. Bissell (A.B. Yale College).

Biology — Reception Room — 8 to 9 (College Extension)
Dr. Hardie (A.B. University of Toronto).
(The two subjects above alternate weekly.)

Arithmetic — Dining Room — 7 to 9
I Division, Mr. Seymour Coman.
II Division, Mr. Ernest Geoghegan.

Algebra-Advanced — Upper Hall — 7 to 8 (College Extension)
Miss Isabel Stone (B.A. Wellesley College).

Thursday

Shakespeare (Hamlet) — Drawing Room — 7 to 8 (College Extension)
Miss Ellen Gates Starr.

Algebra — Dining Room — 7 to 8 (College Extension)
Mr. R. M. Bissell (A.B. Yale College).

Lecture or Concert — Drawing Room — 8 to 9

PROGRAM FOR TWELVE WEEKS.

Jan. 14	"Socrates"	Mr. Chas. F. Bradley, Prof. of Biblical Exegesis, Northwestern University.
Jan. 21	"Psychology and History"	Mr. John Dewey, Prof. of Psychology, University of Michigan.
Jan. 28	"Classic Art" (*Illustrated by Stereopticon*)	Mr. Lorado Taft.
Feb. 4	"Concert" — Schubert	Songs, Miss Eleanor Smith. Piano, Miss Katharine Lyon.
Feb. 11	"The French Metric System"	Mr. Sam'l S. Greeley.
Feb. 18	"American Politics Before the Revolution"	Mr. Homer Kingsley.
Feb. 25	"Concert" — Schumann	Songs, Miss Eleanor Smith. Piano, Miss Katharine Lyon.
Mar. 3	"Lilies and Ferns, Their Life Histories"	Mr. C. B. Atwell, Prof. of Biology (Northwestern University).
Mar. 10	"Victor Hugo and His Times"	Mrs. Mary H. Wilmarth.
Mar. 17	"The Influence of French Women in Politics"	Mrs. Charles S. Henrotin.
Mar. 24	Concert — Organ Recital	At the house of Mrs. John C. Coonley, Cor. Division St. and Lake Shore Drive.
Mar. 31	Reception for College Extension Faculty and Students.	

Hull-House Athletic Club — Gymnasium — 7:30 to 9:30

This Club has existed for two years with the same membership under various names. The members, thirty in number, are girls from fourteen to sixteen years of age. After an hour of gymnastics they read and discuss matters of interest to the Club.

Gymnastic Teacher, Miss Savage.

Pianist, Miss Henry.

Miss Farnsworth has charge of the Club.

Cooking Class — Diet Kitchen — 7:30 to 9
Miss Allen.

Friday

Reception to Germans — Drawing Room — 8 to 10
Fraulein Neuschafer and the residents receive. The evening is entirely social in character, music and the reading of German literature, or history, occupying a part of the time. A small German library is at the disposal of the guests.

German-Advanced — Octagon — 7 to 8 (College Extension)
Fraulein Neuschafer.

English Literature — Octagon — 8 to 9 (College Extension)
Miss Julia C. Lathrop (B.A. Vassar College).

Chemistry – with Experiments — Studio — 7 to 8 (College Extension)
Miss Harriet Stone (B.A. Wellesley College).

Electricity – with Experiments — Studio — 8 to 9 (College Extension)
Mr. L. K. Comstock (Ph.D. University of Michigan).

*French – Elementary and Advanced — Dining Room — 7 to 9
(College Extension)*
Mrs. Mary H. Wilmarth.

*German Elementary — Art Exhibit Room, Butler Gallery — 7:30 to 8:30
(College Extension)*
Mrs. Florence Kelley.

Men's Gymnastic Class — Gymnasium — 7:30 to 9
Mr. Arthur Probst (B.L. Cornell University).

Saturday

Clay Modeling — Studio, Butler Gallery — 7:30 to 9
Miss Julia Brachen.

English Class for Italians — Dining Room — 7 to 9
Miss Julia M. Hintermeister.
Receptions for Italians are held from time to time on Saturday evenings. The celebration of Italian holidays is observed.

Meeting of the Shirt-Makers Protective Union — On the second and fourth Saturdays of each month — Drawing Room — 8 to 10

This Union was organized at Hull-House by Miss Mary E. Kenney, President of the "Bookbinders' Union." The second Saturday of each month is devoted to business of the Union; the fourth to lectures.

Women's Gymnastic Classes — Gymnasium — 8 to 9:30 (For members of the Bookbinders' and Shirtmakers' Unions).

Teacher, Miss Willard.
Pianist, Miss Emmert.

AFTERNOONS

Monday

Sewing Classes for Italian Girls — 3:30 to 5

Total membership, one hundred and twenty.

Dining Room

Mrs. Rand; Mrs. Hutchinson; Mrs. Briarly; Mrs. Amory.

Drawing Room

1st Class, Misses Head.
2d Class, Miss Barnum; Miss Ashton.
3d Class, Mrs. Bideleaux.
4th Class, Miss Peasley; Miss McCormick.
5th Class, Miss Woolfolk.
6th Class, Miss Booth.

Boys' Class in Gymnastics — Gymnasium — 4:30 to 5:30

Mr. Edward Bideleaux.

Class Lesson on Piano — Day Nursery

Miss Lyon.

Tuesday

School Boys' Clubs — 3:30 to 5

Average membership in each Club and Division — twenty.

Fairy Story Club — Octagon

Miss Farnsworth.

Jolly Boys' Club — Dining Room
Miss Trowbridge.

Kindergarten Club — Reception Room
Miss Dow.

Red Stars — Drawing Room
I Division, Miss Howe.
II Division, Mrs. McCabe.
III Division, Miss Kales.
IV Division, Miss Baker.

Reading Party — Upper Hall — 4 to 5 (Hawthorne)
Miss Miller.

Latin Class-Ovid — Octagon — 5 to 6 (College Extension)
Miss Alice M. Miller (B.A. Smith College).

Drawing Class — Studio, Butler Gallery — 3:30 to 5
Miss Barnum.

Wednesday

History of Mediæval Art — Drawing Room — 4 to 5 (Teachers' Class)
Miss Starr.

Thursday

Hull-House Woman's Club — Drawing Room — 2 to 3:30
The members of this Club meet weekly. The object is the discussion of household economics, and the study of child nature. They hope to collect statistics in regard to the comparative costs of food, fuel, etc.

Class Lessons on Piano — Drawing Room — 3:30 to 5
Miss Lyon.

Friday

Classes and Clubs of School Girls — 3:30 to 4
Total membership, one hundred and fifty.

Darning Class — Octagon
Miss Antisdel; Miss Runnels.

Sewing Class — Dining Room
Miss Cook; Mrs. Exstromer.

Pansy Club — Reception Room
Miss Addams.

Gymnastic Classes — Gymnasium
Teacher, Miss Sproat.
Pianist, Miss Adams.

Cooking Class — Diet Kitchen
Miss Kinnear.

Crocheting Class — Drawing Room
Miss Higginson.

Story-Telling Club
Miss Dow; Miss Caroline Howe.

Saturday

Painting (Oil) — Studio, Butler Gallery — 2 to 4 (College Extension)
Miss Price.

Demonstration Lesson in Sick-Room Cooking — Diet Kitchen — 2 to 4:30
Miss Nason.

Sunday

Concerts — Drawing Room — 4 to 5
There have been a series of twenty concerts given by various musicians and musical clubs of the City.

Plato Club — Reception Room — 5 to 6
Miss Lathrop.
This Club has a small membership who meet every Sunday afternoon to read philosophic essays.

The College Extension department is quite distinct from the other departments of Hull-House. It is designed for students who desire the advantages of higher education but whose necessities prevent them from going to colleges or giving the hours of the day to study. A few of the students are preparing for college. Its purpose is identical with that of the

University Extension Movement. The students pay a fee of fifty cents a term, which covers all expenses connected with the course, as the teaching, chiefly by college graduates, is voluntary. The present term is the sixth term of College Extension work at Hull-House. The present number of matriculated students is 182.

The upper floor of the Butler Gallery is divided into an Art Exhibit Room and a Studio. Three art exhibits have been held in the former. The building was opened for the first exhibit in June, 1891, at which time Mr. Barnett, Warden of Toynbee Hall, gave an address on Popular Art Exhibits. The attendance at these exhibits has averaged three hundred persons a day, the exhibit being on for two weeks and open daily from 3 to 10 P.M. The two exhibits of oil paintings included the works of Corot, Cazin, Watts, Davis, etc, which were loaned by Mr. Charles L. Hutchinson, The Art Institute, Mr. E. B. Butler, Rev. Frank Bristol and others. A valuable collection of etchings and engravings, belonging to Mr. Charles Hamill, has also been exhibited.

The Butler Gallery has the lower floor fitted up for a Public Reading Room. It is a branch station of the City Public Library and is supplied by the Board with 400 books, with 60 periodicals and the services of two librarians. It is subject to the usual regulations of branch reading rooms and books are taken to and received from the Central City library twice a day. It is open daily from 9 A.M. to 10 P.M., on Sunday from 10 A.M. to 10 P.M.

A Summer School was held in Rockford Seminary, Rockford, Ill., during the month of July, 1891. The faculty and students, with few exceptions, were members of the Hull-House College Extension Course, and many of the usual classes and lectures were continued. The course was diversified by the outdoor study of birds and botany, lessons in lawn tennis, etc. The trustees of Rockford Seminary gave the use of the buildings and appurtenances free of rent. A charge of two dollars a week covered the boarding expenses with an average attendance of seventy-five students.

A Kindergarten of thirty-five children is held every morning in the Hull-House drawing-room.

Director, Miss McDowell.

Five Bathrooms have been erected in the wing of Hull-House. They are open daily for the use of those who have no bathing facilities in their own houses.

A Stamp Station of the Penny Provident Fund has lately been opened for the benefit of the members of the Children's Clubs. Miss Farnsworth is in charge of the station.

The Hull-House Day Nursery occupies a cottage at 221 Ewing Street. The average attendance in 1892 has been 24 children a day. A charge of five cents is made for each child.

Supt. of Nursery, Miss McKee.

Assistant, Mrs. Losfelt.

The Nursery has a daily Kindergarten.

Director, Miss Brockway.

A Hull-House Diet Kitchen has been opened in the rear cottage at 221 Ewing Street. Foods for the sick are prepared daily by Miss Edith Nason, who is a graduate of St. Luke's Training School. Orders are received daily between 9 A.M. and 6 P.M. The foods are divided into broths, gruels, porridges, soups and delicacies, a list of which is supplied to the physicians and nurses of the neighborhood. A charge is made for the materials used. Miss Nason, who lives at Hull-House, spends her mornings in district nursing for the Visiting Nurses' Association. Her afternoons are given to the care of the Diet Kitchen.

Miss Lathrop, a resident of Hull-House, has received an honorary appointment from the Cook County Commissioners as a County Visitor. She reports daily to the County Agency. An effort is made in all the relief work of Hull-House to pursue Charity Organization methods. Mrs. C. H. Walker, Mrs. Thos. Gane and others assist weekly.

A Bureau for Woman's Labor has been opened in an office adjoining Hull-House under the charge of Mrs. Florence Kelley, and is open from 7 A.M. to 9 P.M. It supplies labor for factories, offices and stores, as well as households, but aims to bring the latter under more dignified conditions than at present prevail. In pursuance of this policy, from time to time courses of twelve daily lessons are given in the Hull-House Diet Kitchen. These lessons are designed for young women wishing to use their skill in household labor. Lectures on the proper care of little children are also given in the Day Nursery.

Residents,

JANE ADDAMS,
ELLEN GATES STARR,
ANNA M. FARNSWORTH,
JULIA C. LATHROP.

2

FLORENCE KELLEY

Hull-House

New England Magazine, July 1898

Florence Kelley went to live in Hull-House in the winter of 1891. She brought with her all the skills and ideas gained from life with her father, Philadelphia's pro-labor congressman, William "Pig Iron" Kelley, her undergraduate work at Cornell University, her graduate work at the University of Zurich, and her immersion in the European socialist movement, which included translating Friedrich Engels's The Condition of the Working Class in England *in 1886. Having escaped an abusive marriage, Kelley also brought three small children with her to Hull-House.*

There was an ongoing argument at Hull-House, particularly in the 1890s, about the value of charity work versus broad social action. As a socialist, Kelley favored the latter: labor organizing, legislative lobbying, and political campaigns. But by the time she wrote this article for New England Magazine, *Kelley had lived at Hull-House for seven years and had been persuaded by her experience that a certain amount of charity work was necessary for broad social action.*

The genteel eastern reformers who read this magazine were more comfortable with charity work than socialism. In this article, Kelley employed all the tact and debate skills she learned as a politician's daughter and Cornell student. On the one hand, she wanted to convince her readers of the value of broad social reform without alarming them. On the other hand, she wanted to argue with her socialist allies who often scoffed at the "detail work" performed at Hull-House because they regarded such work as petty philanthropy unrelated to serious social action. In reading Kelley's words, note the argument she made to resolve the genuine conflict between hands-on, daily work in the neighborhood and fundamental political and economic change. Think, as well, about who might have been more persuaded by Kelley's argument, the genteel readers of New England Magazine *or Chicago's socialists. Keep in mind that Kelley was able, during the 1890s, to move Hull-House beyond the neighborhood and into more political and legal lobbying. How does this article show Kelley's appreciation for the importance of "detail work" in building a community base for such lobbying?*

New England Magazine n.s. 18 (July 1898): 550–65.

The object of Hull-House, as stated in its charter and printed at the head of the *Bulletin* issued every month, is "to provide a centre for a higher civic and social life to institute and maintain educational and philanthropic enterprises, and to investigate and improve the conditions in the industrial districts of Chicago."

The question is often asked whether all that the House undertakes could not be accomplished without the wear and tear of living on the spot. The answer that it could not, grows more assured as time goes on. You must suffer from the dirty streets, the universal ugliness, the lack of oxygen in the air you daily breathe, the endless struggle with soot and dust and insufficient water supply, the hanging from a strap of the overcrowded street car at the end of your day's work: you must send your children to the nearest wretchedly crowded school, and see them suffer the consequences, if you are to speak as one having authority and not as the scribes in these matters of the common, daily life and experience. Beyond this, there are many things which you can learn only by way of neighborly contact. For even the resident of longest experience does not suffer hunger and cold because trade is bad and the factories are closed or running half time; does not see the children of the family hungry because the county agent manages the relief funds badly and the county refuses either to give relief if there is an able bodied man in the family or to furnish him work even in the dead of winter.

A settlement neighborhood, like all the humbler life of America, suffers from the continual loss of its abler members. The better educated sons and daughters move away; the more energetic and enterprising immigrants stay but a relatively short time. Virtually a whole street of thrifty Bohemians have moved away out upon the open prairie since the Hull-House maps were made in 1893. The ceaseless inflow of new comers from the countries of southern Europe, the ceaseless settling of residual elements from more prosperous districts, tend to keep the population on a dead level at the foot of the ladder which all are hoping to climb, each for himself, with no thought of any united effort for the common good. Nowhere is the individual so left to himself as in the cosmopolite medley of a great working class district in an American city; and nowhere does the devil clutch more voraciously after the hindmost.

Under these conditions, if the neighbor to whom you are attached is out of work, if you are suffering from the bad alleys, you try not only more unweariedly, but with greater effect, both to get the alleys put right and your neighbor set at work, than you could do if you lived afar and had no common cause. If you go to the mayor and to your alderman to complain of your own grievances, you incidentally voice your inarticulate neighbors' need as you could not do if you were merely on a committee from some other part of the city, self appointed to look after his welfare; and you are in a position to stir your inarticulate neighbor to continue to do the same thing after you are dead and forgotten. The isolation, the apathy, the lack of initiative, the social downdraft, as it has been well called, that unsocialize a great industrial neighborhood, cannot be replaced with light and life by any spasmodic effort. Only when the whole community persistently does its part can the slum be outgrown and transformed, as the ugly stages of the hobbledehoy are outgrown and left behind in growing manhood; while for arousing the whole community to do its part, surely the resident group contributes a stimulus limited in value only by the interpretative skill and wisdom of the residents. . . .

The fact that Miss Addams is already, by virtue of eight years' residence at Hull-House, an older inhabitant than many of the neighbors, and that all feel assured that she is identified for life with the House and the neighborhood, gives the element of permanence to the Settlement, despite the fact that it is made up of shifting relays of sojourners in a district whose population is forever shifting.

An enterprise, started in warm enthusiasm by a resident, goes on long after that resident has dropped it. Perhaps the form may vary if the neighborhood need demands a modification of the original plan; but the difficulties of the initial steps having been met by the temporary sojourner, the undertaking remains, a real gain. . . .

Nor is immediate local work in and for the neighborhood rigidly exacted of the resident. The student, whether a coming doctor of philosophy gathering material for a thesis in sociology by invading the neighboring sweatshops, or a "medical" using the House telephone for communicating with the family of the patient, or a journalist honestly trying to learn whereby the press may make amends for the daily damage wrought by its scareheads, or the laborious gatherer of data bearing upon municipal affairs as they affect the workers,— in whatever capacity students have knocked at the door, and however slight their immediate availability for neighborhood uses, they have been made welcome and bidden stay, because the Settlement believes that the trained mind working upon social problems must in the long run make valuable contribution towards their solution. . . .

Wide hospitality has naturally led to rapid growth. When the House was filled to overflowing, a neighboring tenement served as annex until the roof of the House could be raised and a third story added affording place for seven residents. Another overflow led to the raising of another roof and the addition of five rooms for men in the Butler Gallery wing. During the last winter there have been five and twenty residents, and for the third time a waiting list and the beginnings of a group in a neighboring tenement await the building of more ample quarters. To guard against the spread of misinformation in the name of Hull-House by casual sojourners prone to generalize upon trivial observation, the rule was adopted in 1893 that candidates must first stay six weeks and then, if voted in, not less than six months. In fact, the term of residence varies from the eight years of the founders down through terms of six, four, three and two years, shared by a majority of the residents, to a few newcomers still in their first year.

A curious study might be made of the experiments in hospitality, of which during eight years many have succeeded and few have failed, although as in the case of the Coffee House the final success may have taken a form quite different from that which filled the imagination of the residents who toiled over its beginnings. A good example is the Free Public Bath, direct successor of five tubs which once occupied the cellar and laundry and rendered service to neighbors in search of the purification prescribed by their ritual or seeking a supply of the city water when it failed to rise above the first floor of their houses. The hot water often gave out and when it did not, five tubs were naturally insufficient for the needs of several thousand families living in tubless houses in the soot of a manufacturing district blackened by soft coal. When the Hull-House gymnasium was opened in 1893, a dozen showers for the use of the classes were provided. But the eagerness of the neighbors for bathing facilities was so superabundantly proved by experiment, that it was clearly worth while to spend the effort, time and patience required for getting a free public bath for the use of all. A society had been at work for many months with the general aim of obtaining a free public bath. The mere work of securing its location in the neighborhood after money had been appropriated by the Council cost not less than twenty interviews with the mayor, the Council committee, the city architect, and the landowner, who generously gave his land at a nominal price. In November, 1893, the Carter H. Harrison Free Public Bath was opened about a block away from Hull-House, with seventeen showers, a tub and swimming tank, which latter has unhappily never been used, though no convincing reason has been assigned for the failure to make this great pleasure available. About one hundred thousand baths a year are given in the public bath. After its opening the Hull-House tubs made way for a more spacious dining-room; and to-day only the older residents of the House and the neighborhood have any recollection of one of the most useful forms of hospitality attempted at Hull-House.

The little lending library, from which boys and girls borrowed books in 1889 and 1890, involved not only obtaining and administering the books, but receiving in the House hordes of children, whose comings and goings it was far from easy to keep upon the agreeable footing of hosts and guests. The effort, however, so clearly showed the eagerness of the children and their parents to use books, that a Chicago merchant was found willing to pay for a good brick building for the purpose, if the Free Public Library would furnish the books and librarians for a branch reading room. This was done in 1891, and in three years the number of readers grew so large that the reading room was removed to a store front near by, accommodating twice as many people, its entire maintenance being assumed by the city. Like the bath, the reading room is now a part of the life of the neighborhood, and could not be taken away from it. In neither case did the initiative come from the neighborhood, to whose mind baths and books, however eagerly accepted when offered, had not presented themselves as functions of the municipal life to be induced by agitation. In both cases the offer was made in a small way from neighbor to neighbor, and when the response showed the existence of an active constituency, it was the presentation of the situation by residents of Hull-House which induced the city government to extend its functions into previously neglected territory. . . .

Certain it is, that such work cannot be done from a distance, and that the mixed motives involved in doing one's duty more readily in company with a good friend are very powerful in the neighborhood and must be taken into account in every movement which rests upon an appeal to the abstract sense of right, the abstract conception of duty, civic or otherwise. It is incomparably easier to enlist friends and neighbors than mere fellow citizens in any public work.

The playground, crèche, kindergarten, college extension classes, popular lectures, political campaign meetings in the gymnasium, the thirty clubs of men, women, boys and girls, the Sunday concerts, children's chorus and all the other activities of the House serve their best purpose, perhaps, indirectly. From the very fact that they are concentrated in one place and focus the social, civic and educational life of the ward at a centre to which many individuals are bound by ties of personal attachment they bring into real neighborhood life people who, sharing in common only the narrowing experience of poverty and social disadvantage, are farther held apart by differences of race, religion, traditions, manners and customs.

When the Men's Club circulates petitions for a new school, when the Women's Club sends a delegation to the meeting of the Board of Education to ask for the new school, when they vote money out of their dues to place a good photograph in the nearest primary building, when one of the clubs of older children votes from its treasury money to send a sick member for a long holiday, all these things grow up naturally from the habit of social living. But the habit of social living itself does not grow up spontaneously; it requires an established, recognized social centre, where the current of social life flows strongly and natures inclining to isolation and passivity are swept into the activity of common interests. One key to the growth of the House is probably the fact that many residents have taken active part in those municipal, social and labor movements which bear indirectly as well as directly upon the life of the neighborhood. The Arbitration Congress, the Child Labor law, the garment workers' strike, the Charity Organization Society, the Civic Federation, the Chicago Women's Club and many other elements of the life of the city and state have made heavy demands upon the energies of the House. On the other hand, much of the detail work of the House, which to the uninitiated seems to be its chief reason for being, is forced upon it by the lack of equipment in Chicago for such work. A vast amount of personal charitable endeavor has, of necessity, been done by residents, for which old, established, efficient agencies exist in the older cities.

The persistent, honest effort of the House to do the impossible in its own neighborhood insures a respectful hearing when a resident insists that Chicago can no longer do without some systematic provision for tuberculous patients; that the epileptics have no adequate colony, home or hospital; that the parental school is a crying necessity for the boys who are now naughty, will soon be bad, and must end as criminals, if the city continues to fail in this duty as it has hitherto failed. Because a resident is in daily attendance at the nearest police court, the opinion of the House is founded upon a close acquaintance with the facts; and because this opinion comes from the House, carrying the weight of its reputation for sane and careful statement, the evidence of the individual resident who has gathered it finds a hearing impossible to an investigator from a distance, however patient and careful. This voicing the needs of the neighborhood is more effective in proportion as the residents are men and women of the world, in good standing with all sorts of people, living at peace and on good terms with their kind, and not discounted by offensive allegiance to any ism.

Although at times the House may seem to exist chiefly for its mass of detail work, yet as the years go by the truth grows clearer, that much of this has been chiefly valuable for the fund of experience it yields as a basis for wider social action.

3

WILLIAM G. SUMNER, LL.D.

The Concentration of Wealth: Its Economic Justification

The Independent, 1902

William Graham Sumner was a leading American advocate of Herbert Spencer's philosophy of Social Darwinism. He was a professor of political and social science at Yale University from 1872 until his death in 1910, the year Twenty Years at Hull-House *was published. Sumner wrote several important, scholarly books on political economy and monetary history, but he was also a prolific essayist who believed that scholars should disseminate their views to the public. He often published articles in popular magazines such as* The Independent, *which was a weekly magazine founded in the 1840s as an organ of the Congregational Church. In the Progressive Era,* The Independent *reached the very readers Sumner wished to appeal to: educated, upper-middle-class Americans who were concerned about clean government and social reform, but who opposed labor unions and believed in limited government and laissez-faire economics. Both the magazine and Sumner represented a respected ideology in American life, but one which was being challenged by younger, "progressive" reformers.*

In this editorial, Sumner expresses a positive opinion about the concentration of wealth which Jane Addams and her progressive allies opposed. Sumner believed that the most "fit" members of the society became wealthy and that, by virtue of their fitness, they were best equipped to rule society. Critics like Addams held that many became wealthy through political chicanery, not great ability. What was Sumner's response to such a charge? Faced with the era's heated debate over how best to insure the upward evolution of the human race, would Sumner choose more efficient production of wealth or increases in political and economic democracy? Do you think he and Addams differed simply on the means to human progress or on the ultimate goal and purpose of human progress?

The Independent 54 (Jan.–Dec. 1902): 1036–40.

The concentration of wealth I understand to include the aggregation of wealth into large masses, and its concentration under the control of a few.

In this sense the concentration of wealth is indispensable to the successful execution of the tasks which devolve upon society in our time. Every task of society requires the application of capital, and involves an economic problem in the form of the most expedient application of material means to ends. Two features most prominently distinguish the present age from all which have preceded it; those are, first, the great scale on which all societal undertakings must be carried out; second, the transcendent importance of competent management — that is, of the personal element in direction and control. . . .

Stated in the concisest terms the phenomenon is that of a more perfect integration of all societal functions. The concentration of power (wealth), more dominant control, intenser discipline, and stricter methods are but modes of securing more perfect integration. When we perceive this we see that the concentration of wealth is but one feature of a grand step in societal evolution. . . .

Every age is befooled by the notions which are in fashion in it. Our age is befooled by "democracy." We hear arguments about the industrial organization which are deductions from democratic dogmas, or which appeal to prejudice by using analogies drawn from democracy to affect sentiment about industrial relations. Industry may be republican; it never can be democratic, so long as men differ in productive power and in industrial virtue. In our time joint stock companies, which are in form, republican, are drifting over into oligarchies or monarchies, because one or a few get greater efficiency of control and greater vigor of administration. They direct the enterprise in a way which produces more, or more economically. This is the purpose for which the organization exists, and success in it outweighs everything else. We see the competent men refuse to join in the enterprise, unless they can control it, and we see the stockholders willingly put their property in the hands of those who are, as they think, competent to manage it successfully. The strongest and most effective organizations for industrial purposes which are formed nowadays are those of a few great capitalists, who have great personal confidence in each other, and who can bring together adequate means for whatever they desire to do. Some such nucleus of individuals controls all the great joint stock companies. . . .

There seems to be a great readiness in the public mind to take alarm at these phenomena of growth. There might seem to be rather reason for public congratulation. We want to be provided with things abundantly and cheaply. That means that we want increased economic power. All these enterprises are efforts to satisfy that want. They promise to do it. Especially the public seems to turn to the politician to preserve them from the captain of industry. When has anybody ever seen a politician who was a match for a captain of industry? . . .

In fact, there is a true correlation between (*a*) the great productiveness of modern industry and the consequent rapid accumulation of capital from one period of production to another, and (*b*) the larger and larger aggregations of capital which are required by modern industry from one period of production to another. We see that the movement is constantly accelerated, that its scope is all the time widening, and that the masses of material with which it deals are greater and greater. . . .

It is a consequence of the principle just stated that at every point in the history of civilization it has always been necessary to concentrate capital in large amounts relatively to existing facts. In low civilization chiefs control what capital there is and direct industry. They may be the full owners of all the wealth or only the representatives of a collective theory of ownership. This organization of industry was, at the time, the most efficient and the tribes which had it prospered better than others. In the classical States with slavery, and in the medieval States with serfdom, the great achievements which realized the utmost that the system was capable of were attained only where wealth was concentrated in productive enterprises in amounts, and under management, which were at the maximum of what the system and the possibilities of the time called for. If we could get rid of some of our notions about poverty and equality, and could lay aside this eighteenth century philosophy, according to which human society is to be brought into a state of blessedness, we might get some insight into the might of the societal organization; what it does for us, and what it makes us do. Every day that passes brings us new phenomena of struggle and effort between parts of the societal organization. What do they all mean? They mean that all the individuals and groups are forced against each other in a ceaseless war of interests, by their selfish and mutual efforts to fulfill their career on earth, within the conditions set for them by the state of the arts, the facts of the societal organization, and the current dogmas of world philosophy. . . .

If we are willing to be taught by the facts, then the phenomena of the concentration of wealth which we see about us will convince us that they are just what the situation calls for. They ought to be because they are, and because nothing else would serve the interests of society. . . .

I often see statements published, in which the objectors lay stress upon the great *inequalities* of fortune, and, having set forth the contrast between rich and poor, they rest their case. What law of nature, religion, ethics, or the State is violated by inequalities of fortune? The inequalities prove nothing. Others argue that great fortunes are won by privileges created by law and not by legitimate enterprise and ability. This statement is true, but it is entirely irrelevant. . . .

No man can acquire a million without helping a million men to increase their little fortunes all the way down through all the social grades. In some points of view it is an error that we fix our attention so much upon the very rich and overlook the prosperous mass, but the compensating advantage is that the great successes stimulate emulation the most powerfully.

What matters it then that some millionaires are idle, or silly, or vulgar, that their ideas are sometimes futile, and their plans grotesque, when they turn aside from money-making? How do they differ in this from any other class? The millionaires are a product of natural selection, acting on the whole body of men, to pick out those who can meet the requirement of certain work to be done. In this respect they are just like the great statesmen, or scientific men, or military men. It is because they are thus selected that wealth aggregates under their hands — both their own and that intrusted to them. Let one of them make a mistake and see how quickly the concentration gives way to dispersion. They may fairly be regarded as the naturally selected agents of society for certain work. They get high wages and live in luxury, but the bargain is a good one for society. There is the intensest competition for their place and occupation. This assures us that all who are competent for this function will be employed in it, so that the cost of it will be reduced to the lowest terms, and furthermore that the competitors will study the proper conduct to be observed in their occupation. This will bring discipline and the correction of arrogance and masterfulness.

4

An Oft-Told Tale

The New York Call, April 25, 1912

The Lamb Tags on to the Lion

The New York Call, August 11, 1912

As Twenty Years at Hull-House *makes clear, Jane Addams had a difficult relationship with socialists. Her pro-labor views were close enough to theirs to invite the expectation of alliance, but both Addams and the socialists typically emerged disappointed from such attempts at cooperation. The two editorials included here, both from the socialist newspaper* The New York Call, *show the socialists' impatience with Addams. The first editorial is a response to a speech Addams gave on the "social evil" of poverty in April 1912 to a group of ministers. The second editorial, written four months later, is in response to Jane Addams's choice to support Theodore Roosevelt's third-party run for the presidency on the Progressive Party ticket, rather than to support Eugene Debs on the Socialist ticket. Her speech nominating Roosevelt at the Progressive Party convention in Chicago in August 1912 marked the first time an American woman had seconded the nomination of a presidential candidate.*

The authors of these editorials make no attempt to hide their disgust with Addams. Is their anger directed at her motives or her methods? What evidence do they use to show that she had been ineffectual as a reformer? Why do they find her support of Roosevelt particularly galling? Apart from the political differences these editorials identify, how might the comments made in them be helpful in describing Addams's style of dealing with people and conflict?

An Oft-Told Tale

There is much truth in the statement that what are known as "good" people are very often tiresome. Most of them have contracted the habit of "vain repetition," which now, as in the days of Christ, passes current for righteousness.

The New York Call, April 25, 1912.

We confess that when we hear for the millionth time the statement that "the church must take hold of the 'social evil' and stamp it out of existence," or words to that effect, it makes us very tired.

Just why our "good" people should keep on with the eternal reiteration of this flatulent phrase is difficult to understand except on the hypothesis that righteousness is usually developed at the expense of brains.

Here, for instance, is Miss Jane Addams, the well-known Chicago reformer, addressing the Christian Conservation Congress on this subject at Carnegie Hall, and repeating over and over again what she and thousands of other reformers have repeated weekly perhaps for the last thirty years.

And how was it received? With indifference? Not at all. With "tremendous applause" instead. And the press, what did it do? Did it reprimand Miss Addams for too plain speaking? Did it declare she had "gone too far"? Not at all. It declared she was all right. She didn't "mince words." It commended her therefore.

What will be the result? Will "the church" start out and do what Miss Addams says it should do? Is the "social evil" going to be "stamped out" at last? No, it isn't.

Perhaps it might be more charitable and at the same time a just recognition of Miss Addams' good intentions to answer, "Let us wait and see."

Patience is a virtue, to be sure, but it is possible to exhaust it. We have been waiting year in and year out for this thing to happen, but it hasn't happened. We have listened to Miss Addams in particular for the last twenty years, and a host of other reformers repeating week in and week out this very statement; we have seen innumerable "crusades" suggested, organized, and financed for this purpose, but what has come of it all? Nothing.

Miss Addams is an excellent and well-meaning woman. In fact, "gentle Jane is as good as gold." For her good intentions and desire to elevate humanity we have the sincerest respect. She has given her life and her fortune to this work. If the self-sacrifice of an individual could accomplish anything of value, her work should have told effectively. But what has her effort accomplished? We will not say it has accomplished nothing. Some of her handiwork remains, but what does it amount to? A speck in an ocean of misery, suffering, and poverty. And none know it better than Miss Jane Addams when she casts a retrospective glance at her life-work and compares it with the existing and ever swelling volume of evil conditions which she sought to remove. . . .

The Lamb Tags on to the Lion

In the strange political conjunction of the Gentle Jane Addams of Hull House with the Roaring Bull Moose of Oyster Bay, there is very much more than a mere additional confirmation of the increasing entrance of woman into political life. Miss Addams has been in politics of a small and quiet kind for many years, and apparently detested the noisy and explosive features of that interesting game. In seconding the nomination of the Turbulent One she has certainly made a wide departure from her heretofore calm and placid course, and to all appearances burned behind her many convenient little bridges which in the olden days secured her safe retreat after frequent little excursions into the wild and savage wastes of small radicalism.

Well do we remember those peaceful evenings at Hull House when some well-known, rampant, rip-snorting Socialist was invited to address the assemblage of timid reformers, and how the grim-visaged warrior of the red revolution always had his wrinkled front smoothed down by the mollifying little artifices of the Gentle Jane as a preliminary to his appearance on the platform.

No matter how resolutely the fighting man had determined to fright the souls of fearful reform adversaries, he found it a difficult, if not impossible, task to hand it to them raw and straight as he had intended, once Jane had got through with him. She could always, without actually saying so, manage to leave the impression that it was very bad manners to make a noise and scare timid people, and the would-be fire-eater usually found himself roaring as gently as any sucking dove instead of making the Hull House welkin ring as he had originally resolved. Jane had a curious little way of her own of clipping claws and extracting fangs in those days, and she and all her associates detested noise of all sorts, especially political, to all appearances, more than anything else in the world. And now she has hooked up with the Biggest Noise of all, and actually nominated him for the Presidency, and seemed not only to tolerate the yelling and general uproar but to actually enjoy it. Perhaps the only explanation is that after all the Socialists couldn't roar loud enough and she has been waiting all these years for Theodore the Thunderer to take the center of the stage. . . .

JANE ADDAMS

If Men Were Seeking the Franchise

Ladies' Home Journal, June 1913

Jane Addams was not known for writing satirical pieces, so this editorial in the Ladies' Home Journal *is rather unique. It appeared as one of a series of monthly columns Addams wrote for the popular women's magazine in 1913, when she was vice-president of the National American Woman Suffrage Association. In that series, Addams took a number of political risks, arguing against immigration restriction and in favor of labor unions and explaining to her middle-class readers that economics, not morality, motivated young women's involvement in prostitution. The* Ladies' Home Journal *was on record in opposition to woman suffrage, so it is a testament to Addams's stature that the magazine invited her to write a pro-suffrage article, "Why Women Should Vote," for its pages in 1910 and published this biting critique of antisuffragists in 1913.*

Does this editorial suggest that Addams believed women were more moral, generous, and peace-loving than men because of their innate nature? Or does her choice of words indicate that Addams believed progressive women's anticapitalist, antimilitarist political values derived from female duties and experience?

No woman in America today is so closely in touch with those great social and economic movements that are outside of the home and yet vitally touch the home as Jane Addams, of Hull-House, Chicago. The home-sheltered woman often hears about child labor, the working-girl's wage, labor strikes, convict labor, the emigrant problem, etc., but a comprehensive, authoritative explanation of what these vital questions really mean has not often come her way. Miss Addams will, month by month, on this page explain what they mean and in what direction lie their remedies — often in the hands of the American women themselves.

If any point in this article does not seem perfectly clear any questions will be answered by mail if a stamped, addressed envelope is enclosed. Address Miss Addams in care of the Ladies' Home Journal.

Ladies' Home Journal 30 (June 1913): 21.

Let us imagine throughout this article, if we can sustain an absurd hypothesis so long, the result upon society if the matriarchal period had held its own; if the development of the State had closely followed that of the Family until the chief care of the former, as that of the latter, had come to be the nurture and education of children and the protection of the weak, sick and aged. In short let us imagine a hypothetical society organized upon the belief that "there is no wealth but life." With this Ruskinian foundation let us assume that the political machinery of such a society, the franchise and the rest of it, were in the hands of women because they had always best exercised those functions. Let us further imagine a given moment when these women, who in this hypothetical society had possessed political power from the very beginnings of the State, were being appealed to by the voteless men that men might be associated with women in the responsibilities of citizenship.

Plagiarizing somewhat upon recent suffrage speeches let us consider various replies which these citizen women might reasonably make to the men who were seeking the franchise; the men insisting that only through the use of the ballot could they share the duties of the State.

If Men Were Seeking the Franchise

First, could not the women say: "Our most valid objection to extending the franchise to you is that you are so fond of fighting — you always have been since you were little boys. You'd very likely forget that the real object of the State is to nurture and protect life, and out of sheer vainglory you would be voting away huge sums of money for battleships, not one of which could last more than a few years, and yet each would cost ten million dollars; more money than all the buildings of Harvard University represent, although it is the richest educational institution in America. Every time a gun is fired in a battleship it expends, or rather explodes, seventeen hundred dollars, as much as a college education costs many a country boy, and yet you would be firing off these guns as mere salutes, with no enemy within three thousand miles, simply because you so enjoy the sound of shooting.

"Our educational needs are too great and serious to run any such risk. Democratic government itself is perilous unless the electorate is educated; our industries are suffering for lack of skilled workmen; more than half a million immigrants a year must be taught the underlying principles of republican government. Can we, the responsible voters, take the risk of wasting our taxes by extending the vote to those who have always been so ready to lose their heads over mere military display?"

Second, would not the hypothetical women, who would have been responsible for the advance of industry during these later centuries, as women actually were during the earlier centuries when they dragged home the game and transformed the pelts into shelter and clothing, say further to these disenfranchised men: "We have carefully built up a code of factory legislation for the protection of the workers in modern industry; we know that you men have always been careless about the house, perfectly indifferent to the necessity for sweeping and cleaning; if you were made responsible for factory legislation it is quite probable that you would let the workers in the textile mills contract tuberculosis through needlessly breathing the fluff, or the workers in machine shops through inhaling metal filings, both of which are now carried off by an excellent suction system which we women have insisted upon, but which it is almost impossible to have installed in a man-made State because the men think so little of dust and its evil effects. In many Nations in which political power is confined to men, and this is notably true in the United States of America, there is no protection even for the workers in white lead, although hundreds of them are yearly incapacitated from lead poisoning and others actually die.

"We have also heard that in certain States, in order to save the paltry price of a guard which would protect a dangerous machine, man legislators allow careless boys and girls to lose their fingers and sometimes their hands, thereby crippling their entire futures. These male legislators do not make guarded machinery obligatory, although they know that when the heads of families are injured at these unprotected machines the State must care for them in hospitals, and when they are killed, that if necessary the State must provide for their widows and children in poorhouses."

Some Things That Women Would Do

These wise women, governing the State with the same care they had always put into the management of their families, would further place against these men seeking the franchise the charge that men do not really know how tender and delicate children are, and might therefore put them to work in factories, as indeed they have done in man-made States during the entire period of factory production. We can imagine these women saying: "We have been told that in certain States children are taken from their beds in the early morning before it is light and carried into cotton mills, where they are made to run back and forth tending the spinning frames until their immature little bodies are so bent and strained that they never regain their normal shapes; that little children are allowed to work in canneries for fifteen and seventeen hours until, utterly exhausted, they fall asleep among the débris of shells and husks."

Would not these responsible woman voters gravely shake their heads and say that as long as men exalt business profit above human life it would be sheer folly to give them the franchise; that, of course, they would be slow to make such matters the subject of legislation?

Man's Indifference to Human Life

Would not the enfranchised women furthermore say to these voteless men: "You have always been so eager to make money; what assurance have we that in your desire to get the largest amount of coal out of the ground in the shortest possible time you would not permit the mine supports to decay and mine damp to accumulate, until the percentage of accidents among miners would be simply heartbreaking? Then you are so reckless. Business seems to you a mere game with big prizes, and we have heard that in America, where the women have no vote, the loss of life in the huge steel mills is appalling; and that the number of young brakemen, fine young fellows, every one of them the pride of some mother, killed every year is beyond belief; that the average loss of life among the structural-iron workers who erect the huge office buildings and bridges is as disastrous in percentages as was the loss of life in the Battle of Bull Run. When the returns of this battle were reported to President Lincoln he burst into tears of sorrow and chagrin; but we have never heard of any President, Governor, or Mayor weeping over the reports of this daily loss of life, although such reports have been presented to them by Governmental investigators; and this loss of life might easily be reduced by protective legislation."

Having thus worked themselves into a fine state of irritation, analogous to that ever-recurrent uneasiness of men in the presence of insurgent women who would interfere in the management of the State, would not these voting women add: "The trouble is that men have no imagination, or rather what they have is so prone to run in the historic direction of the glory of the battlefield, that you cannot trust them with industrial affairs. Because a crew in a battleship was once lost under circumstances which suggested perfidy the male representatives of two great Nations voted to go to war; yet in any day of the year in one of these Nations alone — the United States of America — as many men are killed through industrial accidents as this crew contained. These accidents occur under circumstances which, if not perfidious, are at least so criminally indifferent to human life as to merit Kipling's characterization that the situation is impious."

Certainly these irritated women would designate such indifference to human life as unpatriotic and unjustifiable, only to be accounted for because men have not yet learned to connect patriotism with industrial affairs.

These conscientious women responsible for the State in which life was considered of more value than wealth would furthermore say: "Then, too, you men exhibit such curious survivals of the mere savage instinct of punishment and revenge. The United States alone spends every year five hundred million dollars more on its policemen, courts and prisons than upon all its works of religion, charity and education. The price of one trial expended on a criminal early in life might save the State thousands of dollars and the man untold horrors. And yet with all this vast expenditure little is done to reduce crime. Men are kept in jails and penitentiaries where there is not even the semblance of education or reformatory measure; young men are returned over and over again to the same institution until they have grown old and gray, and in all of that time they have not once been taught a trade, nor have they been in any wise prepared to withstand the temptations of life.

"A homeless young girl looking for a lodging may be arrested for soliciting on the streets, and sent to prison for six months, although there is no proof against her save the impression of the policeman. A young girl under such suspicion may be obliged to answer the most harassing questions put to her by the city attorney, with no woman near to protect her from insult; she may be subjected to the most trying examination conducted by a physician in the presence of a policeman, and no matron to whom to appeal. At least these things happen constantly in the United States — in Chicago, for instance — but possibly not in the Scandinavian countries where juries of women sit upon such cases, women whose patience has been many times tested by wayward girls and who know the untold moral harm which may result from such a physical and psychic shock."

Men Are Not Punished for the Social Evil

Then these same women would go further, and, because they had lived in a real world and had administered large affairs and were therefore not prudish and affected, would say: "Worse than anything which we have mentioned is the fact that in every man-ruled city the world over a great army of women are so set aside as outcasts that it is considered a shame to speak the mere name which designates them. Because their very existence is illegal they may be arrested whenever any police captain chooses; they may be brought before a magistrate, fined and imprisoned. The men whose money sustains their houses, supplies their tawdry clothing and provides them with intoxicating drinks and drugs, are never arrested, nor indeed are they even considered lawbreakers."

Would not these fearless women, whose concern for the morals of the family had always been able to express itself through State laws, have meted out equal punishment to men as well as to women, when they had equally transgressed the statute law?

Did the enfranchised women evoked by our imagination speak thus to the disenfranchised men, the latter would at least respect their scruples and their hesitation in regard to an extension of the obligation of citizenship. But what would be the temper of the masculine mind if the voting women representing the existing State should present to them only the following half-dozen objections, which are unhappily so familiar to many of us: If the women should say, first, that men would find politics corrupting; second, that they would doubtless vote as their wives and mothers did; third, that men's suffrage would only double the vote without changing results; fourth, that men's suffrage would diminish the respect for men; fifth, that most men do not want to vote; sixth, that the best men would not vote?

I do not believe that women broadened by life and its manifold experiences would actually present these six objections to men as real reasons for withholding the franchise from them, unless indeed they had long formed the habit of regarding men not as comrades and fellow-citizens, but as a class by themselves, in essential matters really inferior although always held sentimentally very much above them.

Woman Should Adjust Herself to Changing Demands

Certainly no such talk would be indulged in between men and women who had together embodied in political institutions the old affairs of life which had normally and historically belonged to both of them. If woman had adjusted herself to the changing demands of the State as she did to the historic mutations of her own household she might naturally and without challenge have held the place in the State which she now holds in the family.

When Plato once related his dream of an ideal Republic he begged his fellow-citizens not to ridicule him because he considered the coöperation of women necessary for its fulfillment. He contended that so far as the guardianship of the State is concerned there is no distinction between the powers of men and women save those which custom has made.

6

EDWARD ALSWORTH ROSS

Racial Consequences of Immigration

The Century Magazine, February 1914

E. A. Ross was a highly respected sociologist at the University of Wisconsin between 1906 and 1931. He is regarded as one of the founders of modern sociology and associated with the establishment of professional social science in the Progressive Era. Indeed, Ross was affiliated with many progressive causes, especially the cause of labor and greater regulation of capitalism. This article is a reminder that many champions of American workers viewed immigrant workers as employers' threatening tool for labor exploitation. It is one of dozens of articles that Ross published in popular magazines to warn of the dangers of unrestricted immigration by the southern and eastern Europeans who dominated the immigrant flow to America after 1900. Ross published many of his anti-immigration articles in Century Magazine, which had a large circulation among the comfortable, native-born Americans of the era. It was a respectable, high-toned magazine that supported "good government" and "civic improvement," but was not part of the muckraking movement in Progressive-Era journalism.

Ross and Addams shared both a concern for workers and the Progressive-Era conviction that human beings could be the architects of their own environments. Where do their ideas on class and race differ? Who has more faith in the power of the environment to shape people? What would Addams say to Ross's claim that "American stock" is becoming weak and sterile because of foreign immigrants?

The Century Magazine 87 (February 1914): 615–22.

This paper frankly and fearlessly states the lamentable consequences to the American people, as Professor Ross sees them, that must follow upon the continuance of our open-door policy toward the "sub-common" millions of the least desirable nationalities recently pouring into our land. He earnestly combats arguments against restricted laws which have been advanced by interests that favor turning this country into the melting-pot for the backward and outcast of the earth.—THE EDITOR.

The submergence of the "American" pioneer breed goes on apace. In Atlanta still seven out of eight white men had American parents; in Nashville and Richmond, four out of five; in Kansas City, two out of three; and in Los Angeles, one out of two; but in Detroit, Cleveland, and Paterson one man out of five had American parents; in Chicago and New York, one out of six; in Milwaukee, one out of seven; and in Fall River, one out of nine. Certainly never since the colonial era have the foreign-born and their children formed so large a proportion of the American people as at the present moment. I scanned 368 persons as they passed me in Union Square, New York, at a time when the garment-workers of the Fifth Avenue lofts were returning to their homes. Only thirty-eight of these passers-by had the type of face one would find at a county fair in the West or South.

In the six or seven hundred thousand strangers that yearly join themselves to us for good and all, there are to be found, of course, every talent and every beauty. Out of the steerage come persons as fine and noble as any who have trodden American soil. Any adverse characterization of an immigrant stream implies, then, only that the trait is relatively frequent, not that it is general.

In this sense it is fair to say that the blood now being injected into the veins of our people is "sub-common." To one accustomed to the aspect of the normal American population, the Caliban type shows up with a frequency that is startling. Observe immigrants not as they come travelwan up the gang-plank, nor as they issue toil-begrimed from pit's mouth or mill gate, but in their gatherings, washed, combed, and in their Sunday best. You are struck by the fact that from ten to twenty per cent are hirsute, low-browed, big-faced persons of obviously low mentality. Not that they suggest evil. They simply look out of place in black clothes and stiff collar, since clearly they belong in skins, in wattled huts at the close of the great ice age. These oxlike men are descendants of those *who always stayed behind*. Those in whom the soul burns with the dull, smoky flame of the pine-knot stuck to the soil, and are now thick in the sluiceways of immigration. Those in whom it burns with a clear, luminous flame have been attracted to the cities of the home land and, having prospects, have no motive to submit themselves to the hardships of the steerage.

To the practised eye, the physiognomy of certain groups unmistakably proclaims inferiority of type. I have seen gatherings of the foreign-born in which narrow and sloping foreheads were the rule. The shortness and smallness of the crania were very noticeable. There was much facial asymmetry. Among the women, beauty, aside from the fleeting epidermal bloom of girlhood, was quite lacking. In every face there was something wrong — lips thick, mouth coarse, upper lip too long, cheekbones too high, chin poorly formed, the bridge of the nose hollowed, the base of the nose tilted, or else the whole face prognathous. There were so many sugar-loaf heads, moon-faces, slit mouths, lantern-jaws, and goose-bill noses that one might imagine a malicious jinn had amused himself by casting human beings in a set of skew-molds discarded by the Creator.

Our captains of industry give a crowbar to the immigrant with a number nine face on a number six head, make a dividend out of him, and imagine that is the end of the matter. They overlook that this man will beget children in his image, — two or three times as many as the American, — and that these children will in turn beget children. They chuckle at having opened an inexhaustible store of cheap tools and, lo! the American people is being altered for all time by these tools. Once before captains of industry took a hand in making this people. Colonial planters imported Africans to hoe in the sun, to "develop" the tobacco, indigo, and rice plantations. Then, as now, business-minded men met with contempt the protests of a few idealists against their way of "building up the country."

Those promoters of prosperity are dust, but they bequeathed a situation which in four years wiped out more wealth than two hundred years of slavery had built up, and which presents to-day the one unsolvable problem in this country. Without likening immigrants to negroes, one may point out how the latter-day employer resembles the old-time planter in his blindness to the effects of his labor policy upon the blood of the nation. . . .

The Northerners seem to surpass the southern Europeans in innate ethical endowment. Comparison of their behavior in marine disasters shows that discipline, sense of duty, presence of mind, and consideration for the weak are much more characteristic of northern Europeans. The southern Europeans, on the other hand, are apt, in their terror, to forget discipline, duty, women, children, everything but the saving of their own lives. In shipwreck it is the exceptional Northerner who forgets his duty, and the exceptional Southerner who is bound by it. . . .

Among all nationalities the Americans bear the palm for coolness, orderly saving of life, and consideration for the weak in shipwreck, but they will lose these traits in proportion as they absorb excitable blood from southern Europe. . . .

Many things have decided whether Europe should send America cream or skimmed milk. Religious or political oppression is apt to drive out the better elements. Racial oppression cannot be evaded by mere conformity; hence the emigration it sets up is apt to be representative. An unsubdued and perilous land attracts the more bold and enterprising. The seekers of homesteads include men of better stuff than the job-seekers attracted by high wages for unskilled labor. Only economic motives set in motion the sub-common people, but even in an economic emigration the early stage brings more people of initiative than the later. The deeper and smoother the channels of migration, the lower the stratum they can tap. . . .

The fewer brains they have to contribute, the lower the place immigrants take among us, and the lower the place they take, the faster they multiply. In 1890, in our cities, a thousand foreign-born women could show 565 children under five years of age to 309 children shown by a thousand native women. By 1900 the contribution of the foreign women had risen to 612, and that of the American women had declined to 296. From such figures some argue that the "sterile" Americans need the immigrants in order to supply population. It would be nearer the truth to argue that the competition of low-standard immigrants is the root cause of the mysterious "sterility" of Americans. Certainly their record down to 1830 proved the Americans to be as fertile a race as ever lived, and the decline in their fertility coincides in time and in locality with the advent of the immigrant flood. In the words of General Francis A. Walker, "Not only did the decline in the native element, as a whole, take place in singular correspondence with the excess of foreign arrivals, but it occurred chiefly in just those regions"—"in those States and in the very counties," he says elsewhere — "to which those new-comers most frequently resorted."

"Our immigrants," says a superintendent of charities, "often come here with no standards whatever. In their homes you find no sheets on the bed, no slips on the pillows, no cloth on the table, and no towels save old rags. Even in the mud-floor cabins of the poorest negroes of the South you find sheets, pillow-slips, and towels, for by serving and associating with the whites the blacks have gained standards. But many of the foreigners have no means of getting our home standards after they are here. No one shows them. They can't see into American homes, and no Americans associate with them." The Americans or Americanized immigrants who are obliged to live on wages fixed by the competition of such people must cut somewhere. If they do not choose to "live in a pig-pen and bring up one's children like pigs," they will save their standards by keeping down the size of the family. Because he keeps them clean, neatly dressed, and in school, children are a burden to the American. Because he lets them run wild and puts them to work early, children are an asset to the low-standard foreigner.

When a more developed element is obliged to compete on the same economic plane with a less-developed element, the standards of cleanliness or decency or education cherished by the advanced element act on it like a slow poison. William does not leave as many children as 'Tonio, because he will not huddle his family into one room, eat macaroni off a bare board, work his wife barefoot in the field, and keep his children weeding onions instead of at school. Even moral standards may act as poison. Once the women raisin-packers at Fresno, California, were American born. Now the American women are leaving because of the low moral tone that prevails in the working force by reason of the coming in of foreigners with lax notions of propriety. The coarseness of speech and behavior among the packers is giving raisin-packing a bad name, so that American women are quitting the work and taking the next best job. Thus the very decency of the native is a handicap to success and to fecundity.

As they feel the difficulty of keeping up their standards on a Slav wage, the older immigrant stocks are becoming sterile, even as the old Americans became sterile. In a generation complaint will be heard that the Slavs, too, are shirking big families, and that we must admit prolific Persians, Uzbegs, and Bokhariots, in order to offset the fatal sterility that attacks every race after it has become Americanized. Very truly says Professor Wilcox, in praise of immigration: "The cost of rearing children in the United States is rapidly rising. In many, perhaps in most cases, it is simpler, speedier, and cheaper to import labor than to breed it." In like vein it is said that "a healthy immigrant lad of eighteen is a clear $1000 added to the national wealth of the United States."

Just so. "The Roman world was laughing when it died." Any couple or any people that does not feel it has anything to transmit to its children may well reason in such fashion. A couple may reflect, "It is simpler, speedier, and cheaper for us to adopt orphans than to produce children of our own." A nation may reason, "Why burden ourselves with the rearing of children? Let them perish unborn in the womb of time. The immigrants will keep up the population." A people that has no more respect for its ancestors and no more pride of race than this deserves the extinction that surely awaits it.

7

HILDA SATT POLACHECK

I Came a Stranger:
The Story of a Hull-House Girl

When she was about ten years old, Hilda Satt Polacheck and her family escaped the Russian pogroms in Poland in 1892. Though her father had been a skilled artisan in his home country and the family had been economically secure, the family of six children endured poverty in America — especially after Hilda's father died in 1894. In the autobiography Polacheck wrote in the 1950s, she credited Jane Addams with giving her the skills and opportunities necessary to regain the bourgeois status into which she had been born. The excerpt printed here focuses on the years between 1900 and 1910, when Addams introduced Polacheck to the world of writing and publishing. This led Polacheck into artistic and political circles — and into a marriage — which would assure her a life of progressive activism as a respectable middle-class matron in Milwaukee.

Some critics of Hull-House have charged the settlement with providing intellectual, artistic, and political avenues of social mobility that were irrelevant to the lives of the neighbors. What would Hilda Polacheck say to those critics? Polacheck was active in leftist politics in Milwaukee between 1912 and 1950. What would she say to her socialist friends who felt Jane Addams made activists like herself too respectable and too refined? Finally, note that Polacheck wrote her memoir in the anticommunist 1950s, when historical figures like Jane Addams were politically suspect. Indeed, Polacheck could not get her book published in that repressive decade. What message was Polacheck trying to convey, in the 1950s, about progressive activism, prosperity, and American patriotism?

After a span of fifty years, I look back and realize how much of my leisure time was spent at Hull-House and how my life was molded by the influence of Jane Addams. I was not only hungry for books, music, and all the arts and crafts offered at Hull-House, but I was starved for the social stimulus of people my own age. All this was to be found at the house on Halsted and Polk streets.

My family had moved to Bunker Street near Des Plaines Avenue. The street was covered with small two-family houses with cottages in the rear of each house. . . . Our family lived in four small rooms. Half of each week, during the winter, the rooms were filled with wet laundry. Since the clothes were all wrung by hand, it took several days to get the clothes dry. It was no place in which to entertain friends, so while I ate and slept there, I really lived at Hull-House.

There were few activities that I allowed to slip by me. How well I remember the exciting news that a prince was to visit Hull-House. I created a mental picture for myself of a prince. He would wear blue satin knee breeches, a silk shirt with many ruffles, a purple velvet coat with golden buttons, and a big hat with an ostrich plume.

I was at Hull-House when the prince arrived and I dashed out to see him alight from the royal carriage.

I saw a one-horse hack, somewhat spattered with Chicago mud, stop in front of Hull-House and Miss Addams stepped out. She was followed by a short, round-shouldered man with a gray beard. He wore a battered old hat and a Prince Albert coat which was much too large for him. It sort of hung on his shoulders. But he was a prince. He was Prince Peter Kropotkin of Russia, who had come to America to lecture, and while he was in Chicago he stayed at Hull-House as the guest of Jane Addams.

I attended the lecture that he gave the next day. His subject was "Factories, Fields, and Workshops," and I can still remember his vivid description of girls working in match factories. The girls had to carry large pans of sulphur on their heads to supply the match dippers. After a few years of this kind of work, the girls lost all their hair and became bald. Many of the girls died while very young as a result of this work. He was sure that matches could be made of some substance that would not be so destructive to human life.

I had the great privilege of speaking to him during his stay at Hull-House. He was a gentle, kind old man, and I loved him. I told him that I had heard his lecture and that I was deeply touched by what he had said. He said he was glad to see young people interested in the important things of life. Then he leaned forward and kissed me on the forehead. . . .

Not all events at Hull-House centered around celebrities. I began to see weeping women sitting in the reception room. They were always shabbily dressed, with black shawls tied on their heads. On several occasions I acted as interpreter, if the women were Jewish and could not speak English. On one of these occasions I asked a bewildered woman what she wanted. She told me that a policeman had come to her house and had taken her little boy to the police station and that she did not know what to do. When I told this to Miss Addams, she told me to ask the woman how old the boy was and what he had done. The boy was seven years old, and here the woman began to cry hysterically. He was about to take a bottle of milk from a neighbor's doorstep when the neighbor came out and pulled the boy into the house and called a policeman.

I found out later that the little boy had heard his mother tell his father that she had no money for milk, and he merely wanted to help.

The grief-stricken woman told me that another neighbor had told her that no matter what troubles came, you could always get help at Hull-House. When I told this to Miss Addams, her kind eyes and warm smile assured the woman that she had come to the right place.

The very next evening, while we were eating supper, a neighbor came in and told Mother in Polish that her small grandson had been taken away by a policeman. I left my supper uneaten and took the poor woman to Hull-House. I found out later that the eleven-year-old boy had stolen some coal from a freight car which had been left on a siding. When later he had been asked why he did it, he said that his grandmother was cold and that anyway there was a lot more coal in the train, that he had only taken a little bit. . . .

Jane Addams was never condescending to anyone. She never made one feel that she was a "lady bountiful." She never made one feel that she was doling out charity. When she did something for you, you felt she owed it to you or that she was making a loan that you could pay back.

The most forlorn scrubwoman received the same warm welcome as the wealthy supporters of the house. I remember one day the daughter of a wealthy family had come to Hull-House to help in the reception room, and an old shabby woman came in and asked for Miss Addams. Looking down at the poor woman, the young lady started to tell her that Miss Addams was busy and could not be disturbed, just as Miss Addams was coming down the stairs. She quickly told the young lady that perhaps she had better go home. Then she took the old woman by the arm and said she was just going to have a cup of tea and would she join her. Then she led her to the coffeehouse, where she listened to a tale of woe.

America has not yet awakened to the realization of what it owes to Jane Addams. No one will ever know how many young people were helped by her wise council, how many were kept out of jail, how many were started on careers in the arts, in music, in industry, in science, and above all in instilling in their hearts a true love of country — a love of service. . . .

Her presence was felt everywhere in the house. Whether we were reading Shakespeare, or working in the Labor Museum, or dancing in the dancing class, or listening to a lecture or concert, whenever she appeared, the room became brighter. Every time I saw her the thought came to me that if it had not been for her, I would not be enjoying all these things.

I remember Miss Addams stopping me one day and asking me if I had joined the dancing class. She thought I worked too hard and needed some fun. So I joined the dancing class and learned the waltz, two-step, and schottische. By this time I was able to pay the dollar that paid for ten lessons.

The dancing class was in the charge of a beautiful, understanding woman. Her name was Mary Wood Hinman and we all loved her. She was always dressed in a gray accordion-pleated skirt, with a blouse of the same material, a red sash, and gray dancing shoes. She floated around that room like a graceful bird. We danced once a week in this carefree class, all winter. In June, the class closed for the summer with a gay cotillion, every bit as gay, if not as elaborate, as the ones staged today to introduce debutantes to society. No matter where the members of the dancing class came from, dingy hovels, overcrowded tenements, for that one night we were all living in a fairyland.

My sister and I next joined the gymnasium. We managed to scrape together enough money to buy the regulation gymnasium suit — wide bloomers and blouse — though if anyone could not afford the suit, she could attend anyway. Miss Rose Gyles was the teacher, and she put us through the paces once a week.

The gymnasium was like an oasis in a desert on Halsted Street. Hundreds of boys, who had no other means of recreation, could go to the gymnasium and play basketball till they were so worn out that they could only go home and go to bed.

One evening, as I entered the reception room, Miss Addams called me into the residents' sitting room and asked me to join a class in English composition. The class was just being organized and the instructor was to be Henry Porter Chandler, of the University of Chicago. Not many students had applied, and Miss Addams asked me to register for the class as she did not want Mr. Chandler to feel that people were not interested in such a class.

I told Miss Addams that I had never written anything. But she insisted, and so I went into the dining room where four or five people were gathered. She introduced me to Mr. Chandler. Mr. Chandler outlined a course of work. He asked us if we had ever written anything. Most of us had not. He then told us that there were certain kinds of writing, such as book reviews, short stories, arguments, criticisms, and some others. He asked each of us to write anything that we wanted and to bring it to the class the following week. He then dismissed the class.

Mr. Chandler was the secretary to William Rainey Harper, the first president of the University of Chicago, and an instructor in English composition.

I could not sleep that night. Why was it that he did not tell us how to write? How could a person just write? Then the thought came to me that if you had something to say, perhaps you could write it down on paper. I kept thinking, Have I something to say? . . .

The next time the class met, I brought the masterpiece, over which I had sweated five nights and a whole day Sunday, to Mr. Chandler. Each member of the class had brought a composition. Mr. Chandler did not look at the papers. He told us he would let us know the following week what he thought of our efforts. . . .

The week that followed will ever stand out in my memory as a turning point in my life. The one thought that ran through my mind was, What would Mr. Chandler think of my composition? Would he toss it in the wastebasket? Would he laugh at it? Whatever the outcome, the fact that I had put my thoughts down on paper made a deep impression on me. Walking to work, sitting all day at the sewing machine sewing those endless cuffs, my thoughts were always with Mr. Chandler. . . .

After a miserable day at the factory, when everything seemed to happen, my machine had broken down and I had lost several hours of work, I arrived at Hull-House. The composition class was to meet that night. What would Mr. Chandler think of my composition? Would he pay any attention to it? He had probably thrown it into the wastebasket. It couldn't possibly be worth anything, I kept telling myself.

The class assembled and Mr. Chandler opened his briefcase and pulled out a mass of papers. He handed them to the various authors, without any comment.

My heart missed several beats.

Then he handed me my paper and said: "Very good." I do not remember anything else that he said that night. But as the class was being dismissed, Miss Addams came into the room and said that she wanted to talk to me, that I was to wait for her. She talked for a few minutes with Mr. Chandler, then she took me into the octagon and said these magic words: "How would you like to go to the University of Chicago?" She was very calm, as if she had asked me to have a cup of tea.

She did not realize that she had just asked me whether I wanted to live. I just sat there looking at her.

"Did you say the University of Chicago?" I finally gasped.

"Yes," she said. "Mr. Chandler told me that your paper shows promise, and he will make all the arrangements."

"But that is impossible," I said.

"Nothing is impossible," said Jane Addams.

For some time I could not talk. I kept thinking, I did not graduate from grammar school. How could I hope to go to the great university?

Miss Addams, with her infinite patience, sat there holding my hand. I know she was living through my thoughts.

If this could happen, then all sorts of miracles could happen. But then, did not miracles happen in Hull-House all the time?

"But what about a high school diploma?" I asked. "I heard that no one can go to college without a high school diploma."

"Mr. Chandler said that you could come as an unclassified student," she said.

"But what about money?" I was beginning to lose hope.

"You will be granted a scholarship," she said. "It will cost you nothing."

"But I must contribute to the support of the family," I said. "My wages are needed at home."

"Well, I thought of that, too," she said smiling. "We will make you a loan of the amount that you would earn, and whenever you are able, you can pay it back."

By this time tears were running down my cheeks. What had I done to deserve all this? She took my hand and said: "I know how you feel, my dear. I want you to go home and talk this over with your mother, and let me know what you want to do. But I want you to go, remember that."

I went home and found Mother and my sister sitting at the kitchen table, drinking tea. I sat down without removing my coat. My sister looked at me.

"What's happened to you?" she said.

I just sat there staring — then I blurted out: "Miss Addams wants me to go to the University of Chicago."

"But how can you?" my sister asked.

Then I poured out my soul. I told them what Miss Addams had said about a loan, how my tuition would be free, how my life would be changed.

"This can happen only in America," Mother said.

"Yes," I said, "because in America there is a Jane Addams and Hull-House."

The exciting events of the night before did not keep me from going to work the next day. I sewed cuffs all day. As soon as I had finished eating supper, I dashed off to Hull-House. I waited for Miss Addams to come out of the dining room.

She saw me at once and took me into the octagon. The walls were covered with the photographs of the great humanitarians of the world: Leo Tolstoy, Abraham Lincoln, Henry Demarest Lloyd, John Peter Altgeld, Susan B. Anthony, Peter Kropotkin, Eugene V. Debs, and a host of others. And while these faces were looking down at us, I told Miss Addams that my mother and sister had consented to my going.

It was with a great deal of satisfaction that I told the foreman of the shirtwaist factory that I was leaving.

Memories keep coming back. It must have been the winter term when I matriculated at the University of Chicago. I remember that it was very cold traveling to the university early in the morning. . . .

When the university closed for the summer, I evaluated my work. The English literature course had opened all sorts of vistas to me. But I think I did not pass. The jump from the fifth grade in the grammar school to Chaucer was a little too much for me. But the course gave me an everlasting desire to read and study, so it was not a loss. I did pass in German and I think I fared well in the composition class.

That term at the University of Chicago opened a new life to me. And I have never stopped being grateful for having been given the opportunity to explore the treasures to be found in books.

I often wonder what sort of a life I would have lived if I did not have that short term in the university made possible by Jane Addams.

After the short but eventful term at the University of Chicago, I must confess I was at loose ends. I was determined not to go back to the factory to sew cuffs. But I knew that I had to earn my living and help support the family. I now felt prepared to do more interesting and stimulating work. The question was, What could I do?

The answer came sooner than I dared hope. Miss Addams was preparing to go to Bar Harbor for the summer and she suggested that I take the job of answering the doorbell and the telephone. In those days the door was locked and everyone who wanted to come in had to ring the doorbell. This work was usually done by volunteers, but most volunteers were leaving the city for the summer and I may have been the first paid worker to have had that job. I worked from four o'clock in the afternoon till nine at night, five days a week. On Saturday I did "toting."

The word "toting" I think was invented at Hull-House. In Webster's dictionary the word "tote" is given, and it means "to carry or bear on the person, as a burden." But at Hull-House it did not mean that at all. Toting meant showing people through the house. And let me say right here that I never found it a burden.

I came in contact with people from all over the world. It seemed as if everybody who came to Chicago from some part of the country or the world came to see Hull-House. I know that there are people in Chicago who had not been there, but tourists came. I never tired of showing the wonders of the house on Halsted and Polk streets.

I was asked and answered thousands of questions. I would not be able to count the times that I was asked why Miss Addams had never married. At that time, I did not know. But if I had known, I would have felt that it was nobody's business.

Most of the classes were discontinued during the hot summer months. But there had been a great demand for English classes for adult foreigners. A delegation of the students called on Miss Addams and asked her to allow the classes to continue during the summer. Miss Addams agreed to try one class if a teacher could be found. I volunteered.

As I look back on that momentous event, I realize how presumptuous it was of me to offer to teach a class at Hull-House, where the standards were very high. I had no training in teaching. But English had fascinated me from the start; I had worked very hard to learn it, so why could I not teach the immigrants what I had learned? I offered to teach the class and was overjoyed when my offer was accepted. I had a feeling that, after all, there was no one else around who was willing to take the class. So the people who wanted to continue studying during the summer were told that the class would not close.

Being allowed to teach English to immigrants at Hull-House did more for me than anything that I imparted to my students. It gave me a feeling of security that I so sorely needed. What added to my confidence in the future was that my class was always crowded and the people seemed to make good progress. From time to time Jane Addams would visit the class to see what I was doing, and she always left with that rare smile on her face; she seemed to be pleased. . . .

My students were now beginning to confide in me. Classes at Hull-House were never just classes where people came to learn a specific subject. There was a human element of friendliness among us. Life was not soft or easy for any of them. They worked hard all day in shops and factories and made this valiant effort to learn the language of their adopted country. At times they needed real help, and they knew that somewhere in this wonderful house on Halsted Street they would get it. . . .

Hull-House had a unique arrangement for getting work done. No teachers or attendants were paid. It was all volunteer work. The residents of Hull-House were occupied with outside work during the day, and each gave a certain number of evenings to teaching and directing clubs. The only people who were paid were those who devoted their full time to the house. . . .

So in the fall, when volunteers returned, I decided to look for a job. I had learned to use a typewriter, so I decided to look for more "genteel" work. . . .

Miss Addams suggested that I might try A. C. McClurg & Co., a publishing house and at the time the largest bookstore in Chicago. With a letter of introduction from Jane Addams, I was given a very friendly interview and got the job.

Working among books was almost as good as taking a course in literature. It gave me the opportunity of knowing what books were being published. I was keenly interested in what books people were reading. And I had the great privilege of working at McClurg's when *The Quest of the Silver Fleece* was published. It was the first time that I came across the name of W. E. B. Du Bois. This book aroused a keen interest in the growth of cotton in the South and the part that the Negro played in the industry.

I still spent my evenings at Hull-House, and one evening Miss Addams asked me to help organize a social and literary club for young men and women about my age. We all needed an outlet for recreation. About thirty young people joined the club, which was named the Ariadne Club. I don't know who suggested the name, but like the mythological daughter of Minos, who led Theseus out of the labyrinth by a thread, the club led many of us out of a labyrinth of boredom.

I now had the opportunity to come into contact with young men. The club met once a week, and how I looked forward to those meetings. The first order of business, after officers were elected, was to appoint a program committee, whose duty it would be to arrange weekly programs. Since this was a social and literary club, one week was devoted to dancing and the next to study. For the more serious evening, a member was usually assigned to write a paper and to read it before the club. This was followed by a discussion.

And what subjects we discussed.

Papers were written on the collection of garbage, grand opera, clean streets, single tax, trade unionism, and many others. I think our subjects were influenced by what was going on at Hull-House.

The Ariadne Club soon branched out and launched a series of debates. We would try to find another club that would accept a challenge. If we could not find a club, the members would form opposing teams. The subjects of these debates come back to me: Which is mightier, the sword or the pen? Should women be allowed to vote? Which is stronger, the desire for fame or riches?

We also had music in the Ariadne Club. The members who could play an instrument, or sing, would perform; we heard some very good concerts. Many of the members who worked all day would study music at night. I recall when a piano lesson could be had for twenty-five cents. Some of the members attended the Hull-House Music School, and I venture to say that not a few became successful musicians.

The Ariadne Club also produced plays. I recall taking part in *David Garrick,* in which I played a fussy and obnoxious old maid.

My interest in the theater was a direct outgrowth of the dramatics at Hull-House. It was a preparation for life.

An Addams Chronology
(1860–1935)

1860   Laura Jane Addams born, September 6, in Cedarville, Illinois, the fifth child of John Huy Addams and Sarah Weber Addams.

1863   Jane Addams's mother, Sarah, dies in January from complications of pregnancy.

1868   Anna Hostetter Haldeman marries John Huy Addams in November and becomes Jane Addams's stepmother. Anna Haldeman has two sons: Harry Haldeman, age 20, and George Haldeman, age 7.

1875   Sarah Alice Addams, Jane Addams's sister, marries Harry Haldeman, her stepbrother.

1877–1881   Jane Addams attends Rockford Female Seminary in Rockford, Illinois. In her first year there, becomes friends with Ellen Gates Starr and is voted president of her class, an office she holds for all four years.

1880–1881   Editor of the *Rockford Seminary Magazine*. Makes the magazine independent of the school's headmistress by selling advertising to businesses in town.

1881   Graduates as valedictorian from Rockford Female Seminary. Six weeks later, her father dies. Enters Woman's Medical College of Philadelphia, Pa., in the fall and lives with stepmother, sister, and stepbrother/brother-in-law in Philadelphia.

1882   Leaves Woman's Medical College after one semester. Undergoes medical treatment with Dr. S. Weir Mitchell of Philadelphia. Having given up on ever attending Smith College, agrees to return to Rockford Female Seminary to be among the first from that institution to receive an A.B. degree.

1883–1887   Spends winters in Baltimore with Anna Haldeman Addams and George Haldeman; travels in Europe with Anna Haldeman Addams, 1883–85.

1887–1888   Travels in Europe with Ellen Gates Starr and their teacher from Rockford, Sarah Anderson. Visits Toynbee Hall in June, 1888.

1887   Is appointed to the Board of Trustees of Rockford College (formerly Rockford Female Seminary). Serves in that post until 1908.

1889   Opens Hull-House in September with Ellen Gates Starr. Serves as Head Resident of that institution until her death in 1935.

1890   Meets Mary Rozet Smith, lifelong partner.

1891   Opens Butler Art Gallery, the first building added to the Hull-House settlement.

1892   Gains national notice when two speeches delivered at the Plymouth School of Ethics Conference appear in *Forum* magazine as "Hull-House, Chicago: An Effort toward Social Democracy" and "A New Impulse to an Old Gospel." These were subsequently published under the titles, "The Objective Value of a Social Settlement" and "The Subjective Necessity for Social Settlements" in *Philanthropy and Social Progress,* ed. Henry C. Adams (New York: Crowell Publishing Company, 1893), 1–26, 27–56.

1893   Participates on numerous committees to design and host congresses of labor, social settlements, university extension, and women held in conjunction with the World's Columbian Exposition in Chicago.
Embarks on first major lecture tour, speaking at women's colleges on east coast.
Lobbies, successfully, for creation of Illinois Factory Inspector office.
Opens a second addition to Hull-House, a building housing the coffeehouse and gymnasium.

1894   Opens first public playground in Chicago on land adjoining Hull-House, having gained the land by convincing the owner of dilapidated housing to tear it down and donate the land to the settlement.
As a member of the Chicago Civic Federation, attempts to arbitrate the Pullman strike.

1895   Publishes *Hull-House Maps and Papers.*
Opens third addition to Hull-House site, the Children's Building (also known as the Smith building because Mary Rozet Smith's family contributed the funds).
Takes first and only paid position of her career: as the garbage inspector for the Nineteenth Ward in Chicago.

1895–1900   Engages in a series of unsuccessful political campaigns to unseat Alderman Johnny Powers and replace him with male candidates more in line with progressive ideology and practices.

1896   European tour with Mary Rozet Smith includes a meeting with Count Leo Tolstoy at his farm in Russia.

1899   Opens fourth addition to Hull-House site, the Jane Club, a cooperative apartment building for working women. Later in the year, opens fifth building for theater and new coffeehouse.

Teaches a summer school course at University of Chicago with Florence Kelley.

Lobbies successfully for creation of Cook County, Illinois, Juvenile Court.

1900   Renovates old coffeehouse and gymnasium building as new Hull-House Labor Museum and new gymnasium.

1902   Publishes *Democracy and Social Ethics.*

Opens sixth and seventh building additions to the Hull-House complex, a new apartment building for the Jane Club and the Men's Club building.

1903   Campaigns for passage of Illinois Child Labor Law.

1904   Becomes first woman to deliver convocation address at the University of Chicago.

1905–1909   Serves as a member of the Chicago Board of Education; chairs the School Management Committee.

1905   Opens eighth building addition to Hull-House complex, the Women's Club building.

1907   Publishes *Newer Ideals of Peace.*

Opens ninth building addition to Hull-House complex, the Boys' Club building, and begins work on new Residents' Dining Hall. Opens tenth building addition, the Mary Crane Nursery building, at the end of the year.

1908   Named America's foremost living woman by *Ladies' Home Journal.*

1909   Publishes *The Spirit of Youth and the City Streets.*

1909–1910   Serves as first woman president of the National Conference of Charities and Corrections.

1910   Publishes *Twenty Years at Hull-House.*

Becomes first woman to receive an honorary degree from Yale University.

Is first woman elected to the Chicago Association of Commerce.

Serves as mediator in Hart, Shaffner and Marx strike in Chicago.

1911–1914   Serves as a vice-president of the National American Woman Suffrage Association.

1912   Publishes *A New Conscience and an Ancient Evil.*

Establishes Bowen Country Club, Hull-House summer camp at Waukegan, Illinois.

Seconds the nomination of Theodore Roosevelt as Progressive party candidate for president.

1913   Speaks at Seventh Congress of International Alliance for Suffrage and Equal Citizenship in Budapest, Hungary.

1915   Elected chair of newly organized Woman's Peace Party.

Presides at First International Congress of Women, The Hague, Netherlands; elected president of International Committee of Women for a Permanent Peace.

Travels with other representatives of International Congress of Women to capitals of belligerents in World War I to present mediation plans.

Co-authors *Women at the Hague* with Emily Greene Balch and Alice Hamilton as part of effort to lobby for peace in early days of World War I.

Is castigated in U.S. press for speaking out against the war upon her return from Europe.

1916   Publishes *The Long Road of Woman's Memory*.

1917–1918   United States Food Administration under Herbert Hoover engages Addams to lecture on food conservation in wartime despite her outspoken, controversial stance against the government's wartime policies on espionage.

1919   Listed on the "Traitors List" presented to Senate Judiciary Committee during post–World War I Red Scare.

Elected president of the Women's International League for Peace and Freedom, which she helps to establish at Second International Congress of Women in Zurich, Switzerland.

1919–1929   Serves as president of Women's International League for Peace and Freedom.

1921   Presides at Third International Congress of the Women's International League for Peace and Freedom in Vienna, Austria.

1922   Publishes *Peace and Bread in Time of War*.

1924   Supports presidential campaign of Robert M. LaFollette, Sr., who ran on the Progressive party ticket.

Presides at Fourth International Congress of the Women's International League for Peace and Freedom in Washington, D.C.

Presides at Fifth International Congress of the Women's International League for Peace and Freedom in Dublin, Ireland.

1927   Joins unsuccessful efforts to prevent execution of Sacco and Vanzetti, Italian anarchists on trial for armed robbery and murder in Massachusetts.

1928   Presides at Pan-Pacific Women's Association, Honolulu, Hawaii Territory.

Supports Herbert Hoover for president.

1929   Attends Sixth International Congress of the Women's International League for Peace and Freedom in Prague, Czechoslovakia; is named president for life of the WILPF.

1930   Publishes *The Second Twenty Years at Hull-House*.

1931   Becomes the first American woman to be awarded the Nobel Peace Prize.

1932   Publishes *The Excellent Becomes Permanent*.

1934   Mary Rozet Smith dies of pneumonia in Chicago.

1935   Honored at twentieth anniversary celebration for Women's International League for Peace and Freedom.

Dies from abdominal cancer following surgery in Chicago.

My Friend, Julia Lathrop published posthumously.

Selected Bibliography

BY AND ABOUT JANE ADDAMS

Addams, Jane, *Hull-House Maps and Papers: A Presentation of Nationalities and Wages in a Congested District of Chicago.* New York: Thomas Y. Crowell, 1895.

————, *Democracy and Social Ethics.* New York: Macmillan, 1902.

————, *Newer Ideals of Peace.* New York: Macmillan, 1907.

————, *The Spirit of Youth and the City Streets.* New York: Macmillan, 1909.

————, *Twenty Years at Hull-House.* New York: Macmillan, 1910.

————, *A New Conscience and an Ancient Evil.* New York: Macmillan, 1912.

————, *Women at the Hague.* New York: Macmillan, 1915.

————, *The Long Road of Women's Memory.* New York: Macmillan, 1916.

————, *Peace and Bread in Time of War.* New York: Macmillan, 1922.

————, *The Second Twenty Years at Hull-House.* New York: Macmillan, 1930.

————, *The Excellent Becomes Permanent.* New York: Macmillan, 1932.

————, *My Friend, Julia Lathrop.* New York: Macmillan, 1935.

Davis, Allen F., *American Heroine: The Life and Legend of Jane Addams.* New York: Oxford University Press, 1973.

Deegan, Mary Jo, *Jane Addams and the Men of the Chicago School, 1892–1918.* New Brunswick: Transaction Books, 1990.

Linn, James Weber, *Jane Addams: A Biography.* New York: D. Appleton-Century Company, 1935.

THE PROGRESSIVE ERA

Carson, Mina, *The Settlement Folk: Social Thought and the American Settlement Movement, 1885–1930.* Chicago: University of Chicago Press, 1990.

Cashman, Sean Dennis, *America in the Age of the Titans: The Progressive Era and World War I.* New York: New York University Press, 1988.

Danbom, David B., *"The World of Hope": Progressives and the Struggle for an Ethical Public Life.* Philadelphia: Temple University Press, 1987.

Diner, Steven J., *A Very Different Age: Americans of the Progressive Era.* New York: Hill and Wang, 1998.

Feffer, Andrew, *The Chicago Pragmatists and American Progressivism.* Ithaca: Cornell University Press, 1993.

Kloppenberg, James T., *Uncertain Victory: Social Democracy and Progressivism in European and American Thought, 1870–1920.* New York: Oxford University Press, 1986.

Lasch-Quinn, Elisabeth, *Black Neighbors: Race and the Limits of Reform in the American Settlement House Movement, 1890–1945.* Chapel Hill: University of North Carolina Press, 1993.

Link, Arthur, and Richard L. McCormick, *Progressivism.* Arlington Heights, Ill.: Harlan Davidson, Inc., 1983.

Luker, Ralph E., *The Social Gospel in Black and White: American Racial Reform, 1885–1912.* Chapel Hill: University of North Carolina Press, 1991.

Patterson, James T., *America's Struggle against Poverty, 1900–1985.* Cambridge, Mass.: Harvard University Press, 1986.

Rodgers, Daniel, "In Search of Progressivism," *Reviews in American History* 10 (December 1982): 113–32.

Sklar, Kathryn Kish, "Who Funded Hull House?" in *Lady Bountiful Revisited: Women, Philanthropy and Power,* ed. Kathleen D. McCarthy. New Brunswick: Rutgers University Press, 1990.

Trattner, Walter I., *From Poor Law to Welfare State: A History of Social Welfare in America.* New York: Free Press, 1989.

Westbrook, Robert, *John Dewey and American Democracy.* Ithaca: Cornell University Press, 1991.

Wiebe, Robert C., *The Search for Order, 1877–1920.* New York: Hill & Wang, 1967.

WOMEN AND SOCIAL REFORM

Baker, Paula, "The Domestication of Politics: Women and American Political Society, 1780–1920," *American Historical Review* 89 (June 1984): 620–47.

Blair, Karen, *The Clubwoman as Feminist: True Womanhood Redefined, 1868–1914.* New York: Holmes & Meier, 1980.

Brown, Victoria, "Jane Addams, Progressivism, and Woman Suffrage," in *One Woman, One Vote: Rediscovering the Woman Suffrage Movement,* ed. Marjorie Spruill Wheeler. Troutdale, Or.: NewSage Press, 1995.

Buechler, Steven M., *The Transformation of the Woman Suffrage Movement: The Case of Illinois, 1850–1920.* New Brunswick: Rutgers University Press, 1986.

Dye, Nancy Schrom, *As Equals and as Sisters: Feminism, the Labor Movement, and the Women's Trade Union League of New York.* Columbia: University of Missouri Press, 1980.

Flanagan, Maureen A., "Gender and Urban Political Reform: The City Club and the Woman's City Club of Chicago in the Progressive Era," *American Historical Review* 95 (October 1990): 1032–50.

Gordon, Linda, "Social Insurance and Public Assistance: The Influence of Gender in Welfare Thought in the United States, 1890–1925," *American Historical Review* 97 (February 1992): 19–54.

Koven, Seth, and Sonya Michel, eds., *Mothers of the New World: Maternalist Politics and the Origins of Welfare States.* New York: Routledge, 1993.

Muncy, Robyn, *Creating a Female Dominion in American Reform, 1890–1935.* New York: Oxford University Press, 1991.

Scott, Anne Firor, *Natural Allies: Women's Associations in American History.* Urbana: University of Illinois Press, 1992.

Sklar, Kathryn Kish, *Florence Kelley and the Nation's Work: The Rise of Women's Political Culture, 1830–1900.* New Haven: Yale University Press, 1995.

Wheeler, Marjorie Spruill, *One Woman, One Vote: Rediscovering the Woman Suffrage Movement.* Troutdale, Or.: NewSage Press, 1995.

IMMIGRATION, LABOR, AND CHICAGO

Barrett, James R., *Work and Community in the Jungle: Chicago's Packinghouse Workers, 1894–1922.* Urbana: University of Illinois Press, 1987.

Bodnar, John, *The Transplanted: A History of Immigrants in Urban America.* Bloomington: Indiana University Press, 1985.

Cumbler, John T., *Working-class Community in Industrial America: Work, Leisure, and Struggle in Two Industrial Cities, 1880–1930.* Westport, Conn.: Greenwood, 1979.

Gilbert, James, *Perfect Cities: Chicago's Utopias of 1893.* Chicago: University of Chicago Press, 1991.

Glenn, Susan A., *Daughters of the Shtetl: Life and Labor in the Immigrant Generation.* Ithaca: Cornell University Press, 1990.

Holli, Melvin G., and Peter d'A. Jones, *Ethnic Chicago: A Multicultural Portrait,* 4th ed. Grand Rapids, Mich.: Wm. B. Eerdmans, 1995.

Katznelson, Ira, *City Trenches: Urban Politics and the Patterning of Class in the United States.* Chicago: University of Chicago Press, 1981.

Lindsey, Almont, *The Pullman Strike: The Story of a Unique Experiment and of a Great Labor Upheaval.* Chicago: University of Chicago Press, 1967.

Miller, Donald L., *City of the Century: The Epic of Chicago and the Making of America.* New York: Touchstone Books, Simon & Schuster, 1997.

Montgomery, David, *The Fall of the House of Labor: The Workplace, the State, and American Labor Activism, 1865–1925.* Cambridge: Cambridge University Press, 1987.

Nelli, Humbert S., *Italians in Chicago, 1880–1930: A Study in Ethnic Mobility.* New York: Oxford University Press, 1970.

Oestreicher, Richard, *Solidarity and Fragmentation: Working People and Class Consciousness in Detroit, 1875–1900*. Urbana: University of Illinois Press, 1990.

Salvatore, Nick, *Eugene V. Debs: Citizen and Socialist*. Urbana: University of Illinois Press, 1982.

Smith, Carl, *Urban Disorder and the Shape of Belief*. Chicago: University of Chicago Press, 1995.

Index

Abbott, Edith, 132*n*
Abbott, Grace, 28, 30, 132
absentee landlords, 149–50
Addams, Anna Haldeman, 7, 11–12, 13, 253
Addams, George, 8
Addams, James, 45
Addams, Jane, 204 (illus.)
  as absentee landlord, 149–50
  baptized as Presbyterian, 74
  belief in compromise, 36, 38
  birth of, 4, 253
  characteristics of, 245–46
  childhood, 4–7
  childhood self-image of, 44–45
  concern for world affairs, 43–44, 50
  considered a saint, 2
  considered a socialist, 65–66
  death of father and, 7–8, 63
  early ambitions, 6
  early impressions, 42–51
  elitism/egalitarianism views, 8–10, 14
  farm owned by, 75–76, 149–50
  father's influence on, 5–7, 13–14, 43–48
  fear of death, 43
  female activists and, 33–34
  graduates from Rockford College, 67–68
  health of, 8, 44, 68–69, 148
  as leader of Progressive Era, 31–38
  life plan, 8
  Lincoln's influence on, 51–59
  love for father, 45–46
  male model of heroic stewardship, 6–7
  medical study by, 66, 68
  as 19th Ward garbage inspector, 154, 254
  Nobel Peace Prize, 38
  nominating speech for Theodore Roosevelt, 229, 231
  nonpartisanship of, 36
  opens Hull-House, 10, 20
  opposition to World War I by, 38
  personal anecdotes, vii–viii
  philanthropic approach, 9
  Hilda Satt Polacheck and, 244–52
  political philosophy, 2
  publications, vii–viii, 254–57
  reputation of, 2–3
  Rockford College experiences, 59–68
  role of, at Hull-House, 28–30
  self-description of, 12–13
  self-mockery by, 14
  socialism and, 35–36, 37, 229–31
  Tolstoy visit, 148–52
  visibility of, 29
  writing abilities, vii, viii
Addams, John Huy, 253
  background, 4
  bribery and, 53–54
  death of, 7, 53, 63
  influence on Jane, 5–7, 13–14, 43–48
  Lincoln and, 51–53
  marriage to Anna Haldeman, 7
  mention in "autobiographical notes," 11, 13–14
  mills, 45–46
  professes to be a Quaker, 48
Addams, Sarah Alice, 253
Addams, Sarah Weber, 253
adolescents. *See* young people
aestheticism, 51*n*
aging. *See* elderly people
Albert, Prince, 73
alcohol
  saloons, 97, 160, 180
  as temptation for young women, 125
Altgeld, John P., Governor, 126
American Academy of Political and Social Science, 58
American Academy of Science, 160
American Federation of Labor, 127
American Journal of Sociology, 25
American Railway Union, 101*n*
anarchists
  factory legislation and, 126
  free speech and, 114–15
  Hull-House associated with, 191–96
  Hull-House discussion of, 116
  legal rights of, 192–93
  policies toward, 194–95
  public suspicion of, 191–96
  rights of, 194–96
  Sunday school, 80
  violence against, 195–96

263

ethnicity of, 18
houses, 83–84
population, 24–25
poverty in, 83–84
representation of, 224
sweating system, 83
Hull-House Social Club, 208
Hull-House Social Science Club, 118–21
Hull-House Weekly Program, viii, 26, 207–18
Hull-House Woman's Club, 215
    investigation of garbage collection violations by, 153–54
    organization of, 153
humanitarianism, 57, 94–95
human traits, 88
Huxley, Thomas Henry, 93

ideals, 67
idleness
    of elderly women, 107
    unemployment, 110
If Christ Came to Chicago (Stead), 108
Illinois
    Board of Education, 169
    Child Labor Law, 122–23, 125–26, 159–60, 255
    employment agencies, 132
    labor legislation, 122–36
    Legislature, 123
    State Board of Charities, 163
    State Bureau of Labor, 123
    State Immigrants' Commission, 132n
    Supreme Court, 125
immigrants, 136–47. *See also* Bohemian immigrants; Canadian French immigrants; German immigrants; Greek immigrants; Hull-House neighborhood; Italian immigrants; Jewish immigrants; Russian immigrants
    Addams's attitudes toward, 20
    Americanization of, 137
    attitudes of, 24
    child care skills taught to, 145–46
    class consciousness of, 118
    cultural traditions, 23–25, 136, 137–42, 141, 146–47
    educational programs for, 20
    employment bureaus and, 132
    English-language classes for, 199–200, 250
    fertility of, 241
    fidelity to parents, 142
    first generation, 136
    garbage disposal discussed with, 153
    household skills taught to, 145–46
    Hull-House Labor Museum and, 137–42
    in Hull-House neighborhood, 82–83
    intellectuals' concerns about, 24
    interest in the arts, 181
    isolation of, 88
    juvenile delinquency, 143–45

numbers of, 23
nutrition of, 96–97
Old Settlers' Party, 87
opposition to, 87
parental control of children by, 122–23, 142–45
perception of women's work by, 154–55
second generation, 136
social activities, 136–37
standards of, 241–42
success of, 2
as teachers, 139–40
theater interests, 186–87
third generation, 136
value of Hull-House to, 136–37
wine-drinking by, 85
women's services, 111–12
Immigrants' Protective League, 132n
immigration
    dangers of, 238
    racial consequences of, 238–43
incinerators, 153, 154
income
    maldistribution of, 16
    poverty line, 16
    unequal distribution of, 18–19
Independent, The, 3, 225–28
industrial cities
    attraction of workers to, 17
    inner cities, 17
industrial development
    concentration of wealth and, 226–28
    immigration and, 240
industrial diseases, 158n. *See also* disease
inequality. *See also* equality
    Addams's childhood experiences with, 47
    concentration of wealth and, 227–28
infant mortality, 160
intellectuals, 199
    Addams's attitude toward, 20
    concerns about immigrants, 24
    living in Hull-House neighborhood, 84
    manual labor by, 150–52
intellectual stimulation
    Hull-House clubs and, 173–74
    need for, 90–93
    Settlements and, 205–6
    for working people, 150
International Alliance for Suffrage and Equal Citizenship, 255
International Committee of Women for a Permanent Peace, 255
International Congress of Women, 255, 256
internationalism, 160–61
International League for Labor Legislation, 135–36
Irish immigrants, 83
Isaaks, Abraham, 191n
isolation
    of immigrants, 88
    theater and, 185